THE FLIGHT OF THE
INTELLECTUALS

PAUL BERMAN

 MELVILLEHOUSE
BROOKLYN, NEW YORK

Melville House Publishing
145 Plymouth Street
Brooklyn, NY 11201

www.mhpbooks.com

ISBN: 978-1-933633-51-0
First Melville House Printing: April 2010

Book design by Kelly Blair

Library of Congress Control Number: 2010921188

CONTENTS

To Marty Peretz and Leon Wieseltier:

A few years ago, in the course of a book called *Terror and Liberalism*, I happened to mention a soon-to-be fashionable and already interesting Islamic philosopher from Switzerland named Tariq Ramadan, whose writings had caught my eye. I devoted a couple of pages to discussing Ramadan's ideas, and the couple of pages seemed to me adequate. But then, as time passed, I came to suspect that I had underestimated my theme, and Ramadan was turning out to be far more interesting than my couple of pages had allowed.

The philosopher from Switzerland, I began to think, has become a representative man of our age. Destiny has delivered him to the very spot where half a dozen major conflicts and controversies converge. The man is a collision point. Entire publics project upon him their own ideas. He attracts attention in the intellectual magazines. And the press coverage, some of it, has likewise proved to be all too representative of our moment—a coverage animated by earnest good intentions, but, then again, by squeamishness and fear. And by less-than-good intentions. Or so I found myself thinking, as I leafed through the magazines. And I concluded that, out of loyalty to my readers, or out of devotion to the god of lucidity, or merely out of obeisance to the spirit of the times, I ought to say a little more about Tariq Ramadan and his peculiar image in the press.

Marty, you have been presiding over *The New Republic* for quite a while now, and Leon, in your capacity as the literary editor, you have been presiding over my own contributions to the magazine for nearly as long —and, during all this time, your magazine has stood for a grand unwavering principle. This is the principle of complexity. It is the recognition that some things cannot be understood at all if they are not explained in full. Most magazines simplify. Your magazine elaborates. Therefore I came to you with my thoughts.

I wrote a long, intricate, and not-always sweet-tempered essay. You published every pointed word. And, at once, I was struck by a marvelous reality that is sometimes overlooked in our age of giant televisions and mammoth search-engines. The world is full of serious-minded readers, and the readers are perfectly willing to follow the lengthiest and most complicated of arguments, if the argument seems to them apt. People in far corners of the earth read my essay and responded to it variously. Thumbs pointed up, and pointed down. Either way, though, the responses convinced me that, on one issue at least, I was entirely right.

This was in my choice of themes. I had found my way to a central debate of our moment—the debate over Islamist ideas in the Western countries, and over the reluctance of journalists and intellectuals from Western backgrounds to grapple seriously with the Islamist ideas. Then again, the responses to my essay convinced me that, on a number of controversial points (in this present debate, *every* point, or very nearly, turns out to be controversial), I ought to say still more.

And so, I have said more. I have presented some additional historical details, which I draw from the archival discoveries just now of several talented historians. I have pondered a couple of medieval texts, which bear on our own non-medieval difficulties and which, in any case, have proved to be, in their inscrutability, a delight. I have disentangled ambiguities. I have commented on some admirable personalities of our time, and on the critics who admire them not at all. I have updated the outdated. I have corrected errors. The modest essay that originally appeared in your magazine has, in these several ways, thickened, at last, into a book. And now I press the book, printed and bound, into your hands, inscribed to you.

Paul Berman
February 2010

You have asked me, dear brother—and may Allah decree for you the quest of man's chiefest bliss, make you candidate for the Ascent to the highest height, anoint your vision with the light of Reality, and purge your inward parts from all that is not the Real!—you have asked me, I say, to communicate to you the mysteries of the Lights Divine, together with the allusions behind the literal meaning of certain texts....

—al-Ghazali

Chapter One
THE PHILOSOPHER AND THE PRESS

Tariq Ramadan is a charismatic and energetic Islamic philosopher in Europe who, during the last
fifteen years or so, has become popular and influential among various circles of European Muslims—
originally in Geneva, where his father founded the
Islamic Center in 1961 and where Ramadan grew
up; then in Lyon, the French city closest to Switzerland, where Ramadan attracted a following of
young people from North African backgrounds; then
among French Muslims beyond Lyon; at the Islamic
Foundation in Leicester, in England, where he spent
a year on a fellowship; among still more scattered
Muslim audiences in Western Europe, who listened
to his audio recordings and packed his lecture halls,
typically with the men and the women sitting demurely in their separate sections; among Muslims in
Francophone regions of Africa—and outward to the
wider world.

Ramadan possesses a special genius for shaping cultural questions according to his own lights

and presenting those questions to the general public. He has demonstrated this ability from the start. As early as 1993, at the age of thirty-two, he campaigned in Geneva to cancel an impending production of Voltaire's play *Fanaticism, or Mahomet the Prophet*. The production was canceled, and a star was born—though Ramadan has argued that he had nothing to do with canceling the play, and to affirm otherwise is a "pure lie." Not every battle has gone his way. He taught at the college of Saussure. His colleagues there were disturbed by his arguments in favor of Islamic biology over Darwin. This time, too, Ramadan shaped the debate to his own specification. He insisted that he had never wanted to suppress the existing biology curriculum—merely to complement it with an additional point of view. A helpful creationist proposal. But the Darwinians, unlike the Voltaireans, were in no rush to yield.

That was in 1995, and by then Ramadan had already established himself in Lyon, at the Union of Young Muslims and the Tawhid bookstore and publishing house. These were slightly raffish immigrant endeavors, somewhat outside the old and official mainline Muslim organizations in France. Even so, the mainline organizations welcomed the arrival of a brilliant young philosopher. He built alliances. He attended conferences. His op-eds ran in the newspapers. He engaged in debates. Eventually his face appeared on French television and on the covers of glossy magazines, which introduced him to the general public in France, a huge success. And yet—this is the oddity about Tariq Ramadan—as his triumphs became ever greater and his thinking more widely known, no consensus whatsoever emerged regarding the nature of his philosophy or its meaning for France or Europe or the world.

Some mainstream journalists in France were drawn to him from the start. The Islam-and-secularism correspondent at *Le Monde*, full of admiration, plugged him regularly and sometimes adopted his arguments. At *Le Monde Diplomatique*, Ramadan became a cause, not just a story. The editor lionized him. *Politis* magazine promoted him. On the activist far left, some of the anti-globalist radicals and the die-hard enemies of McDonald's saw in Ramadan, because of his denunciations of American imperialism and Zionism and his plebian agitations, a tribune of progressive Islam, even if his religious severities grated on left-wing sensibilities. The Trotskyists of the Revolutionary Communist League forged something of an alliance with him. A number of Christian activists regarded him with particular fondness: a worthy partner for inter-religious dialogue. A dike against the flood tides of secular materialism. An inspiration for their own revived spirituality. A religiously motivated social conscience similar to their own, laboring on behalf of the poor and the oppressed. Ramadan might even have seemed, in some people's eyes, stylishly trendy at one moment or another—a champion of Islam who, because Islam has been so badly demonized, held out a last dim hope for shocking the bourgeoisie. Then again, some of the French experts on Islam likewise found something commendable in him: a thoughtful effort to modernize Islam for a liberal age. The distinguished scholar Olivier Roy, who had no interest in shocking anyone, looked on Ramadan in an admiring light.

Still, in France other people recoiled, and did so without much hesitation, and recoiled at the people who had failed to recoil. The critics insisted that Ramadan's friends and admirers in the press were deluding themselves, and that alliances with him were bound to backfire, and that, beneath the urbane surface, he represented the worst in Islam, and not the best. Some of the critics were Christian conservatives and political right-wingers and nativists, whose hostility might have been predicted. Then again, the most prominent of Ramadan's left-wing Christian allies turned against him, and did so in a fury, as if betrayed. Some mainline Muslim leaders in France grew reserved. Even the French anti-globalists proved to be of two minds about him. A good many militants of the anti-globalist cause watched with dismay as Ramadan's pious followers filled the seats at anti-globalist meetings, and veiled women thronged the podium. Muslim liberals reviled him. His loudest enemies in France turned out to be left-wing feminists, who took one look and shuddered in alarm. Feminists from Muslim backgrounds denounced him in *Libération*, the left-wing newspaper. The Socialist Party politicians in France, who had every reason to seek out Arab and Muslim voters, showed not the slightest interest in him.

Dark rumors spread. The Spanish police inquired into his Lyon networks. In 1995 the French minister of the interior denied him permission to re-enter France—which sparked a mobilization of petition-signers until the ministry, confessing error, rescinded the order. His detractors in the press—initially at *Lyon Mag*, the city magazine in Lyon—speculated grimly about his personal connections. He responded with a double lawsuit, against *Lyon Mag* and against one of his critics, who was Antoine Sfeir, a Lebanese historian. The verdict ended up split: against the magazine but in favor of Sfeir. The magazine kept on hammering nonetheless. So did Sfeir.

Books about Ramadan tumbled into the bookstores at a remarkable pace. Caroline Fourest's *Frére*

Tariq appeared in France in 2004 (and in English translation, as *Brother Tariq*, in 2008) and has proved to be the most influential: an angry book, alarmed, energetic in tabulating the naïve tropes and clichés of the French press, indignant at the journalists who keep falling for the same old manipulations, indignant at the progressives who view Ramadan as a progressive. But Fourest's book was only the first, followed by at least six more books in France in the last several years—among them Paul Landau's *Le Sabre et le Coran*, or *The Saber and the Koran* (no less hostile and accusatory than Caroline Fourest's); Aziz Zemouri's *Faut-il faire taire Tariq Ramadan?*, or *Should Tariq Ramadan Be Silenced?* (which affords Ramadan a fair-minded chance to have his own say, at length); and Ian Hamel's *La vérité sur Tariq Ramadan*, or *The Truth About Tariq Ramadan* (mildly sympathetic to Ramadan, sometimes skeptical, indignant at the hostility expressed by Caroline Fourest and Paul Landau). And the books, too, having contributed to the controversy, contributed to his popularity.

Ramadan seems to have known instinctively how to respond to accusations and innuendos, and his rejoinders succeeded in turning each new setback into an advance. He suggested a bigotry against Islam on his critics' part, amounting to a kind of racism, which any decent person ought to condemn. He argued that criticisms of him represented a holdover from the colonialist mentality of the past. He was dignified, self-controlled, unflappable; and also a man with a polemical knife. He accused Caroline Fourest of being a militant for Zionism, and a liar. He was angry. Sometimes his anger proved effective in the conscience-stricken atmosphere of modern post-imperial France. Some people, listening to his responses, grew pensive. His supporters waved their fists. And his critics became still more fretful—not just about Ramadan, but about the people who, in applauding or merely in growing pensive, seemed to have accepted his categories of analysis, as if in a stupor.

His entrance into the Anglophone world began quietly enough. The Islamic Foundation in Leicester, where he studied and wrote in 1996–97, enjoys the distinction of having been the first and most vociferous Muslim institution in Britain to campaign against Salman Rushdie and his novel *The Satanic Verses* back in 1988—before even Ayatollah Khomeini had issued a fatwa authorizing Rushdie's assassination. Ramadan was not vociferous, though. He attracted no attention. In 1999 he published his book *To Be a European Muslim* with the Islamic Foundation. The book enjoyed a modest success. It was regarded as a thoughtful argument for healthy new relations between old-stock non-Muslim Europe and the new-stock immigrant Muslim population. Daniel Pipes in the United States, a sharp critic of Islamist radicalism, was among the expert observers who broke into applause at *To Be a European Muslim*—though, if you visit Pipes's website, you will see that, ever since his initial review, Pipes has been posting additional remorseful observations about how wrong he was, and what could possibly have gotten into him? (You will also see that Ramadan, together with a like-minded journalist or two, has responded by promoting Pipes into the center of an anti-Ramadan conspiracy on behalf of the Jews.)

In 2001 the Islamic Foundation brought out Ramadan's *Islam, the West and the Challenges of Modernity*. The new book was a philosophical study,

California Press edition of *Five Tracts of Hasan Al-Banna (1906-1949)*, translated by Charles Wendell, published in typescript in 1978.) He cited some additional events in the history of Islam. And he cited two examples from modern history, which seemed to him more astonishing yet. "For who would have imagined that King 'Abd al-'Aziz Al-Su'ud"—he means the person more commonly known as Ibn Saud, the founder of modern Saudi Arabia— "whose family had been banished, whose people had been persecuted, and whose kingdom had been stolen, would win back that kingdom with twenty or so men; and that afterwards he would become one of the hopes of the Islamic world for a restoration of its grandeur and a recreation of its unity? And who would have believed that that German workingman, Hitler, would ever attain such immense influence and as successful a realization of his aims as he has?" Hitler was the only non-Muslim name in al-Banna's list of exemplary models.

The inspirational quality was evidently great, though. Al-Banna's Muslim Brotherhood prospered. By 1936 there were eight hundred members. In Palestine that year, an uprising—the "Arab Revolt"—broke out against the Zionists and the British imperialists. The most violent and intransigent of the Palestinian leaders was the Grand Mufti of Jerusalem, Haj Amin al-Husseini. Al-Banna revered the mufti. He pledged support. He launched a solidarity campaign. The campaign proved to be massively successful, at least within Egypt. By 1938, the Muslim Brotherhood's membership had swollen to two hundred thousand. The Brotherhood became a political force. It was also more than political. It was a religious movement, pious and observant. It was intellectually vigorous. It was educationally active. The of his life he wrote: "Degradation and dishonor are the results of the love of this world and the fear of death. Therefore prepare for jihad and be the lovers of death." And, in this manner, al-Banna and his followers created the original institutional model for what has come to be known as "Islamism"—with the suffix "ism" trailing after Islam to distinguish al-Banna's political and more-than-political twenti-eth-century renewal movement from the ancient re-ligion itself. The model, having begun to prosper in Egypt, spread elsewhere—to the mufti's Palestine, to Syria, to the Sudan, to the North African Maghreb and other places. Inspirations from the Brotherhood spread to Iran (via the Shiite variation on al-Banna's idea elaborated by Ayatollah Khomeini and later by Ali Shariati) and to the Shiite zones of Lebanon, and even to India and what eventually became Pakistan (via a sister movement founded independently by Abul Ala Mawdudi, al-Banna's South Asian counter-part) and beyond.

The Muslim Brotherhood spread in a small way even to Europe. This was under the leadership, even-tually, of al-Banna's loyal lieutenant and secretary, Said Ramadan, known as "the little Hassan al-Ban-na," a proud honorific. Said Ramadan played a big role in the Brotherhood. As a very young man, he took on the responsibility for propagating the Broth-erhood's message in Palestine (where he fought in 1948 in the war against Israel and where, in the my-thology created about him by al-Banna, he played a central role in rescuing Jerusalem from the Zion-ists) and to South Asia (where he coordinated affairs with Mawdudi's sister movement). Said Ramadan edited al-Banna's magazine. The magazine published al-Banna's remarks about being the lovers of death. Said Ramadan founded his own magazine, a monthly at the airport. The European platitudes flourished, too, in their new American home. By the time Buruma's defense of Ramadan had appeared, Timothy Garton Ash had already hinted at the entire line of argument in *The New York Review of Books*. Garton Ash is a rightly admired journalist, famous for having reported accurately and in depth from the Soviet bloc countries during the years of repression. His dispatches from East Germany and other communist countries used to run in those same pages, *The New York Review of Books*. He used to applaud the anti-communist dissidents. In 2006 he applauded Ian Buruma's journalism on Islamist themes. And, in passing, he applauded Tariq Ramadan, too. He applauded Ramadan precisely along Buruma's lines, except without the cautionary remarks.

A third journalist stepped forward. This was Stéphanie Giry, an editor at *Foreign Affairs*. Ramadan published a biography of the Prophet Muhammad. The biography came out in Britain under the title *The Messenger* and, in the United States, under the title *In the Footsteps of the Prophet*. Oxford University Press published the American edition, and *The New York Times Book Review* invited Giry to evaluate the book. Her evaluation was positive. She invoked the profile of Ramadan by Buruma that had just then appeared in *The New York Times Magazine*. She joined her applause to Buruma's. She seconded Buruma's dismissal of Ramadan's critics. She looked on Ramadan's book on the Prophet Muhammad as politically progressive: a book that "can help reconcile Islam with Western liberalism today"—which echoed Buruma's verdict on Ramadan exactly.

It is not obvious to me that Buruma, in preparing his profile for *The New York Times Magazine*, had read very much by Ramadan, nor that Giry, in working up her evaluation for *The New York Times Book*

Review, had read more than a single book, though she had met the man. As for Garton Ash, he intimated in *The New York Review of Books* that he based his estimation of Ramadan on having heard him speak at Oxford, where Garton Ash and Ramadan have been colleagues—which suggests that Garton Ash may have read nothing at all. Even so, a conventional wisdom had plainly convened. The conventional wisdom looked on Tariq Ramadan as a long-awaited Islamic hero—the religious thinker who was going, at last, to adapt Islam to the modern world. This was the reigning opinion in the New York intellectual press, back in 2006 and 2007. In the years since then, a number of subtler and more cautious judgments have made their way into print. Ramadan's critics and skeptics have added their own pointed remarks, here and there. Still, those original American portraits of Ramadan, the ones in the New York magazines in 2006 and 2007, expressed a set of instincts and assumptions, and the instincts and assumptions have turned out to be enduring and influential—instincts and assumptions that are bound to go on shaping the ways that a great many people in the Western countries look on the Islamist movement, and how they look on the Muslim liberals, too, who are the Islamist movement's greatest enemies.

And so, Tariq Ramadan, by acquiring a brilliant fame and refracting its rays in one country after another, has succeeded in brightly illuminating a twin development in the world of modern ideas. He has illuminated a large new trend among select circles of pious Muslims in Europe and in many other places around the world. And he has illuminated an equally remarkable trend among the normally impious journalists of the Western countries. A new twist in the modern history of Islam; and likewise in the history of the Western intellectuals.

Chapter Two
MEMORIES OF FASCISM

Tariq Ramadan is nothing if not a son, a brother, a grandson and even a great-grandson—family relations that appear to shape everything he writes and does, and that certainly shape how other people perceive what he writes and does. The most famous member of his family was his grandfather. This was Hassan al-Banna, who is a giant of modern history. Hassan al-Banna was born in northern Egypt in 1906, and he died in Cairo in 1949—assassinated by the Egyptian government's secret police as he exited the Young Men's Muslim Association (though Ramadan, in a book devoted largely to his grandfather, has taken the position that al-Banna was assassinated on British orders, "in association with the Americans and the French").

Al-Banna's father, Ramadan's great-grandfather, wrote books on Islamic law and tradition, and al-Banna naturally inherited a thorough Islamic education in an old-fashioned style. At a very young age, though, al-Banna came up with the idea of modernizing the creaky old doctrines. His idea drew on some older inspirations. He gazed back on a couple of lively personalities from the late nineteenth century, his modernizing predecessors—on a vigorous Islamic reformer from Iran (or, in some accounts, from Afghanistan) named Jamal al-Din al-Afghani, and on al-Afghani's Egyptian disciple, Muhammad Abduh. Al-Afghani and Abduh had given sufficient thought to these matters to end up publishing a magazine. They had worked up some grand ambitions. They wanted to overthrow the European imperialists— and, at the same time, to end the stagnation of the Muslim world. Their ideal was to join reason to faith, modernity to tradition, the European breakthroughs of their own age to the Islamic achievements of the glorious past. They called for an Islamic rejuvenation that was going to return to the pure seventh-century roots of Islam, and, at the same time, was going to retain a spirit of innovation—which made sense on the grounds that, back in the seventh century, Islam itself was forcefully innovative.

Some ambiguous notes may have crept into those nineteenth-century ideas. It has even been suggested that Jamal al-Din al-Afghani, in his eagerness for progress and modernization, invoked Islam mostly for rhetorical purposes, and not really out of any sincere religious conviction. Al-Afghani and Abduh were keen on overthrowing the cultural domination of the Western world—and yet, in the 1880s, when they labored together over their magazine, they published it in Paris, the capital of the Western world. A latent ember of Western rebellion may have warmed their anti-Western rebellion from the start. Nothing in those ambiguities ought to surprise us. In several places around the world in the late nineteenth and early twentieth centuries—in India, China, Latin America—nationalist-minded intellectuals toiled earnestly to graft the latest innovations from Europe and North America onto their own autochthonous traditions, in the hope of producing a new kind of political-and-cultural doctrine, capable of overthrowing the Western imperialists. That was an irresistible idea in those days. It is irresistible even now. Only, it was never obvious how to do anything of the sort. Al-Afghani and Abduh were unable to work up a practical formula. Hassan al-Banna came up with some suggestions, though. He proposed to take al-Afghani and Abduh's Islamic renewal movement from the nineteenth century and to convert the whole thing into a forward-looking political force in the style of his own time. His own time was the 1920s, '30s, and '40s.

Political tendencies of a new and unusual sort were prospering almost everywhere in continental Europe during those years—authoritarian and hierarchical movements of the ultra-left under Soviet command, or else movements of the ultra-right, wilder and more fanciful than any of the conservative or old-school right-wing currents of the past. The left-wing movements were keenly revolutionary. So were the right-wing movements. Only, instead of picturing their revolutionary goal as a leap into the utopian future, the right-wing movements pictured a utopian leap into the glories of the past—the resurrecting of ancient empires and antique virtues, in a modernized version. The right-wing movements pictured the glories of the past in several different ways, depending on the local mythologies and traditions. But everywhere the right-wing movements conformed to the same style. They celebrated a cult of their own leaders, whom they deemed to be messianic figures, semi-divine. They pursued the satisfactions of philosophy, poetry, the graphic arts, and conspiracy-theorizing. They were movements of the artistic avant garde. They cultivated a hyper-agitated and violent tone. They organized militias. They put young people into uniforms and marched them around in paramilitary sports organizations. They took a kind of erotic pleasure in the joys of hatred. And, almost everywhere in Europe, they prospered.

Al-Banna glanced in those directions. The right-wing successes impressed him. Then again, he glanced at the educational theories of Maria Montessori and the avant garde of European pedagogy, and those ideas, too, seemed to him worthy of emulation. His stroke of genius was to borrow freely from those several European developments and yet to bend the borrowings to his own purposes, which he conceived as narrowly Islamic. Was that a feasible project on al-Banna's part—to insert a series of up-to-date European innovations into his proposed revival of the Islamic seventh century? The question is naïve. The Mediterranean Sea has always been a trader's paradise. Its southern and northern littorals have been exchanging goods and concepts ever since there were goods and concepts. And so, in 1928, Hassan al-Banna, already abuzz with novel instincts and intuitions, founded an organization. He was in his early twenties, and his new organization was the Muslim Brotherhood. The Brotherhood was minuscule. This did not discourage him.

In one of his seminal tracts, "To What Do We Summon Mankind?", he confidently pointed out that, over the course of history, tiny movements led by charismatic figures have triumphed more than once. He cited the example of the Prophet Muhammad and his Companions in ancient times. "Who would have believed that the Arabian peninsula, that dry and infertile desert, would ever produce enlightenment and learning, and, through the spiritual and political influence of its sons, rule over the mightiest states in the world?" (I am quoting from the University of

Muslims, having fled to Europe precisely in order to escape the Muslim Brotherhood and its organizational progeny and its cultural and political influences, are bound to gaze with instinctive dread at the European descendants of Hassan al-Banna). Tariq Ramadan himself, Swiss-born and Swiss-educated, has always exulted in his family legacy, discretely or boastfully, sometimes presuming the right to speak for his long-gone revered grandfather, sometimes carrying himself with the wounded air of a man who, through his father, knows in the flesh the sting of persecution and exile.

And yet Tariq Ramadan's august background generates, all by itself, still more controversy, and has done so from the start of his career, not just among anti-Islamist immigrants from the Muslim countries. At the University of Geneva, Ramadan wrote a doctoral dissertation on his grandfather al-Banna's ideas—and the academic committee judged the work to be a partisan apologia, unworthy of commendation. Ramadan protested. Switzerland's best-known socialist intellectual, Jean Ziegler, rose to Ramadan's defense. A second committee was convened, a rare occurrence. Even then, his thesis barely passed—accepted without honors. The dispute over his dissertation was an academic quarrel, but also more than academic—a dispute, ultimately, over the meaning of al-Banna's Islamic renewal movement in the past and its legacy for today.

I have not read Ramadan's thesis. In 1998, however, he published a book called *Aux Sources du renouveau musulman: D'al-Afghani à Hassan al-Banna, un siècle de réformisme islamique*, which I will render into English as *The Roots of the Muslim Renewal: From al-Afghani to Hassan al-Banna, A Century of Islamic Reformism* (though if the book ever gets translated into English, it could well end up bearing another title entirely). This I have read. It is the most tightly disciplined and rigorous of Ramadan's full-length books—the most pleasing to read, from a strictly literary standpoint. I think this one book is the key to everything else that Ramadan has written. The book recounts the intellectual history, from the mid-nineteenth century to the mid-twentieth, of the philosophical current within modern Islam that Ramadan regards as his own. And, at the heart of the book, stretched across some two hundred pages, is a portrait of the single most influential figure within that history, who is, of course, Hassan al-Banna—the man whose ideas Ramadan has adopted for himself and has set out to preserve, which also means: to adapt.

Ramadan's two hundred pages on al-Banna are a gusher of adulation. Al-Banna is presented as a champion of anti-colonial rebellion—which he certainly was, at least in regard to the European empires in the Muslim world. Then again, al-Banna is presented as the leader of a magnificent religious reform within Islam, akin to Protestant reform within Christianity—which is a more controversial point. He is presented as the leader of an equally magnificent movement for social conscience, akin to Catholicism's liberation theology, except that al-Banna anteceded the Catholic liberation theologians by a few decades. He is presented as a visionary, ahead of his own time. A man of democratic temperament. A man committed to rational judgment and scientific truth. A peaceful man, patient and practical. A man whose ideals would benefit the world, and not just its Muslim portion, if only his principles were enacted. Reading those two hundred pages, you could find yourself supposing that Hassan al-Banna was the

Mahatma Gandhi of the Arab and Muslim world. A severe and pious man. A friend of the oppressed. An inspiring man. A man who, from the evidence presented by his grandson, never once made a major error and scarcely any minor ones. (His gravest misjudgment, to judge by Ramadan's account, was a naïve optimism that led him to suppose that decolonization would, all by itself, lead to economic development—a completely understandable error.) Does the portrait of al-Banna in *The Roots of the Muslim Renewal* resemble in any significant way Ramadan's university dissertation? Then I can understand why the academic committee would have balked. To read through Ramadan's account of his grandfather you have to pick your way carefully past the omissions and gaps, as if tiptoeing down a potholed road.

To cite a single difficult matter, al-Banna's Muslim Brotherhood in the past did, after all, enjoy, if that is the word, a reputation for assassinations and bombings—though the Muslim Brothers have always sharply contested any such imputation. Ramadan himself is adamant: "It is necessary to say or to recall that, despite the rumors or the accusations produced by the different Egyptian or English governments to justify the arrests, repression and finally the dissolution of the organization, no act of violence can be attributed to the association, and the documents prove that al-Banna never ordered even the slightest political assassination." Even so, the Egyptian and English governments have not been alone in thinking otherwise.

Al-Banna's more insistent detractors are bound to point out that, in Palestine, the Muslim Brotherhood goes under the name of Hamas. Now, I realize that some people believe that Hamas has evolved in recent years into a kind of civil-rights organization, perhaps a little gruff in its methods, which is principally devoted to advancing the human rights and welfare of the Palestinian population of Gaza and the West Bank—and therefore is no longer an organization that ought to be described as terrorist. Still, in other people's eyes, Hamas remains the world's most famous celebrant of the cult of suicide bombings—an organization known for its attacks on random crowds at pizza parlors and dance halls, and known, too, for a veneration of suicide so intense as to descend into morbid children's cartoons and the Hamas kindergarten motto, "The Children are the Holy Martyrs of Tomorrow." And yet Hamas, for all its emphasis on death and terror, does not appear to have deviated in any respect whatsoever from the principles of its parent organization—merely to have continued marching down the original road. Even the specialized concern with early-childhood education reflects the Islamist movement's earliest emphases. The Muslim Brotherhood in Egypt itself and everywhere else has always stood united in awe and admiration for their brothers in Hamas. And in active solidarity—which makes sense, given that, back in 1936, solidarity with the mufti of Jerusalem and his wing of the Arab Revolt served as the principal engine of al-Banna's early successes.

Hamas venerates, in turn, the founding Supreme Guide of the Muslim Brotherhood. Hamas adopted its organizational charter in 1988, and the opening passage of that charter consists of a quotation from the Koran, as you would expect from an Islamist group. But the Koran is followed directly by a quotation from Hassan al-Banna, even if al-Banna never set foot in Palestine (though Ramadan does leave the suggestion, in the final pages of *The Roots of the*

Muslim Renewal, that al-Banna's opposition to the proposed partition of Palestine in 1948 was one of the factors behind his assassination in 1949—which would make al-Banna something of a Palestinian martyr, after all). Al-Banna condemned, on religious grounds, the notion of any partition of Palestine, regardless of where the border was drawn, and he did so from the first moment that such an idea was seriously proposed, in 1937. He was intransigent. The Hamas charter quotes him saying: "Israel will be established and will stay established until Islam nullifies it, as it nullified what was before it." In some translations the word *nullify* is rendered as *obliterate*. Either way, no one who reads the Hamas charter will suppose that Hassan al-Banna was a champion of peaceful compromise.

Quite a few militias and insurgent groups in the Middle East have earned a reputation for terrorism (a vexed word, to be sure, though not so vexed that people fail to understand its Middle Eastern meaning: the practice of murdering civilian populations for political or scriptural purposes, or for no reason at all). Some of those militias and groups descend from the radical wing of Arab nationalism. Others descend from the Marxist left. And yet, a preponderance of the organizations with terrorist reputations do seem to descend from al-Banna's Muslim Brotherhood, either directly and overtly, like Hamas, or schismatically. Al Qaeda figures as merely one among the many schismatic offshoots, a splinter group whose genealogy traces back to factions within the Muslim Brotherhood of Egypt itself in the 1970s—though Al Qaeda, because of its global reach and its unusually inclusive notion of who merits death, commands an outsized attention in the Western countries.

The controversy over terrorism and its historical link to Hassan al-Banna has raised a persistent
question for Ramadan, which he has had to address
more than once in the years since September 11,
2001—most prominently (for American readers, at
least) in the interview that he granted to Ian Buruma
and *The New York Times Magazine* in 2007. Buruma
quite properly inquired about Al Qaeda. Ramadan
responded. He acknowledged that Al Qaeda's history does trace back to the Muslim Brotherhood,
in times gone by. But—this was Ramadan's contention—Al Qaeda's history owes nothing at all to al-
Banna. Al Qaeda draws its inspiration instead from
a Muslim Brother named Sayyid Qutb, who enrolled
in the movement only after al-Banna had been assassinated. Or so Ramadan told Buruma—though
Buruma might have noted that, in *The Roots of the
Muslim Renewal*, Ramadan has proposed a different
explanation.

In *The Roots of the Muslim Renewal*, Ramadan
argues that Islamism's violent strain got its start
among Qutb's followers, the "Qutbists," but this
was not because of anything that Qutb himself had
written or done. The followers wrongly interpreted
Qutb's doctrines. Then again, in Ramadan's interpretation of Islamist violence in Egypt, not even the
Qutbists were to blame. The ultimate responsibility for Islamist violence belonged to Egypt's president in the 1950s and '60s, Jamal Abdel al-Nasser,
who brought about a violent resistance by cruelly
repressing the Islamists. Nasser's successor, Anwar
Sadat, did some repressing of his own, though not
as cruelly; and Sadat, too, bore a responsibility for
encouraging the violence. The enemies of the Muslim
Brotherhood—those were the blameworthy parties,
in Ramadan's interpretation. But not the Brother-

hood itself, nor its philosophical doctrines and its variegated political legacies. In any case, on the topic of Hassan al-Banna and his relation to Sayyid Qutb, Ramadan explained to Buruma and the *Times Magazine*, "They didn't even know each other." This observation was correct, in a narrow sense (though, as I will explain, it was entirely misleading). And Ramadan went on to describe al-Banna's political ideals, if only to demonstrate how great was the philosophical gap separating al-Banna from Sayyid Qutb. Al-Banna, in Ramadan's account, "was in favor of a British-style parliamentary system, which was not against Islam."

Was this likewise an accurate observation, even narrowly? Egypt in Hassan al-Banna's time already possessed a multi-party system, though of course the multiple parties reflected the influence of Britain's colonial domination. Everyone agrees that al-Banna wanted to throw out the British, but some people would add that he also wanted to throw out the parliamentary system. He wanted to create, instead, a single national council to rule over Egypt in conformity with the dictates of Islam, as interpreted by himself or by the Islamic scholars whom he chose to revere. Ramadan acknowledges in *The Roots of the Muslim Renewal* that al-Banna's idea of a national council might be regarded as an Islamically-guided one-party state. Al-Banna's own description of this—I find it in his tract "Toward the Light"—does appear to support such an interpretation. His goal: "An end to party rivalry, and a channeling of the political forces of the nation into a common front and a single phalanx." In Ramadan's analysis, though, the proposed new phalanx was nonetheless going to be tantamount to a multi-party system, owing to the fundamentally democratic nature of Islam. I glean additional details from another study sympathetic to al-Banna. This is a book by the Norwegian scholar Brynjar Lia, *The Society of the Muslim Brothers in Egypt: The Rise of an Islamic Mass Movement, 1928–1942*, which comes with an admiring preface by Hassan al-Banna's younger brother, Jamal al-Banna, who is Ramadan's great-uncle.

In the Norwegian scholar's interpretation, Hassan al-Banna did want to establish something resembling a constitutional and representative system, except with a twist. The representative system was going to rest, in the Norwegian scholar's description, "on the unity of power without any division between the civil and religious powers." It was going to be a theocracy, then. Rule by prelates. Political opposition? Not in al-Banna's proposed new phalanx. There was going to be room, instead, for something called "consultation." Lay people would have their say. And al-Banna entertained a grander ambition. In the Norwegian scholar's account, "Finally, when an Islamic government had gained power in Egypt, it should expand its cooperation with other Muslim countries with a view to founding a 'League of Islamic Nations,' which would subsequently appoint a Caliph, thereby re-establishing the Caliphate." And what was *that* going to mean, the re-established Caliphate, as imagined by Hassan al-Banna?

The Norwegian study offers no details on this point. Ramadan himself, in *The Roots of the Muslim Renewal*, merely tells us that al-Banna postulated the resurrected Caliphate as his goal and wrote nothing more about it, which leaves us to wonder. I don't know why Ramadan says this, however. In the course of his book he makes plain that, in his estimation, the greatest of scholarly authorities on al-Banna and his thinking is Sheikh Yusuf al-Qaradawi, a distinguished figure in the history of the Islamist movement, who devoted a book to expounding al-Banna's ideas. The book is *Islamic Education and Hassan al-Banna*, which was translated somewhat imperfectly into English in a Beirut edition in 1984. Qaradawi explains that al-Banna taught the Muslim Brotherhood to engage in Islamic education, to be followed by a massive struggle or jihad, to be followed, ultimately, by worldwide domination. Al-Banna's message to the Muslim Brothers, in Qaradawi's summary: "He breathed into them the hope of uniting under the banner of Islamic caliphate and taking the responsibility of fulfilling the whole world's leadership and guidance, but never forgot to mention the deep trenches, dangerous abysses, rivers and mountains of difficulties and calamities."

But you don't have to rely on Qaradawi, either. In the portions of his own writing that have been translated into English, al-Banna himself spelled out quite a few ideas. I will cite his tract "Toward the Light," which he wrote in 1947, two years before his death—a mature work. Al-Banna explains that he wants to encourage the liberation of the Islamic fatherland. And he neatly defines the fatherland. The Islamic fatherland should be regarded in stages as: (1) the particular Muslim country in which an individual Muslim might find himself living; (2) all the other Muslim countries; (3) all the lands that used to be ruled by the Islamic Empire of the past—which, as he specifies in a different tract, included Spain, part of France, southern and northern Italy, and so forth. And al-Banna lays out, in "Toward the Light," the Islamic fatherland's fourth and final stage, to wit: "(4) Then the fatherland of the Muslim expands to encompass the entire world. Do you not hear the words of God (Blessed and Almighty is He!): 'And fight them till sedition is no more, and the faith is God's!'"—with a citation to the Koran.

The Caliphate, then—this was a more than Egyptian idea, and more than Palestinian. The Caliphate was a project to encompass the world. And how would life be organized under its global command? I will give the flavor of al-Banna's proposals by quoting a few phrases from "Toward the Light": "an end to the dichotomy between the private and the professional spheres," "the imposition of severe penalties for moral offenses," "the recognition of fornication, whatever its circumstances, as a detestable crime whose perpetrator must be flogged," "the prohibition of dancing and other such pastimes," "the expurgation of songs," "the confiscation of provocative stories and books that implant the seeds of skepticism in an insidious manner," "punishment of all who are proved to have infringed any Islamic doctrine or attacked it," "active instigation to memorize the Koran in all the free elementary schools," and so on. Al-Banna calls for an Islamic militarism, which, he says, will be superior to the militarism of Mussolini's Fascism, Hitler's Nazism, and Stalin's Communism because, while those other movements favor pure force, the militarism of Islam prefers peace. Al-Banna calls for rights for non-Muslim minority groups—though, as he specifies in some other writings, the non-Muslims will be required to pay tribute in a spirit of "humility," which means that, in the future reign of the Caliphate, non-Muslims will enjoy the rights of being a subjugated population. And he goes on—but I think I have offered a sufficient impression.

So, then—how to describe al-Banna's larger ideal, his world-dominating Caliphate? The question plunges us back into the more-than-academic debate that got started at the University of Geneva. Ramadan's interpretation of his grandfather as the champion of "a British-style parliamentary system" occupies a distinctive pole of opinion within the larger debate. But an alternative interpretation also exists. And the alternative interpretation has been expounded in a literature of its own, which is a fairly old literature by now, and has lately grown substantially bigger. I will describe the alternative interpretation.

Al-Banna's movement, in the alternative view, aimed at establishing a new sort of society—orderly, serene and authoritarian, based on obedience and conformity in all areas of life (or, to quote al-Banna himself, "social solidarity between ruler and ruled, in both custodianship and obedience"). The new society was going to roll back any recent progress in women's rights, quash individuality and erase human differences. The intention was to cultivate a spirit of unyielding rage against supernaturally evil enemies. And the intention was to generate a popular enthusiasm for a politics not just of ultra-conservative communitarian obedience but of violence and war: the kind of politics that regards terror as a goal in itself, and not just a tactic, and regards death as desirable—qualities, in short, that have hardly anything to do with British-style political traditions, and not much to do with Catholic liberation theology, either, in its 1968-ish style. These are the qualities of an altogether different political tradition, which is recognizable from the 1930s and '40s—the political impulse that used to be known in Europe as (but here is another vexed word, requiring an elaborate and patient commentary of its own) fascism. A terrible word. There is no avoiding it, though.

The Tunisian-French writer Abdelwahab Meddeb has offered a discussion of this most controver-

sial of words in its connection to the Islamist movement, and I find his commentary to be exceptionally
keen and clarifying—a useful counterweight to Tariq
Ramadan's apologetics for his grandfather and his
grandfather's political legacy. The mass media long
ago made Ramadan a celebrity in the Francophone
world, and have lately been doing so in the Anglophone world, and I am sorry to report that no such
development has overtaken the literary and cultural
career of Abdelwahab Meddeb. Even so, Meddeb is
a distinguished intellectual. He has won prizes and
acclaim of a sort that have never descended upon
Ramadan—the Prix François Mauriac, the Prix Max
Jacob, and so forth, which add up to a considerable
luster in the Francophone literary world. Meddeb
is a champion of Islam, too. He boasts of a glorious Islamic background of his own, though his own
background, instead of being radical and insurgent
like Ramadan's, is conventional and old-fashioned:
a family history of Islamic scholarship and jurisprudence in Tunis, culminating in a proper education at
one of North Africa's ancient mosque-universities.
Abdelwahab Meddeb's version of Islam points in a
different direction from Tariq Ramadan's or Hassan
al-Banna's, though. Meddeb's version is liberal.

   In 2008 Meddeb published a book of essays in
France under the title, *Sortir de la Malédiction*, or *To
Escape the Curse*. One of those essays, which laid out
sundry aspects of the curse in question, was called
"On Islamic Fascism." Meddeb recalled that, back in
2006, during the administration of George W. Bush,
America's president and his secretary of defense,
Donald Rumsfeld, took to speaking about "Islamic
fascism." The sound of that phrase, intoned with a
Bush administration snarl, vibrated disagreeably in
Meddeb's ear. By attaching the word "fascism" to

"Islamic," the White House in those days seemed to have converted "Islamic" into an epithet. Or so Meddeb judged, though I think he was less than fair on this point, and neither Bush nor Rumsfeld meant to insult Islam. The Bush administration never did learn to control its own message, though. A catastrophic failing. Bush went multisyllabic: "Islamofascism." Meddeb winced.

The Bush administration spoke about "Islamic fascism" with Al Qaeda in mind, though also with an implied reference to some of the other currents on the radical side of the Islamist movement—the Palestinian Hamas, the Lebanese Hezbollah, the Iranian theocrats, and so forth. The administration's habit of rhetorically lumping those several groups together struck Meddeb as still another mistake, tactically speaking—a formula for committing the crudest of foreign-policy blunders. One of Bush's keenest supporters among the American intellectuals was Norman Podhoretz, a founding father of the neo-conservative movement. Meddeb noticed that, in 2007, Podhoretz published a book called *World War IV: The Long Struggle Against Islamofascism*, together with an op-ed in *The Wall Street Journal* called "The Case for Bombing Iran." Meddeb eyed Podhoretz. The mixture of dogmatism and bellicosity struck Meddeb as disastrous. All in all, Meddeb, from his home in France, detected in the rhetoric of the Bush administration and its supporters a bombast of a dubious sort—a useful bombast, maybe, for pounding the table and threatening America's enemies, and useful (he granted this) for reminding Americans of their own country's glorious struggles and achievements in the anti-fascist and anti-totalitarian campaigns of the twentieth century. But the Bush administration bombast seemed to him not at all useful for working up a subtle foreign policy in our present-day world, and altogether harmful for pleading the liberal cause to people in the Muslim countries.

And yet—a complexity, here—Abdelwahab Meddeb did think that Al Qaeda, Hamas, Hezbollah and the Iranian theocrats shared some traits. The traits merited a name. And in Meddeb's judgment, this name was indeed *fascism*. Meddeb himself, in the past, had pasted a fascist label across the radical Islamist movement, and, upon reflection, he was in no rush to peel the label off again just because in the United States, the hamhanded politicians and ideologues of the Republican Party had lately taken to using a similar language. From Meddeb's standpoint, the fascist label, if deployed with proper delicacy and nuance, offered, in regard to Islam, a stout and necessary defense, instead of an insult—a way of insisting that Islam was one thing, a vast and ancient religion, his own religion, with intricate and contradictory roots which he was happy to discuss. And fascism, the Islamists' fascism, was something else entirely: a political exploitation of the old religion, thoroughly detestable, intent on imposing a more-than-ordinary despotism over everyday life.

Meddeb was wholly in favor of making careful political distinctions, and his purpose in speaking about Islamic fascism was precisely to offer two of his own—a couple of analytic subtleties that, absent a word like *fascism*, might disappear from view. The difference between Islam and the Islamists marked only the first of those subtle distinctions, and a crucial subtlety it was. The second point bore on the question of dictatorships. In modern times, there have been plain old dictatorships—and *fascist* dictatorships. Dictatorships whose grandest goal adds up to keeping the dictator in power—and dictatorships that aim at something more: the dictatorships that yearn to colonize every last corner of private life, the dictatorships that dream of exterminating whole sectors of the population. An Islamist dictatorship, Meddeb wished to observe, is all-encompassing in its ambitions. He recoiled, and, in his choice of words, he found a simple and emphatic and even classic way of speaking and spitting at the same time.

Still, this choice of words—was it the best of all possible choices? Someone could share Meddeb's indignation, and sympathize with his two big points, as well—his refusal to accept the Islamist movement as the authentic voice of Islam and his alarm over Islamism's ambitions—and, even so, wonder about his vocabulary. It is easy to imagine that a different word could express those same objections, and do so without running quite as grave a danger of being misunderstood. I cite a counter-vocabulary proposed by Bassam Tibi, the Syrian-German political philosopher, who has lately been a professor at Cornell. Tibi and Meddeb belong, in a sense, to the same philosophical party, if I can call it a party—the school of thought whose adherents affirm Islam as their personal religion, and whose adherents also affirm the liberal principles and culture of human rights. Tibi and Meddeb, the faithful Muslim liberals, take umbrage at the same thing—at well-meaning observers from outside the world of Islam who, in a misplaced effort to sympathize with oppressed and stigmatized Muslims, agree to regard the heritage of Hassan al-Banna as the authentic and respectable voice of Islam.

Tibi is not a literary man, though. He is an old student of Max Horkheimer's and the Frankfurt School, which is to say, a political theorist. And, in his theory-minded punctiliousness, he has preferred to invoke the fustier and more academic word *total-*

itarian—at least in regard to the more radical wing of the Islamist cause. I notice a similar usage in the writings of still another professorial Muslim liberal, Abdullahi Ahmed An-Na'im of Emory University, who presents his thinking in a much more pious light. An-Na'im traces his own intellectual lineage back in still another direction, into the traditions of Islamic philosophy in Sudan. And, with those traditions in mind, An-Na'im makes the case that Islam, properly understood, requires in our modern age a secular and liberal political system. The argument appears in his book *Islam and the Secular State*, which came out in 2008. He erects a philosophical wall between mosque and state. And, in the course of doing this, An-Na'im inveighs against what he calls "the totalitarian post-colonial claims of an Islamic state"—which is a pretty severe way of describing the Islamist alternative.

You might suppose that here is a semantic quibble of truly tiny proportions. The difference between *fascist*, as employed by a literary man like Abdelwahab Meddeb, and *totalitarian*, as employed by professors like Bassam Tibi and Abdullahi Ahmed An-Na'im, is anything but vast. Etymologically speaking, the two words are practically the same. *Fascist* was coined, or at least popularized, by Benito Mussolini, to describe his own political party, the capital-F Fascists of Italy. And *totalitarian* was likewise coined, or at least popularized, by Benito Mussolini, in this case to describe the political ideal of his capital-F Fascists: the total revolution that Mussolini and his comrades dreamed of bringing about—the revolution that was going to be political, economic, cultural and even spiritual. (Fascism in Mussolini's concept was a religion, and not just a politics. Fascism celebrated a cult of the movement and the leader, Il Duce, who turned out to be himself.) The two words, *fascist* and *totalitarian*, are Mussolinian twins. But that was in the 1920s and '30s. Then the years wore on, and the semantic twins went their separate ways.

Totalitarian became a philosophers' word. It denoted a new kind of society, totally oppressive, which might assume a fascist shape, or then again a communist shape. Hitler was a totalitarian, and Stalin was no less of one—which left open the possibility that, in the future, still more variants of the totalitarian impulse might spring to life, as different from the mid-twentieth century European variants as fascism and communism were to one another. Or so the philosophers argued, and Bassam Tibi has picked up on the argument. In an online debate over Tariq Ramadan at the *Signandsight.com* website, Tibi wrote: "In my research, I come to the conclusion that al-Banna is the spiritual and political source of Jihad Islamism, which represents totalitarianism in its latest manifestation"—Tibi's contention that Islamism, on its most radical wing, is not, in fact, an expression of ancient Islam or an anthropological quirk of Middle Eastern life, but is altogether modern and recognizable, deserving of a modern label. Anyway, the reference to al-Banna catches my attention. I stumble on a similar remark by the Iranian scholars Ladan Boroumand and Roya Boroumand in an anthology called *Islam and Democracy in the Middle East,* edited by Larry Diamond, Marc F. Plattner and Daniel Brumberg. The Boroumands, who are sisters, flatly declare: "The man who did more than any other to lend an Islamic cast to totalitarian ideology was an Egyptian schoolteacher named Hassan al-Banna"— which, apart from pointing to al-Banna, emphasizes again the argument about Islamism as a variation of totalitarian ideology.

The word *fascist* has trod a different path. In the 1930s and '40s people began to attach the word *fascist* not just to Mussolini's political party but to political movements of the revolutionary far right in Spain and other places in Europe, and especially to Hitler's National Socialists, or Nazis—the several parties and movements that ended up rotating around what was called the "Fascist Axis," together with a few movements that remained nominally independent. And then, once Hitler and his Axis had been defeated, the word *fascist* attached itself to still more parties and movements—to the many violent political tendencies around the world whose enthusiasm for group hatreds and apocalyptically paranoid ideologies and hygienic utopias conjured a memory of the classic fascists of yore. The word *fascist* proved to be flexible, in that respect. Usefully flexible—a word that allowed people to identify and denounce a new kind of political tendency on the far right, different from the old-fashioned conservative and even reactionary movements of the past. Then again, *fascist* turned out to be, after a while, too flexible by half—an elastic word that, through repeated stretching and the dessicating effects of time, eventually snapped and crumbled, such that younger generations have hardly known what *fascist* used to mean, in the days of their grandparents. This was George W. Bush's problem back in 2006, when he gave the word a try. Entire publics had no idea what Bush was talking about.

And yet, some writers, with an eye on the political legacies that descend from al-Banna, do go on speaking about dangers that are not just *totalitarian* but *fascist*—even if *totalitarian* conveys pretty much the same idea. Abdelwahab Meddeb is a distinguished example, but he is hardly the only one. And why is that? Why would talented writers of our own time, people who do have a way with language, stick to the more controversial and archaic of those two words? It is because *totalitarian*, being abstract, is odorless. *Fascist* is pungent. To hear that emphatic f-sound and those double different *s*'s is to flair your nostrils. And *fascist* is a memory word. *Fascist* conjures the past. Not in everyone's mind, it is true—hence the difficulty in putting the word to use. Still, some people do harbor a few memories of North Africa and the Levant from long ago—recollections of their own experience, or recollections gleaned from relatives and friends, or gleaned merely from their readings or research over the years. A sense of the past, in any case. And what are those recollections—the memories that abruptly stir to life, as if awakening from sleep, at the sound of that one terrible word, *fascist*?

I will answer this question, and my answer will wend its way back to our present-day controversies over Tariq Ramadan and his interpretation of Islamism and its history. But first, a glance at the remembered past from the days of Hassan al-Banna.

Chapter Three
THE CAIRO EMBASSY FILES

The attacks of September 11, 2001 inspired ten thousand scholarly inquiries into the terrorist movements of the Middle East and their historical roots, and most of the inquirers did the obvious thing and set about digging into the history of Arab politics and Islamist political doctrine. A handful of scholars and journalists sunk their spades in a different direction, though, slightly to the side, and investigated a topic that might seem, at a glance, less than central. This is the history of German foreign policy in the Middle East during the 1930s and '40s. The topic is old, and it has been excavated in the past, and you might suppose that, by 2001, every last remaining relevant artifact would have been exhumed long ago and laid out to dry in the scholarly sun. But that is not the case. Nazi foreign policy, taken as a field for scholarly inquiry, has the misfortune of being larger than anyone might wish it to be. And so, a number of historians and journalists have spent the last several years poking about to see if anything else might be discovered, and from time to time they have come up with a dismal new finding. And there is much to be learned, and all of it is depressing.

Germany's foreign policy in the Nazi era rested on a puzzling ideological contradiction, and the difficulty in squaring the circle proved to be, for the Nazi theoreticians and propagandists, oddly stimulating—a spur to creative thought within the peculiar world of Nazi doctrine. Germany under Hitler needed to attract friends and supporters around the world, not to mention outright allies. The acquiring of friends, supporters and allies was Germany's main foreign-policy goal, and, in principle, it ought to have been easily achieved. According to the Nazi interpretation of world events, German was fighting a titanic battle against three enormous and frightening forces at the same time. These three terrible forces were the British imperialists to the west; the Soviet Union and the communists to the east; and, everywhere at once, something called "international Jewry." Eventually the United States turned out to be yet another sinister enemy, across the sea. The Nazis proposed to defeat all three of those enemies, and then all four of them, and to crush their lesser allies, and to remake the world. This was a project with an obvious potential for popular appeal, if only because Germany's enemies were everywhere, and the enemies had enemies of their own, who likewise were everywhere, and Germany promised to be a victorious friend.

The colonial subjects of the British Empire, to begin with them, wanted nothing more than to dismantle the imperial edifice brick by brick. Why not look to Hitler and the Axis powers for a little help in undertaking this mighty project? That was a tempting thought to people in a great many unhappy corners of the worldwide empire. Soviet Communism in those days was entering its most gruesome phase. Whole populations in Eastern Europe and Central

Asia dearly hoped that Communism and all its works and champions could be eradicated from top to bottom. Why not look for Axis support in this project, as well, now that Hitler seemed to be growing ever more powerful?—another obvious line of argument, in some people's minds. The United States enjoyed the kind of relations with Latin America that more or less guaranteed a round of applause for anyone at all who stood a chance of demolishing America's power. The combined powers of the Wehrmacht and the Japanese imperial navy definitely stood a chance.

As for the Jews, they were roundly disliked around the world, except maybe in places where no one had heard of them. Anti-Semitic doctrines of one sort or another—nationalist, right-wing, conservative, populist and left-wing—found homes nearly everywhere along the political spectrum in those days. A high-brow anti-Semitism prospered in the world of the literary and artistic avant garde. A theological anti-Semitism prospered in some of the tradition-minded and right-wing corners of conservative Christianity, unto the Vatican. And the various anti-Semitic doctrines had the perverse effect of igniting still more animosity against the Jews for reasons that were not at all doctrinal. The modern era of persecuting the Jews got underway in the years after 1881 in czarist Russia. Pogroms and persecutions broke out, and continued to break out, and were accompanied all the while by a growing strength among anti-Semitic political factions in Poland and other countries further to the west.

The persecutions in Eastern Europe sent a few million Jews fleeing to all points. And, wherever large numbers of those people came to shore, they aroused new kinds of rancor among their new neighbors, as was only natural—the cultural resentments

and political and economic grievances that typically
follow in the wake of mass immigrations. Normal
grievances and fantastical doctrines fed on one another. And, under those circumstances, the Nazi idea
of postulating the Jews as an enemy of mankind began to seem, in the eyes of more than a few people
around the world, plausible, or, at minimum, acceptable—one more reason to think of Hitler's Germany
as a well-aimed gun in a violent world. Anyway, op-
portunism is history's strongest law, and, until 1944,
a pro-fascist politics seemed like a reasonable bet.

A complication, though: the Nazi leaders, being
Nazis, were keenly committed to pursuing a second
foreign-policy objective, as well, which consisted of
promoting their own most dearly-held doctrines and
principles. Here was the puzzling difficulty. Nazi
doctrines were not entirely compatible with the goal
of attracting friends and supporters. The part about
Aryan supremacy, for instance—this particular theory might have appealed to anyone who figured that
he himself was a superior Aryan. But what were
other people, the non-Aryans, to think? It was not
entirely obvious what sort of apology or explanation
Germany's diplomats could possibly offer those other people, who, somewhat awkwardly for Germany,
constituted most of the world's population.

The part about the Jews raised a further difficulty. The Jews, in the Nazi concept of them, were
more than annoying and odious. The Jews were terrifying. They were an invisible and sinister conspiracy that had festered for centuries, as revealed in *The
Protocols of the Elders of Zion* and other staples of
Nazi propaganda. International Jewry, in the Nazis'
estimation, was the unseen power behind the Soviet
Union. International Jewry was likewise the power
behind the British imperialists. When America en-

tered the war, international Jewry turned out to be the secret power dominating the White House. International Jewry was threatening to annihilate the superior Aryans, which meant that, from a Nazi standpoint, to exterminate the Jews was a matter of simple self-defense.

The Nazis were out of their minds. They subscribed to a supernatural theory of their Jewish enemy. They could not distinguish between their own emaciated victims and a frightening conclave of all-powerful cosmic demons. And this element of the Nazi imagination, the simple dottiness of it all, was bound to arouse still other worries among anyone around the world who, on grounds of conventional enemy-of-my-enemy realism, might have considered enlisting in the fascist alliance. The strongest possible argument in favor of joining with the Nazis rested, after all, on the belief that Germany's leaders knew what they were doing. But what if the Nazis were incapable of identifying the world before their eyes? Even a mildly anti-Semitic person, or even somebody who shuddered with loathing at Jews and Jewishness, yet who nonetheless prized his sense of practical reality, might think twice before striking up an alliance with leaders like those.

In Europe, as it happened, a good many people with solid right-wing instincts, Nazism's instinctive sympathizers in one country after another, struck up alliances, even so. The sympathizers seem to have figured that, if the Fascist Axis ended up ruling the earth, their own racial status would surely turn out to be biologically superior, and good riddance to the inferior races. Or the sympathizers shrugged off the racial theories in the belief that no one could possibly be so foolish as to act on a foolish ideology. Or the sympathizers merely hoped for the

best. As for the mania about Jews, Nazism's sympathizers in Europe could always choose to beam a
benign light over the whole matter, even if they did
not subscribe to every last tenet of the larger anti-
Semitic theory. The sympathizers could gaze back
nostalgically on Europe's hoary old traditions—on
the ancient theological accusation against the Jews
for murdering Christ; on the continuing Christian
doctrine that Jewish guilt was passed millennially
through the generations; on the medieval superstitions about Jews murdering Christian babies for
ritual purposes; and about Jews poisoning the wells
with the Black Death—the weird old theologies and
folklore from long ago that had never entirely lost
their hold over whole regions of the continent. And
Nazism's sympathizers could tell themselves that
tradition is good, even when it is bad.

Anyway, the Nazis, seen in a certain light, were
attractively up to date. *The Protocols of the Elders
of Zion* was composed by the czarist secret police
in Paris at the turn of the twentieth century, on the
basis of a clever French hoax from the 1860s—which
made the *Protocols* one more literary product of the
fancy-free Parisian imagination in the modernist age.
And yet, a damp medieval mold seemed to cover the
modern document, and this was oddly alluring. The
Nazi leaders and ideologues, not too keen on Christianity, plucked crucifixes off the schoolroom walls.
The Nazis wished to eradicate everything that went
under the name of Christian ethics. Their fondest
dream was to revive pagan rites that no one actually
remembered anymore. The Nazis were the pop-eyed
audiences at Wagner operas. Even so, their pagan
ideas, like Wagner's operas, echoed with basso tones
borrowed from Christianity, not only in regard to
ancient superstitions about Jewish conspiracies and
guilt. George L. Mosse, the German-American histo-

rian of Nazism, made the point in one of his classic books, *Masses and Man: Nationalist and Fascist Perceptions of Reality*: "The whole vocabulary of blood and soil was filled with Christian liturgical and religious meaning—the 'blood' itself, the 'martyrdom,' the 'incarnation.'"

And not just the vocabulary. Back in the Middle Ages, the pious Christian warriors of the First Crusade waged war against the infidels and, in their zeal, massacred a full quarter of the Jewish population of Northern Europe, even before moving on to massacre still more Jews and Muslims in Jerusalem—which meant that mass extermination, too, figured among the hoary tropes of European authenticity and tradition, though no one liked to put it that way. And so, in the 1930s and '40s, the Nazis broadcast their insane oratory over the radio, and Nazism's friends and sympathizers in Europe found it possible to respond by gazing thoughtfully at the wall, instead of shamefacedly at the floor. Or the sympathizers could pretend to be lost in their own morally uplifting thoughts, oblivious to the static from the radio. But those were European responses.

Everything about the Nazi doctrines was bound to seem a little different, viewed from the Middle East. Nazi racial theory consigned the Arabs, Turks and Persians to lower rungs of human status. In 1939, as Bernard Lewis recounts, Hitler was reported to have delivered a speech describing the peoples of the Middle East and other non-Europeans as "painted half-apes, who want to feel the whip." German diplomats in the Middle East dutifully reported back to the chancellery in Berlin that Arabs, Turks and Persians responded poorly to this sort of thing. Nazi doctrine on the Jews doubled the problem. The Jews seemed biologically loathsome, in Nazi eyes, because the Jews were deemed to be Semites—but, unfortunately for German diplomacy, the Arabs, being cousins of the Jews, were likewise deemed to be Semites. Nor was this just a matter of cranky theorizing on the part of the Nazi ideologues (though it was certainly cranky theorizing). Anti-Semitism was inscribed in the German legal code, which suggested that, by German law as well as in Nazi opinion, the Arabs, as much as the Jews, were obliged to accept their inferior status. And Nazi anti-Semitism raised still another problem.

In Europe the Nazis railed about real-life complaints against the Jews, but, in truth, the real-life complaints added up to nothing more than minor and local irritations, as with any ethnic minority or immigrant group—which explains why the Nazis, in trying to arouse the sentiments of mass hatred, mostly relied on the medieval superstitions, as modernized by themselves. But no one could say that, in the Middle East, real-life reasons to complain about the Jews were merely irritations. The Jews who came pouring out of Europe in the decades after 1881 arrived at any number of destinations around the world, and one of those destinations turned out to be the dusty Ottoman province of Palestine, which, after the Ottoman defeat in the First World War, evolved into a dusty province of the British Mandate, but which the newly arriving immigrants intended on transforming into a verdant new society called the Jewish National Homeland. The Zionist project was a modest affair, at first. The Jewish flood poured out of Europe, but only a trickle of people made their way to the unlikely new National Homeland.

Still, the European persecutions went on swelling, and the trickles, likewise. And then, once Hitler had come to power, the flood-gates opened at last, and a Jewish tide came pouring southward into Palestine. Jews began to make their way to the proposed new National Homeland from Yemen, too—an early sign of what would become yet another mass flight. Demography in Palestine bobbed up and down oceanically. Jerusalem in the mid-nineteenth century used to be a small town with a slim majority of pitiful and impoverished Jews; then it swelled up, at the end of the nineteenth century, into a big town with a majority Arab population; and then, in the 1920s and '30s, it swelled up yet again into a fullscale city, large, thriving, and overwhelmingly Jewish. And, in Palestine, the Arabs had every reason for alarm.

Only, what was the right way to picture the real-life grievances against the Jews in Palestine? The Nazis, far away in Germany, took a keen interest in this question. The Nazis dispatched weapons and funds to Haj Amin al-Husseini's forces. But the Nazis also wanted—they needed, as true believers in their own cause—to export their own ideological interpretation of events, as well, and to convince entire populations to accept the new interpretations. Here was yet another difficulty, though. Arab grievances against the Jews in Palestine, being authentic, were visible in real life, and there was no need to adorn the grievances with fantastical griffins and horned devils from the European Middle Ages. The grievances, being visible, were visibly limited, too. The Jewish refugee and immigrant tide swept across several corners of Arab land in Palestine, and then across several corners more. But the newly Jewish corners amounted, even then, merely to a portion of the larger Palestine, which itself amounted only to a portion of British Mandatory Palestine, which itself amounted only to the British half of the larger Levant, which amounted to a single region in a far vaster Arab world.

Traditional Jewish communities were scattered throughout the Arab countries, and some of those communities were pretty big—upwards of half a million Jews in Morocco and Algeria, another hundred thousand in Tunisia and still more in Libya, Egypt, Syria Lebanon, Iraq and beyond. And yet the Jews in those many other regions took relatively little interest in the Palestinian conflict. Zionism's Middle Eastern following tended to be minuscule, except in Yemen and in Palestine itself. A larger conflict between Jews and Arabs, something on a regional scale, came into being only at the moment when al-Banna and his followers and allies launched their solidarity campaign for Amin al-Husseini, and the boycotts and riots against the Jews broke out in Cairo and other places. Even then, in the late 1930s, the conflict within Palestine itself continued to reflect the peculiarities of a local battle: the extreme bitterness of the face-to-face, but also the lurking possibility of compromise, neighbor to neighbor. Some of the Arab leaders and intellectuals, not just in Palestine, did speak about compromises with the Zionists, and more than compromises—about a future life of mutual benefits and business opportunities for Arabs and Jews alike. The Islamist movement itself appears to have contained an alternative strain, for a while. Tariq Ramadan devotes a section of *The Roots of the Muslim Renewal* to extolling the Islamist philosopher Rashid Rida, one of al-Banna's predecessors, a venerated figure within the movement—and Rida, back in the 1920s, went so far as to express respect for the Zionist settlers (which I know only by reading a history of the Egyptian Jews by Gudrun Krämer: Ramadan's book makes no mention of this intriguing fact).

From a Nazi standpoint, on the other hand, the notion of Arabs compromising with Zionism or benefiting from Jewish success in Palestine was bound to be anathema, at least to any Nazi who gave the matter a moment's thought. The whole logic of Germany's worldwide struggle made no sense at all if the Jews were not, by nature, a diabolical plot, and one does not compromise with the diabolical. The Nazis figured at first that Jews who fled from Europe to the proposed National Homeland in Palestine would end up being exterminated anyway, by the Arabs, and there was no reason for the Nazis to get in the way. Still, after a while the Nazis had to wonder what might happen if, instead of being exterminated, the Jews somehow succeeded in building a state. Hitler himself figured that any such development would serve as a staging ground for the larger Jewish conspiracy—therefore, would pose a menace to the world. And yet, on what basis could the Nazis argue for their own interpretation of Jewry and its diabolical nature?

The Nazis promoted *Mein Kampf* and *The Protocols of the Elders of Zion* and generally their mad theory of world events. But the mad theory exuded a European odor. The Nazis had to wonder if ancient European ideas, with their Christian origins, were capable of spreading into the Arab world. As it happens, the ancient European ideas were perfectly capable. During the century before the Nazis came to power, some of the European superstitions had visibly begun to flourish in the Arab world—within a few Christian corners of the Levant, to begin with. In Syria in the mid-nineteenth century, under French colonial auspices, Capuchin monks took to promoting the old European folk-beliefs about diabolical Jews and ritual murder. The Christians of Syria were the first people to present the *Protocols* in an Arabic translation. Then the folk-beliefs made their way into Muslim circles—a fateful development. By 1938, *The Protocols* and *Mein Kampf*, in Arabic translation, were already circulating at a Palestinian solidarity conference in Cairo—in plain demonstration that ancient European superstitions, properly updated, could find a receptive welcome among sophisticated Arab and Muslim readers, and not just among the Christian minority. The Nazis must have been delighted.

And yet, the Nazis never imagined that European ideas could possibly sink deep roots in the Muslim world. (They were wrong on this point, of course. *The Protocols of the Elders of Zion* would eventually achieve a genuinely mass popularity in the Arab and Muslim world, and even a full acceptance among the Islamist intellectuals and leaders, as demonstrated by that same Hamas charter, the one with the epigraph from Hassan al-Banna—the charter, which explains the nature of the Jewish enemy by invoking the *Protocols*. But the Nazis were wrong on many points. And it took a long time for the *Protocols* to begin to look, in the eyes of the Islamists, like a properly Islamic document.) Nor did the Nazis expect much from their own closest imitators in other parts of the world.

Their keenest followers in Egypt were the Young Egypt Party, known as the Greenshirts—in the style of Hitler's Blackshirts, meaning the SS, or Mussolini's Blackshirts, the militia that marched on Rome in 1922. Nasser, a young army officer with a future, enrolled in the Greenshirts. But the Greenshirts were judged by their fellow Egyptians to be Nazi imitators, which doomed them to a marginal role in Egyptian politics, or maybe a vanguard role, but, in either case, not a central role. The Nazis seem to have understood pretty well that, if they had any hope of shaping opinion among the vast Muslim majorities and not just among the Christian minorities of the Middle East, they needed somehow to graft their own doctrines onto Muslim stems, if only that were possible.

And so, the Nazis, in pursuit of relatively straightforward foreign-policy goals, found themselves obliged to cope with two large ideological problems, both of them of their own making. They needed to persuade the Arabs and other populations of the Middle East that Nazi theories on race were no reason to hold back from allying with the Fascist Axis—a difficult argument to make, on its face. They needed to persuade a mass Arab and Muslim public that European and Christian superstitions about Jewish conspiracies ought to be regarded as authentically Middle Eastern and Islamic. And on both of these challenging ideological matters, the Nazi leaders turned for useful tips and practical aid to the same capable and energetic person: someone genuinely creative, enthusiastic, talented (in his fashion), indefatigable, knowledgeable and endowed with a soul that Nazis could recognize as sympathetically fraternal. This was not al-Banna himself, but, instead, al-Banna's hero and inspiration, his greatest ally outside of Egypt, to whom he pledged his support and respect—the Grand Mufti of Jerusalem, Haj Amin al-Husseini, who himself, when his time of desperate troubles came, would look to al-Banna, the most powerful of his own comrades, for help, and would receive it, too. And so began a three-way dance—between the Grand Mufti and the Nazi leaders, on one hand, and between the Grand Mufti and al-Banna, on the other.

The several historians and journalists who have lately investigated these matters have mostly dug into the German state archives; but one of the historians has had the inspired idea of poking around in the American government archives, as well. This person is Jeffrey Herf, who is himself American, a profes-

sor at the University of Maryland. Herf's specialty is
the intellectual history of Nazism. In one book after
another he has set out to show how powerful was
the Nazi doctrine—how flexible it proved to be, how
easily it managed to inhabit other ideas and styles,
which rendered the doctrine attractive and persuasive. In his book *Reactionary Modernism* in 1984 he
wrote about Nazism as a philosophical idea. In 2006
he published a study of Nazi propaganda and the
Nazi hatred of the Jews called *The Jewish Enemy*,
which offered a number of eye-opening examples of
the Nazi talent for presenting conspiracy theories. In
Germany he stumbled on a cache of Nazi wall-post-
ers, which many millions of ordinary Germans must
have seen during the Nazi years, but which had never
been examined by the historians—and the posters,
some of which he reproduced in *The Jewish Enemy*,
turned out to be creepily well-designed, examples of
the genius of modern German graphic art. Then Herf
came out with a second study of Nazi propaganda,
this time devoted to the Nazi efforts to recruit friends
and supporters in the Arab countries—his *Nazi Propaganda for the Arab World*, which Yale University
Press brought out at the end of 2009.

Herf reported in this new book on four of the
German scholars who have figured among the post-
9/11 group of researchers—the work of Matthias
Küntzel (who has written a brilliant and fiery essay called *Jihad and Jew-Hatred*); Klaus Gensicke
(who has written a book on the mufti of Jerusalem);
and Klaus-Michael Mallmann and Martin Cüppers
(who have collaborated on book called *Halbmond
und Hakenkreuz: Das "Dritte Reich", die Araber und
Palästina*, or *Crescent and Swastika: The Third Reich,
the Arabs and Palestine*, which came out in Germany
in 2006. The book by Mallman and Cüppers has not

yet been translated into English and, even so, has already aroused a good deal of discussion in books that do exist in English, e.g., in Küntzel's *Jihad and Jew-Hatred* and in Bernard-Henri Lévy's pamphlet on the modern left and Islamic fascism, *Left in Dark Times*. Herf offers a useful summary of those other scholars' recent work. But, as he has done in all of his books, he has also reported on some archival research of his own—which, in this case, has led him not only into the files of the German government but also, as I say, into the American archives. The State Department archives, especially. And he has come up with some extraordinary discoveries, touching above all on the Grand Mufti of Jerusalem and his dealings with the Nazis.

A mufti is a scholar of Islamic law, or sharia, and Haj Amin al-Husseini was this (even if he owed his title to British support, and his scholarly Islamic credentials have sometimes been questioned, in plain demonstration that not a single point in the history I am recounting is uncontroversial). But the mufti was also a political leader—the head of the Supreme Muslim Council in Palestine and, later on, the chairman of the Arab Higher Committee. These were the principal Palestinian Arab political organizations. In the 1920s, he helped lead a series of violent Arab attacks on Zionist settlers and Palestine's traditional Jewish population. The 1929 pogrom in Palestine was one of the mufti's successes—a predecessor of the Arab Revolt of 1936. The mufti was a political thinker, too. He was a master of ideological adaptation. Islamism and Arabism, doctrinal brothers, merged into one in his presentation. He was serious, too, about looking for strategic allies, not just in Palestine or among the Islamists across the Egyptian border. The Nazis came to power in Germany in 1933, and the mufti approached them right away to propose cooperation. He took inspiration from the Nazis, too. One of his organizations in Palestine sponsored a group called, for a while, the "Nazi Scouts"—though no one ever mistook the mufti for a mere Nazi imitator.

He relied on German support during the years of the Arab Revolt. And his activism was more than Palestinian. He played a major role in Rashid Ali al-Gaylani's coup d'état in Iraq in 1941. The coup in Baghdad lasted long enough for the new Iraqi government to sign a pact with the fascist powers in Europe—the only Arab government ever formally to align with the Axis. The mufti, in his capacity as religious leader, issued a fatwa calling on Muslims to wage an anti-British jihad. Then the coup was overthrown, and Rashid Ali and the mufti fled the country—though not before inciting a pogrom in Baghdad, the Farhoud, as it is called (in which some 110 Jews or, by other estimates, several times that number, were killed—an opening event in the series of pressures that would lead, a dozen or so years later, to the mass flight of the Iraqi Jews to Israel). The mufti made his way to Italy.

He met with Mussolini. He proposed to Mussolini the creating of (I lift these words from Bernard Lewis's *Semites & Anti-Semites*) "an Arab state of a Fascist nature, including Iraq, Syria, Palestine, and Trans-Jordan." The mufti went on to Germany. He met with Joachim von Ribbentrop, the foreign minister. He met with Hitler himself. The führer and the mufti posed for a famous photograph in November 1941. The mufti met with Heinrich Himmler, the head of the SS. Another photograph: the SS chief bowing ostentatiously to a serene-looking mufti. And, until 1945, the mufti and Rashid Ali, together with a substantial Arab staff in Berlin, toiled assiduously with three agencies of the German government—Ribbentrop's Foreign Ministry, Joseph Goebbels' Reich Ministry for Public Enlightenment and Propaganda, and Himmler's SS—to advance their mutual cause.

In Bosnia-Herzegovina in 1944, under Himmler's auspices, the mufti helped put together a Muslim division of the Waffen SS, recruited from the Balkans. This was the so-called *Handzar* or "Saber" division. The SS division fought against the Serbs and the antifascist partisans and exterminated Bosnian Jews. But mostly the mufti's efforts bore on the strategic question of winning popular support for the Axis in the Arab world. This required a propaganda campaign. The Nazis and the larger Axis devoted a good deal of energy to working up an Arabic-language propaganda and disseminating it. They produced leaflets and other literature for mass distribution. And they put together an Arabic-language radio campaign, broadcast on shortwave beams that were capable of reaching everywhere in the Arab world.

The Axis broadcast stations were "Berlin in Arabic," "Voice of Free Arabism," "The Arab Nation," "Bari in Arabic" (from southern Italy), and "Athens in Arabic" (once the Germans had conquered Greece). Rashid Ali, the defeated leader of the Iraqi coup, spoke on some of those broadcasts. But the biggest star of all, as Herf explains, was the mufti. The broadcasts reached a relatively small audience in the Arab world. By 1942 there were only sixty thousand shortwave radios in Egypt, according to American government calculations. On the other hand, most people were illiterate, and the radios were played in cafés and public places, and the broadcasts proved to be influential. The Germans thought so, anyway, and so did the US State Department. The shortwave broadcasts introduced the mufti and his ideas to a

larger audience across the Arab world than could ever
have been his in the pre-war past. And those ideas—
what were they, exactly? The general theme of the
wartime Arabic-language broadcasts from the Axis
has always been known. Historians in the past have
quoted some of the more significant speeches. Still,
whole portions of those radio broadcasts disappeared
into thin air long ago. The station managers or the
state agencies in Germany surely must have preserved
tape recordings of the broadcasts, but if any of those
tapes survived the chaos and destruction of the war's
end, no one has been able to find them.

The United States maintained an active embassy
in Cairo, though, under the direction of Alexander C.
Kirk and, later on, S. Pinkney Tuck ("Kippy" Tuck,
to his friends), the ambassadors. The embassy as-
sembled a skillful staff of Arabic speakers. The staff
tuned into the shortwave Arabic-language broadcasts. And the Arabic-speaking staff systematically
set about transcribing in English what was broadcast in Arabic. Ambassadors Kirk and Tuck and the
embassy officers wrote up summary reports of their
own. And, on a weekly basis, the Cairo embassy sent
the transcripts and analyses back to the State Department in Washington. The documents circulated to
the Office of Strategic Services, or OSS (the predecessor of the CIA), the Office of War Information and
other agencies. The documents served their purpose,
or failed to serve their purpose. Then they went into
storage and remained there.

The files from the Cairo embassy were declas-
sified only in 1977—though, by then, nobody was
interested in looking back on the wartime history.
Nor did anybody take an interest in the years to
come, which is somewhat surprising, considering
how much controversy has surrounded the evolution

of radical political ideas in the modern Middle East. Jeffrey Herf turns out to be the first scholar to look into those files and give them a more than cursory glance. And he has recognized a remarkable fact, which someone without his experience in the German government files might never have noticed. The State Department files are thousands of pages long. And they constitute, he tells us, "the most complete record of Arabic-language shortwave radio broadcasts by Nazi Germany and Fascist Italy." Nothing like this has ever been found in Germany. It is a big discovery. Herf has put his discovery to use. With the State Department reports and transcripts in front of him, and with a few glances transatlantically at the German government agencies and their own files, and with some additional glances at the findings of his German colleagues among the historians, he has been able to reconstruct a good portion of what the mufti and the other Arab exiles in Berlin succeeded in doing in the course of their collaboration with the German Foreign Ministry, the Reich Ministry for Public Enlightenment and Propaganda, and the SS.

The mufti and other exiles and their Nazi colleagues accomplished something large. Toiling together, they managed to create a brand new ideological hybrid for Nazi propaganda purposes—a novel set of ideas, different from classic Nazism, yet nicely adapted to Germany's foreign-policy goals among the radio audiences of the Middle East and the Muslim world. Herf calls the new ideas a "fusion" ideology—though, in reading his description and the quotations he provides, I think of it as more of a mishmash: a bit of this and that, in clever combination. The Arab exiles complained to the Nazis about Nazi racism. Rashid Ali, the Iraqi, was vociferous. The Nazis listened respectfully. And, in the face of

the Arab criticism, the Nazi leaders proved to be surprisingly flexible. (Or not so surprisingly: the entire
Nazi doctrine was nonsense, anyway, and there was
no reason not to revise it at whim.)

The Nazi leaders issued a thoughtful clarifica-
tion. In the Nazis' updated theory of racism, the
Jews continued, as always, to be despicable and inferior. But the Arab people, or at least a great many
Arabs, instead of being descended from an inferior
caste, as had previously been supposed, were now
said to be descended from a superior caste. The Nazi
program veered not one inch from anti-Semitism, a
beloved principle, for them. But anti-Semitism, in the
revised definition, no longer applied to the Arabs,
nor to the Turks and the Persians—only to the Jews.
That was an important step to take in the world
of doctrine and diplomacy. In November 1942, *The
New York Times* (as I learn from studying the footnotes of an anthology called *The Legacy of Islamic
Antisemitism*, edited by Andrew G. Bostom) went so
far as to report the development under the headline,
"Nazis Reassure Arabs—Antisemitism Confined to
Jews, Spokesman Explains." And then the mufti and
Rashid Ali discussed with the Nazi leaders an alternative way of despising and denouncing the Jews—a
revised hatred which, unlike the traditional Nazi hatred, had nothing to do with biology and pseudo-
science, nor with updated versions of the medieval
superstitions of Christian Europe, but drew, instead,
on theological currents within Islam.

The Nazis themselves, it must be said, were fas-
cinated by Islam—sometimes out of what appears to
have been a personal quest. After the war, a good
many Nazis fled to Argentina and Chile, where they
could enjoy the long-term protection of ultra-right-
wing politicians, generals and Catholic clerics, and

feel at home among large and sympathetic German immigrant communities. Even so, a large number of other Nazis on the lam preferred the Arab world. Matthias Küntzel reminds his readers in *Jihad and Jew-Hatred* that, after the war, Egypt became, in Küntzel's phrase, "El Dorado." Old Nazis fled there "in droves." They went there because, in Küntzel's judgment, Egypt offered a better opportunity for keeping up their old and never-ending war against the Jews, even after Hitler's defeat. One of the mufti's principle colleagues in Berlin was Johann von Leers, who was Goebbels's adjutant at the Ministry for Public Enlightenment and Propaganda. Von Leers made his way to Egypt after the war and was even able to resume his career. He worked as a propagandist for Nasser, who himself, as an old Greenshirt, went on clinging to his pro-Nazi enthusiasms well into the 1960s.

Von Leers was more than a careerist, though. He converted to Islam. Just last year, in 2009, two *New York Times* reporters, Souad Mekhennet and Nicholas Kulish, together with colleagues from the German television station ZDF, revealed the fate of another Nazi leader, Aribert Ferdinand Heim, a grotesque criminal. Heim worked as an anti-human medical doctor at the Mauthausen camp, conducting monstrous experiments. When he was about to be arrested in Germany, Heim, too, made his way, as the journalists have discovered, to Egypt. And Heim likewise converted to Islam. These men were on a spiritual journey. Their journey may have begun with *Mein Kampf*, but somehow it ended at al-Azhar. They were seekers and adventurers. Romantics, in their fashion.

But the principal Nazi attraction to Islam was, of course, strategic. Even in the early nineteenth century, German strategists recognized that, because of the global power of the British Empire, Germany needed to look around the world for allies, and Islam seemed to them a sea of anti-British opportunity. During the First World War, the German strategists came up with the notion of *Revolutionierungspolitik* (a word I have learned from a book by Laurent Murawiec called *The Mind of Jihad*, from 2008), meaning the policy of stirring up internal revolutions against one's enemies. Germany scored a huge success with *Revolutionierungspolitik* during the First World War. The Germans poured money in Lenin's direction and sent him back to Russia in his sealed train to lead the ultra-revolutionary left. Lenin duly organized a Bolshevik coup d'état and then, having become the new dictator, removed Russia from Germany's list of wartime enemies, exactly as the German strategists had hoped.

The strategists dreamed of similar triumphs in the Muslim world. The Germans in the First World War issued a call for a worldwide Islamic jihad against the British. German propagandists invoked passages from the Koran to demonstrate that Kaiser Wilhelm had been divinely ordained to liberate the Muslim world from its infidel oppressors. In Laurent Murawiec's judgment, this was the first instance of the modern call for a worldwide revolutionary jihad—the beginning of the beginning. The worldwide Wilhelmine jihad failed to take place. The Germans were keen on the idea, though, and during the Second World War they returned to it, their jihadi *Revolutionierungspolitik*.

Jeffrey Herf tells us that Himmler and the SS sponsored the Orient Research Center at the University of Tübingen, which looked into Islam. Scholars pored through the Koran in search of passages that might be interpreted as pro-Hitler, in the hope of presenting the führer, like the kaiser before him, as the fulfillment of Koranic prophecies. Verses from the Koran were matched with *Mein Kampf*, and the results were sent beaming over the shortwave bands to the Middle East. The broadcasters argued that Hitler had been sent by God to defeat the Jews. This one point became a major theme of the Arabic-language propaganda—an Islamically divine justification for the Nazi policy. The idea of presenting Hitler as an agent of God sounds preposterous. And yet, the idea does seem to have taken hold, here and there.

I have been discussing Ramadan's book *The Roots of the Muslim Renewal*, and therefore I will cite someone whose name figures repeatedly in that book. This person is Yusuf al-Qaradawi, the author of *Islamic Education and Hassan al-Banna*. Qaradawi is a hugely admired figure for Tariq Ramadan and for many other people, as well—someone who has more than once been offered the office that used to be al-Banna's, Supreme Guide of the Muslim Brotherhood, though he has never chosen to accept. In the world of the Islamists, Qaradawi is thought to occupy the mainstream of the mainstream. He is revered not just for his life's work and his erudition but for (though some qualities are in the eye of the beholder) his *moderation*: his refusal to yield to pressures from still more radical factions within the Islamist movement. And Qaradawi is revered for his fidelity to al-Banna and al-Banna's political tradition. Tariq Ramadan mentions in *The Roots of the Muslim Renewal* that, at the funeral of his father, Said Ramadan, in Cairo in 1995, Qaradawi directed the funeral prayer. But mostly Qaradawi is famous for preaching on Al Jazeera TV.

In one of his television appearances, in January 2009, as translated by the Middle East Media Research Institute (MEMRI) project, Qaradawi got onto the topic of the Jews. He said, "Throughout history, Allah has imposed upon the [Jews] people who would punish them for their corruption. The last punishment was carried out by Hitler. By means of all the things he did to them—even though they exaggerated this issue—he managed to put them in their place." Which is, I would observe, a testament to the power of propaganda. Those phrases about Hitler doing God's work did not make their way into Qaradawi's oratory from some little-known corner of the Koran. Here was a present-day televised echo of precisely the kind of ranting that Herf has quoted and summarized in his study of Arabic-language Nazi propaganda—the very argument about Hitler and Islam that, in the 1940s, went beaming outward to the shortwave radios of the Arab world.

The Nazis themselves evidently sensed the power in their propaganda. They wondered how far they could go. Could they make still wilder claims about Nazism and Islam, and get away with it? What if— the Nazi researchers pondered this question—Hitler had been granted a new divine revelation, like the prophets of yore? Couldn't Hitler be presented as a new prophet, surpassing Muhammad—even if Islam has always regarded Muhammad as the final prophet? How about presenting Hitler to the Shia of Iran as a Shiite mahdi? Hitler, the Twelfth Imam? Such were the ruminations. They sound wild. And yet, the spirit of the age does seem to have favored this kind of speculation. In Syria in the early 1940s, the ideologues of the Baath movement—the branch of Arabism that most closely followed the European fascist model—set out to produce a doctrine of their own, which could be described as a post-Islam: a new ideology that claimed to stand on the foundations of ancient Islam, even while reaching higher

still into a modern, mystical, national-socialist, revolutionary, anti-Semitic, airy politics-and-more-than-
politics of the future. Baathism prospered, too, after
a while. Baathism was a doctrine with a future. Its
future was in Syria and Iraq, though.

The Nazi scholars at the University of Tübingen in the 1940s were less successful. The scholars
grew disheartened. They reported to their higher-ups
that, because Hitler was not personally a descendant
of Muhammad, he was disqualified from assuming
a messianic role within Islam. Himmler must have
been crestfallen. It was a setback for the new mishmash ideology. The work went on, even so. Germany's *Revolutionierungspolitik* required nothing
less. And, among the workers, no one labored more
assiduously, to judge from the researches by Herf
and his German colleagues, than Amin al-Husseini.
The Grand Mufti of Jerusalem understood very well
that Nazism and Islam were not the same. He was
shrewder than his Tübingen colleagues. Not for one
moment did the mufti believe that God had imparted
a new revelation to Adolf Hitler. Nor did the mufti
dream of creating some kind of post-Islam, in the
style of Baathism. The mufti remained faithful to the
Islamist outlook, and this meant that Islam, in his
eyes, was already self-sufficient. A religion perfect
unto itself, requiring no additional inputs from Nazis
or anyone else. And yet, in the mufti's interpretation,
Islam, in its perfection, ran along a parallel track to
Nazism—which meant that, in the mufti's estimation, pious Muslims and militant Nazis made natural
allies, and a Nazi-sponsored jihad was a good idea.

Matthias Küntzel, in *Jihad and Jew-Hatred*, has
summarized the mufti's presentation of this argument by listing seven values that, as the mufti saw it,
Islam and the Nazis held in common. These were: 1)

Islam's monotheism, which corresponded to the Nazi leadership principle; 2) a shared sense of obedience and discipline; 3) a shared veneration for battle and the honor of dying in battle; 4) a shared veneration for community, and the community's priority over the individual; 5) a shared esteem for motherhood and the rejection of abortion; 6) a shared glorification of work and creativity; and 7) a shared theory about the Jews. The mufti explained, "In the struggle against Jewry, Islam and National Socialism are very close." Numbers one through six among those points are fairly vague and might be shared by an infinity of movements and religions. But the seventh point, regarding the struggle against Jewry, was solid and specific. Here was the nub of the matter.

The entire argument about shared values raises a question, which I had better address head on. The Grand Mufti of Jerusalem—was he on to something? Is it true that, in the matter of hating the Jews, Islam and Nazism could be seen as, in the mufti's words, "very close"? Were Islam and Nazism natural allies on this one issue? Or, if I may whittle the mufti's assertion down to a more reasonable shape, does Islam, in its capacity to unleash hatreds against the Jews, resemble in any large and telling fashion the historic Christianity of Europe? Anti-Jewish traditions on one side of the Mediterranean and on the other, the Muslim side and the Christian side—are they fundamentally the same? Or different? A large question. And an old question. People were already mulling over this question in the Middle Ages.

The notion of coming up with any sort of solid and reliable answer seems to me, on the other hand, slightly absurd. Islam is as vast and liquid as the ocean, and so is Christianity, and the centuries roll by like waves, and sects and heresies bob amidst the waves, and every province of every country has followed a history of its own, and I wonder how anyone, no matter how well-steeped in ancient manuscripts, could arrive at a generalized view on these topics. But, all right, people do ask these questions, and I can at least summarize three of the main answers from the modern age, beginning with Jewish scholars from nineteenth-century Germany. The Jewish scholars knew the history of European Christendom all too well, and, nursing their resentments, they took pleasure in taunting the vanity of enlightened Europe by extolling the civility and decency of Islamic civilization.

In the decades around 1900, every Jewish family in Europe and America with a bookcase and a claim to progressive and liberal values used to own an edition of the magisterial *History of the Jews* by a German Jewish historian named H. (for Heinrich) Graetz, who rehearsed this theme at length. The six plump volumes of H. Graetz's *History*, in their leather-bound Philadelphia edition, constitute my own most-treasured Jewish family heirloom. I open the pages. The historian writes, "The first Mahometans treated the Jews as their equals; they respected them as friends and allies, and took an interest in them even as enemies. The Asiatic and Egyptian Jews consequently treated the Mahometans as their liberators from the yoke of the Christians." "The Jews felt themselves freer under the new rule of Islam than they did in the Christian lands." "This religion"— Graetz means Islam—"has exercised a wonderful influence on the course of Jewish history and on the evolution of Judaism."

A good many historians followed Graetz's example in the course of the twentieth century, and still more have done so in our own age—historians from

various backgrounds who, out of one impulse or another, have painted attractive images of Muslim and
Jewish co-existence and mutual benefit in the long-
ago past: images conceived in a gloriously multicul-
turalist light (we *can* all get along, and used to do
so in Islamic Andalusia, during the medieval Golden
Age), or in a more tepid anti-Zionist light (why did
the Zionists have to wreck a beautiful thing?), some
of which can make for agreeable reading (because
even if we don't get along right now, we *ought* to get
along, and idyllic episodes from the past, recounted
in the present, might inspire us to make better efforts
in the future).

But that is only one view. In the later twentieth century Jewish refugees from the Muslim world
used to scratch their heads in puzzlement over those
admiring accounts and looked in vain for a proper
description of their own bitter and miserable memories of life as a persecuted minority. And the refugee writers worked up a counter-scholarship of their
own. They produced memoirs, sometimes at a very
high level of literary skill, e.g., the Egyptian Jewish memoirs of André Aciman, the American writer.
A gloomier picture emerged. The refugee writings
inspired still other studies by scholars without any
personal connection to the Middle East: a revision-
ist account of Islamic civilization that presented the
Muslim world in colors just as bleak as those of European Christian tradition. Or bleaker—the kind of
picture that you can see in Andrew G. Bostom's fat
anthology, *The Legacy of Islamic Antisemitism*, with
a bracing foreword by the formidably erudite scholar
Ibn Warraq, from 2008. A similar literature, revision-
ist on the topic of Islamic tolerance to the Jews, has
been coming out lately in other languages, too—for
instance, the voluminous and sometimes very insight-

ful writings of the Italian journalist Carlo Panella: his book *Fascismo Islamico* from 2007, together with his *Il 'Complotto Ebraico': L'Antisemitismo Islamico da Maometto a Bin Laden,* or, *The 'Jewish Plot': Islamic Anti-Semitism from Muhammad to Bin Laden*; and other works. And so, a counter-argument has emerged, sometimes in a heated tone, emphasizing the centuries of Muslim cruelty toward the Jews.

And between those two arguments flows still another stream of analysis, bending ever so slightly in the direction of H. Graetz and the benign nineteenth-century view, but without any of the nineteenth-century shimmers of optimism and social uplift or the present-day wistfulness of the multiculturalists. Bernard Lewis has laid out the midstream argument more than once, but I will cite a more recent presentation of it by Lewis's Princeton colleague Mark R. Cohen, from the 2008 edition of his comparative study of Islam and Christendom, *Under Crescent and Cross: The Jews in the Middle Ages.* In Cohen's account, the Jews under traditional Islam labored under a dozen oppressions, imposed on them by Islamic civilization—a status as *dhimmis,* in the Islamic phrase, meaning second-class citizens: people confined to the margins of society, restricted in their rights and obliged to display their own humility. Sometimes the Muslim world, in its centuries of prosperity and power, unleashed against the Jews a violence that resembled the worst of the European persecutions—a massacre of the Jewish population of Granada in the eleventh century, terrible persecutions in Spain, North Africa and Yemen in the twelfth century, and so forth. Mark R. Cohen has figured nonetheless that Jewish suffering under traditional Islam can hardly be likened to the miseries of Jewish life under traditional Christianity. There was "much less persecution" in the Islamic world. "The Jews of Islam did not experience physical violence on a scale remotely approaching Jewish suffering in Western Christendom." Why so? The contrast between Western Christendom's extreme and ever-repeated violence against the Jews, and the Muslim world's violence, less frequent and normally less extreme—what can account for this very striking difference?

Cohen points to the Christian superstitions about supernaturally evil Jews. In his argument, irrational superstitions about Jews never took hold as deeply in the Muslim world, at least not in traditional Sunni Islam. (Cohen puts Shiite Islam in a different category.) Cohen's final judgment, in regard to the Middle Ages: "The absence of the irrational element of Jewish diabolical enmity in Islamic thinking must be considered a salient reason for the dearth of anti-Jewish persecution in Islam."

Is Mark R. Cohen right about this? I will only point out that, if some of the harsher evaluations of Islamic civilization that you can see in the books by, say, Andrew Bostom and Carlo Panella are accurate, then the Grand Mufti of Jerusalem might have been onto something, and the mufti's case for an Islamic-Nazi alliance stood on reasonably solid theological ground. But if Mark R. Cohen is right, the mufti was engaged in a fundamentally perverse and unnatural effort to twist Islam in a new direction. The mufti did give it a try. He and his colleagues scoured the Koran and the sacred scriptures for suitably hostile remarks, and they found them, even if some of those passages were scraped from the bottom, so to speak, of the Islamic barrel. And, by emphasizing the most savage passages from the sacred literature, the mufti and his colleagues found a way to re-express the Nazi theory about the diabolical Jews in a language of pure Islam.

Sometimes the mufti's broadcasts struck a genuinely conventional Islamic note. In one of the transcripts from the State Department archives that Herf has dug up, the mufti assures his Arab radio audience, "Keep in mind that never in history have you contended with the Jews without the Jews being the loser"—and this advice reflected a traditional Islamic self-confidence: the very trait that early Christianity tended to lack, given the Christian dread of Jewish deicide.

But mostly the Axis broadcasts conjured a modern tone of paranoid hysteria. In the mufti's radio presentations, the Jews were not a persecuted people (even if, in reality, the Nazis were at that very moment loading a sizeable percentage of the world's Jewish population onto cattle cars, and Jews all over the Arab world were beginning to contemplate a mass flight). Nor were the Jews any kind of ordinary ethnic population. Nor were the Zionists in Palestine struggling to construct a state on a modest sliver of land, in the hope of offering a refuge to any surviving Jews from other parts of the world. Not at all! The Jews in the mufti's radio presentations were conspiring against Islam and against the Arab nation as a whole, and had been doing so for 1,300 years. Jewry's goal was Islam's annihilation.

The Jews possessed astonishing powers. Zionism's project was gigantic. The Zionists intended to construct an enormous Jewish kingdom extending from British Mandatory Palestine westward into Egypt and eastward to the Persian Gulf—a Jewish kingdom from the Nile to the Euphrates. Or more enormous still: westward through Libya, Tunisia and Algeria, until, at last, Zionism's borders had spilled into the Atlantic Ocean, and even Morocco, the westernmost of the Arab countries, had fallen into Zionist hands. The entire Arab world was doomed.

Or, in still another description, the Algerian Jews and the Moroccan Jews were plotting to "Zionize" their own countries, in Amin al-Husseini's phrase. The Jews, instead of building a single enormous Jewish National Homeland from Morocco to Iraq, were going to construct two separate homelands, with the second of those homelands located in North Africa.

Herf quotes the mufti: "America, which now carries the Jewish flag, wants to create a second Jewish homeland in the Islamic Maghreb and in North Africa, one in which the Jews driven out of Europe and a part of the Jews and Negroes from North America would find refuge." The remark about Negroes from North America seems a little puzzling, I must say. But why should it puzzle us more than anything else in the mufti's theory? The Zionized North Africa was going to serve, in the mufti's phrase, as "the Jewish bridge linking New York to Jerusalem." Anyway, it hardly mattered whether hugely powerful Zionists were building a single enormous Jewish Homeland, or a still more enormous Homeland, or two smaller Homelands with a population of Negroes and Jews from the United States. The intention was, in each case, so vast as to bespeak, on the part of the Jews, a supernatural ability. And, in each case, Zionism's success was going to wreak total catastrophe on the entire Arab world and the whole of Islam. Not the loss of a sliver of land, but the loss of *everything*, unto the rule of God.

Herf quotes a radio speech delivered by the Grand Mufti in 1942, on the occasion of the opening of the Islamic Institute in Berlin. I leave the 1940s spelling intact: "In point of fact world Jewry dictates the war as was the case during the days of Mohammed. The Jews have spread their influence over Britain. They dominate America. The Jews are behind destructive and atheist communism. They have brought people against each other and the catastrophes and tragedies happening now are caused by the Jews. The first enemies of the Moslems are today the Jews and the British and Americans who support them." And so forth. Ambassador Kirk in Egypt, in one of his reports to the State Department, dryly observed that Arabic-language broadcasters on the Nazi shortwave stations ranted "*ad nauseam*" about the Jews.

Ad nauseam added up to an identifiable message, though. A photographer attended the meeting between the mufti and Hitler in 1941, but so did a secretary, who took minutes, and we know exactly what was said. Hitler patiently explained that Germany's war against the British and the Soviets was actually a war against the Jews. The Jews controlled both Britain and the Soviet Union. The struggle against them was a war "for survival or destruction." The mufti was of the same mind. Mufti and führer bonded over apocalyptic phantasmagory. And this, the paranoid interpretation of world events, went beaming over the airwaves, day after day, for years.

The crucial event in the mufti's military career was something that ultimately failed to take place—a turning point in the world war precisely because it failed to turn. In 1941 the Afrikakorps, under Field Marshall Rommel, landed in Libya. By June of the next year, Rommel, with his German and Italian troops, had defeated the British at Tobruk and was advancing westward into Egypt. Rommel was a talented military leader. An Axis triumph over the whole of North Africa and the Middle East became easy to imagine. Rommel merely needed to score a few more victories over the British and Common-

wealth troops in order to conjure, in the public imagination of the region, an image of impending German success on a grand scale. An image of German
success would have aroused an excitement. And, if
everything had gone by plan, excitement would have
burst into flame, in the form of an Arab uprising
on behalf of the Axis—something like Rashid Ali's
coup d'état in Iraq in 1941, except better timed, and
taking place in Egypt and other locations closer to
Rommel's triumphant advance.

The whole point of the Nazi propaganda campaign in the Middle East, together with the material support that Germany had been doling out to
the mufti in Palestine and to al-Banna's organization
and other groups in Egypt, Syria and elsewhere, was
to bring about such an uprising, when the moment
came. The moment should have been summer, 1942.
Rommel advanced. The propaganda organizations
went into a tizzy of activity. Herf tells us that, during
a period of two months, the Germans distributed, or
at least dropped from airplanes, literally millions of
leaflets and pamphlets in Egypt and North Africa,
with titles like "Islam and the Jews" (which Herf
thinks was written by the mufti) and "Rommel, the
Lion of the Desert."

The Greenshirts staged public demonstrations in
support of Rommel. The Greenshirts were in no position to lead an uprising, though. Al-Banna's Muslim Brotherhood, on the other hand, had become
altogether huge by then. Brynjar Lia, the Norwegian
historian of the Brotherhood, quotes a British security document from 1942 reporting that military
preparations in the Brotherhood had drawn on fascist examples in Europe and, in the case of the Brotherhood's "Battalions," on the German SS (which
is easy to imagine: a key figure in establishing the

Brotherhood's military wing was the Grand Mufti of Jerusalem. It was the mufti, with his SS connections, who arranged for military relations between the Brotherhood and the German diplomats). The Battalions prepared what the British document called "suicide squads," which appears to have caught British attention. The British pushed the Egyptian government to round up some of the people who could have been expected to lead an uprising. Hassan al-Banna spent a month in prison. But al-Banna's arrest turned out to be unnecessary.

Rommel's Afrikakorps got as far as El Alemein, west of Alexandria, and collided with the British Eighth Army. The Eighth Army did not collapse. The Afrikakorps and the Eighth Army collided yet again. This time a new British general had assumed command. It was Bernard Montgomery. American-made equipment arrived. Rommel was driven back. Still more American equipment arrived—tanks, this time. Rommel underwent another defeat in Tunisia. Maybe his Afrikakorps was simply running out of energy. My own father—if I may introduce another autobiographical note—served as a policeman in the American army, and he landed in North Africa along with the rest of the Americans in the aftermath of those early British victories, and his principal responsibility was to stand guard over the fearsome captured Germans. Only, the prisoners turned out to be young boys, barely in their teens. My father was amazed. Field Marshall Rommel may not have commanded the best of all possible forces.

Under those circumstances, not even leaflets by the million and radio rants *ad nauseam* in every smoky café in the Arab world could set off an uprising. Egypt remained tranquil (aside from the fact that the Jewish population of Alexandria and northern Egypt had meanwhile fled southward to Cairo, just in case Rommel did manage to win—yet another sign of the impending avalanche of Jewish flight a few years later). The Muslim Brotherhood, instead of risking everything on a desperate uprising, bided its time. Still, the Nazis entertained one more plan. Germany's invasion of the Soviet Union was underway. The German strategists expected that, once they had crushed the Red Army, they would send German forces southward from the Soviet Union through the Caucasus into the Middle East, this time entering from the east instead of the west. The arrival of German troops, victorious over the Red Army, would signal a new occasion for a pro-Axis uprising in the Arab world and Iran—the kind of uprising that Nazi victories did set off in the Ukraine, in the early days of the invasion of the Soviet Union. Hitler revealed this plan to the mufti. But the German invasion of the Soviet Union turned out badly. The Germans never did get to invade the Arab world from the Caucasus. Here was the Grand Mufti's greatest failure, not for lack of effort. The fault was Rommel's, and Hitler's.

Still, we have reason to ask: what if, through the random chanciness of war, the Afrikakorps had managed to punch a hole in the British forces? Or what if the Nazi forces in Eastern Europe had demolished the Red Army, and the Germans had penetrated into the Arab world from the east? What if, under those circumstances, al-Banna had given the word to the battalions and suicide squads of the Muslim Brotherhood, and the mufti's sympathizers among the radio audiences and leaflet-readers of the Arab world had duly risen up in rebellion, together with the out-and-out Nazi imitators like Nasser? What then? This is a question that, owing to the researches by Herf and his German colleagues, can be answered with more specificity today than in the past. A Nazi victory and Husseini's proposed Arab uprising would have meant—we know this, now—a general extermination of the Jews in the Arab world. Everyone knew this in the 1940s, to be sure. The Alexandrian Jews were not foolish to respond to Rommel's advance by fleeing for their lives. But now we know the exact phrases that went beaming outward to the Arab world on the shortwave broadcasts.

The radio station "Voice of Free Arabism" announced, as Herf informs us: "Should we not curse the time that has allowed this low race to realize their desires from such countries as Britain, America and Russia? The Jews ignited this war in the interests of Zionism. The Jews are responsible for the blood that has been shed. Despite this, Jewish impudence has increased to such an extent that they claim that they alone are the sacrifice of this war and that they alone are tasting bitterness. The world will never be at peace until the Jewish race is exterminated, otherwise wars will always exist. The Jews are germs which have caused all the trouble in the world."

Another speech from radio "Voice of Free Arabism," which was broadcast at precisely the moment when Rommel seemed on the brink of victory: "You must kill the Jews, before they open fire on you. Kill the Jews, who appropriated your wealth and who are plotting against your security. Arabs of Syria, Iraq and Palestine, what are you waiting for? The Jews are planning to violate your women, to kill your children and to destroy you." And more: "Kill the Jews, burn their property, destroy their stores, annihilate these base supporters of British imperialism. Your sole hope of salvation lies in annihilating the Jews before they annihilate you."

Radio "Berlin in Arabic" carried a speech by the mufti himself on March 1, 1944—a well-known speech, which has been reported before. Whoever transcribed the speech in English for the American embassy, though, underlined a passage for emphasis, which may suggest that, to the embassy staff listening in Cairo, the mufti appeared to be shouting into the microphone. Or maybe the embassy staff was merely reacting in horror. The mufti said: "Arabs! *Rise as one and fight for your sacred rights. Kill the Jews wherever you find them. This pleases God, history and religion. This serves your honor. God is with you.*" The mufti again, a few days later: "Make every effort possible so that not a single Jew and not a single imperialist remains in the Arab countries." And again: "God will defeat these tyrants and will help us to win, together with our allies, the Germans and the Japanese. We will have an independent Arab state in which no trace of Jewry will be found."

Did any of those ideas or phrases catch hold among radio audiences back in the 1940s? I have already quoted Yusuf al-Qaradawi, Ramadan's admired hero, from one of his television broadcasts in 2009, echoing Nazi shortwave broadcasts about Hitler as a tool of Allah. I will quote another of Qaradawi's broadcasts, likewise from 2009, transcribed and translated by the MEMRI project: "Oh Allah, take this oppressive, Jewish, Zionist band of people. Oh Allah, do not spare a single one of them. Oh Allah, count their numbers, and kill them, down to the very last one"—which suggests anew that, back in the 1940s, when Qaradawi was a young man, something in the mufti's rhetoric and in the larger Arabic-language Nazi propaganda resonated powerfully enough to leave a lasting echo.

How many Jews did the Grand Mufti have in mind? The total Jewish population in the Arab region amounted to well more than a million people by the early 1940s, with most of those people in the zones under British domination. When the mufti said, "Kill the Jews wherever you find them," could he possibly have meant what the Nazis themselves meant in their own broadcasts—namely, kill all of those people? It is tempting to imagine, merely out of human feeling, that Amin al-Husseini's speeches were hyperbolic, in the florid style of a religious scholar—the pulpit-thumping of a preacher with his head in the skies, or drunk on his favorite fire-and-brimstone passages from the ancient scriptures. Unfortunately, there is reason to believe otherwise. Herf quotes the minutes of Hitler's meeting with the mufti. Germany, Hitler told the mufti, was going to achieve "the total destruction of the Judeo-Communist empire in Europe." And Germany was going to liberate the Arab countries. Hitler explained his goal: "Germany's objective would then be solely the destruction of the Jewish element residing in the Arab sphere under the protection of the British power. In that hour, the Mufti would be the most authoritative spokesman of the Arab world. It would then be his task to set off the Arab operation which he had secretly prepared." Herf sums this up: "Hitler's comments to Husseini on November 28, 1941, indicate that given the opportunity, he wanted to extend the Final Solution outside Europe. Doing so was, in his mind, the logical corollary to the idea that an international Jewish conspiracy was waging war against the Third Reich."

Anyway, the mufti did not need to hear this from Hitler himself. The exterminationist wing of the Nazi organization was the mufti's closest ally. He had opinions of his own, as well, and his opinions carried weight among the Axis leaders. The Nazis understood perfectly well that, in the Arab world, the mufti did have supporters, and the supporters were potentially powerful, not just in Palestine, which was a relatively insignificant province. Egypt was the center of the Arab world, and the mufti's support in Egypt included the disciplined and para-military mass organization that al-Banna had put to-gether: the kind of Arab support that would inspire feelings of respect from any Axis leader who paused to make a few strategic calculations. When the mufti spoke, the Axis leaders had every reason to listen. The historians have recorded how the mufti put his influence to use.

I will quote Matthias Küntzel, whose angry tone in *Jihad and Jew-Hatred* seems to me well struck: "The Mufti only ever criticized the Nazi policy when he feared that Jews might escape the Holocaust. He was on friendly terms with Heinrich Himmler, whom he admired. Their friendship was, however, strained when in 1943 Himmler wanted (as a propaganda stunt and in return for the release of twenty thousand German prisoners) to permit five thousand Jewish children to emigrate—and therefore survive. The Mufti, who, ac-cording to a German government official, 'would pre-fer all of them (the Jews) to be killed,' fought tirelessly against this plan. With success! The children were dis-patched to the gas chambers. The mufti showed special interest in reacting to decisions by the governments of Bulgaria, Romania and Hungary to allow some thou-sands of Jewish children accompanied by responsible adults to leave for Palestine. It would be 'appropri-ate and more expedient,' he wrote promptly to the

Bulgarian Foreign Minister, 'to prevent the Jews from emigrating from your country and send them somewhere they will be under strict control, for example to Poland.' Another success! Already issued emigration permits were withdrawn and the salvation of the Jewish children prevented."

And Hitler's intentions for the Middle East, as conveyed in his meeting with the mufti? I have mentioned the book *Crescent and Swastika,* by Mallmann and Cüppers of the University of Stuttgart. Mallmann and Cüppers have made a dismal discovery, worse even than Herf's findings in the State Department archives. Or rather, like Herf in the United States, Mallmann and Cüppers have nailed down a few realities that other historians have always intuited, but that, until now, no one has been able to document. Mallmann and Cüppers have discovered that, in 1942, a Nazi plan to undertake a mass extermination in the wake of Rommel's expected victories had already been drawn up. It was not just a matter of Hitler's vague promises to the mufti. One of the most dreadful commanders of the Holocaust was Walther Rauff, an *Obersturmbannführer* of the SS—which, as Herf remarks, gave him the same high rank as Adolf Eichmann. Rauff's principal wartime achievement was to manage logistics for the *Einsatzgruppen* in the Soviet Union. Rauff organized gassing vans for Germany's conquered territories in the Soviet Union and Serbia.

In 1942 *Obersturmbannführer* Rauff put together yet another unit, the *Einsatzgruppe Ägypten,* consisting of seven SS officers and a larger group of noncommissioned men, who stood by in Athens, ready to depart for Egypt and Palestine. The unit was small. Mallmann and Cüppers observe, however, that in

Eastern Europe small units had already proved effective at bringing about mass and systematic exterminations. The small units mobilized Ukrainians and other people from the region who were eager or at least willing to act on Nazism's program. The local participants provided the manpower. Rauff's new *Einsatzgruppe Ägypten* was designed to put together a similar operation in the Arab world. One of Rauff's SS officers was the liaison and security chief for the mufti.

Rommel's inability to defeat the British Eighth Army, as it happened, scotched the plans. The mass extermination was deferred. Rauff and his *Einsatzgruppe Ägypten* and his commando unit were sent, instead, to Tunisia, where, out of concern for Germany's Italian allies, the unit confined itself mostly to registering Jews and putting them to work as slave laborers. (And then, after the war, Rauff, too, managed to avoid arrest—in his case, by fleeing to Syria, though eventually he made his way to Chile, where he enjoyed the protection of General Augusto Pinochet.) But the *Einsatzgruppe Ägypten* would certainly have followed the Eastern European model, if only the military events in North Africa had turned out more favorably for the Nazis—an aspect of the Holocaust that, until Mallmann and Cüppers produced their study, we had not known for certain.

Those shortwave broadcasts by the mufti and his colleagues to the Arab world, then—those were anything but bluster. The calls by Amin al-Husseini to annihilate the Jews were some of the most shocking speeches of the Holocaust. They were the voice of the SS, hideously translated into the tones of Islamic scripture, preparing the Arab public to join the campaign that Rauff and the *Einsatzgruppe Ägypten* were already planning to conduct.

Here was, on top of Amin al-Husseini's other crimes, surely one crime more. It was a crime against Islam—the crime that had been committed in the course of the ideological discussions and negotiations in wartime Berlin. It was the creating of something monstrous: an infernal blurring of Islam and Nazism—a blurring that drew on authentic elements within Islam, as Islam's harshest critics insist on pointing out. But then again, it was a blurring that offended and betrayed Islam's larger principles of tolerance and civility, as Islam's admirers properly insist on retorting—a corrupting of Islam, a grotesquerie. Here was the victory, within the world of rhetoric and radio, of one Islam over the other. A victory for Himmler's Islam over the entirely different Islam that H. Graetz, back in the nineteenth century, admired in his *History of the Jews*. A victory for the Islam of fanaticism and hatred over its arch-rival, the Islam of generosity and civilization. Here was the crime against which Abdelwahab Meddeb and so many other Muslim liberals, the anti-fascists, have protested from the depths of their souls. A spiritual crime, on top of the material crimes.

Chapter Four
CRIME AND EVASION

Until the last months of the war, every little group of people in occupied Europe knew about their own sufferings and perhaps knew some scraps of information about horrors in other parts of the continent. But very few people appreciated the full scale of what had occurred. Then the Allied armies liberated the camps. Newly liberated newspapers carried the news. Almost everywhere in Europe the moral standing of the extreme right dropped to zero. It became obvious that fascism and civilization were mutually exclusive. The Allies raised a demand for formal and international trials of the chief criminals—a demand not so much for retribution as for the re-establishing of moral and civilized principles. In many places, this demand acquired an instant popularity, or, at any rate, an acceptance. And the demand touched on the fate of Amin al-Husseini.

The mufti was still in Germany. Somehow he escaped to Switzerland. The Swiss extradited him to France. And now a problem arose. The French were keen on settling their own accounts from the war. They set about executing their own Nazi collaborators, not always in a civilized fashion. But what to do about Amin al-Husseini? Large publics in Europe did understand the mufti's role during the war—his Waffen SS division in the Balkans, his prestige among the Nazi leaders, his protests against any softening of measures against the Jews, his propaganda. The man was reviled. Because of the Waffen SS division, his crimes were deemed to fall under Yugoslavia's jurisdiction. The post-war government of Yugoslavia demanded a trial.

The politics of the Arab world raised a complication, though. The Arab world was by no means of one mind on the question of fascism. As far back as the Spanish Civil War, a large force of Moroccans fought under Generalissimo Franco's command on the fascist side—but a number of Muslim soldiers nonetheless fought on the republican side, as well. André Malraux made a point of recording the role of the North African anti-fascists in his book about the Spanish war. During the world war, the mufti and his Arab colleagues in Berlin called for Arabs and Muslims to fight on the Axis side, but their enlistment campaign never got very far, outside of the Balkans. Vastly more Arab soldiers fought on the Allied side, in the British and Free French armies. Even in Palestine, where tens of thousands of Jews fought under British command, so did several thousand Arabs. Some forty thousand African and North African soldiers in the Free French armed forces are said to have died in the liberation of Europe in 1944 and '45 alone—a huge statistic, if you give it any thought.

The mufti and his colleagues among the profascist Arabs called for murdering the Jews and, in the course of the war, quite a few murders did take place, even if the opportunity to engage in a full scale massacre never arose. Still, other people in the Arab world put up an active resistance to that kind of thing. In Tunisia during the Nazi occupation, a number of very brave Arabs took hair-raising risks to conceal their Jewish neighbors and save them from arrest. Abdelwahab Meddeb has drawn attention to this point, with a citation to the research of the American historian Robert Satloff. The enemies of fascism within the Arab world began to achieve political successes, too. Early in 1945 the Egyptian government abandoned its official neutrality and, with the approval of a small majority in parliament, declared war on Germany—even if Britain, the imperial master, was likewise at war with Germany.

Egypt's declaration of war was conceived in an opportunistic spirit, given Germany's impending defeat. Still, better late than never. And the Egyptians had reason to know right away that, from a moral point of view, their decision was the right thing. It was because of the news about the extermination camps. Two Israeli historians, Meir Litvak and Esther Webman, have conducted a meticulous survey of the Arab journalism on Holocaust themes, under the title *From Empathy to Denial: Arab Responses to the Holocaust*, which Columbia University Press brought out in 2009. And Litvak and Webman demonstrate quite clearly that whatever appeared in the European newspapers likewise appeared in the Arab newspapers. The leading newspaper in Egypt was and is *al-Ahram*, published in Cairo. Litvak and Webman have poured through *al-Ahram*'s archives, and they show that *al-Ahram* kept its readers fully up to date. The Nazi gas chambers, the "selections," the decision by Hitler himself to commit a mass extermination, the destruction of a full third of the world's Jewish population, the statistic of five million seven hundred thousand murdered Jews that Harry Truman had adopted—every one of those details was reported in *al-Ahram*'s pages. The journalists at *al-Ahram* wrote about the Nazi crimes in a tone of moral condemnation, too. Nazi criminals were described as Nazi criminals.

Still—here was the complication—everyone understood during the war that, if a good many Arabs and Muslims condemned the Axis and even fought on the side of the Allies, an even larger number, in some regions an overwhelming number, cheered the Axis on, actively or passively. The Axis was especially popular among the Iraqi Arabs, for some reason. Everyone who reported from the region knew that Amin al-Husseini was widely admired. The war ended, but Husseini's supporters did not turn against him. Nor did his wartime supporters find their own prestige or power slipping away in the aftermath of the Axis defeat. Far from it: the mufti's supporters flourished. Hassan al-Banna was their most powerful leader. Al-Banna's power grew. Al-Banna had demonstrated a canny realism, back in 1942 and '43, in choosing to sit out Rommel's march across North Africa. The Afrikakorps went down to defeat, and the Muslim Brotherhood suffered not a whit. By 1946 the Brotherhood could claim perhaps a million members. The Brotherhood's secret military apparatus swelled into something enormous—forty thousand members, it is said, by 1948. Egyptian army officers like Nasser continued to maintain Brotherhood affiliations. (Nasser's break with the Islamists would take place only later, in the 1950s, after the Muslim Brotherhood had attempted to assassinate him, or was thought to have done so.) And the Brotherhood demonstrated its violent capacities.

Even Tariq Ramadan, who denies that al-Banna was associated with "even the slightest political assassination," acknowledges that his grandfather made a practice of at least threatening violence. And assassinations did take place. Also riots and bombings. A new series of anti-Jewish attacks got started in November 1945 in Cairo, Alexandria, Suez, Port Said and other Egyptian towns—originally as peaceful demonstrations. But peacefulness descended into riots. At the earliest of those riots, al-Banna, who did not picture himself as the leader of a mob, appealed to the crowd to disperse. In vain. The crowd sacked the Jewish quarter of Cairo, together with some Christian sites. Ultimately the Brotherhood stood behind that kind of violence, though. Still more violence against the Jews broke out in 1947—and, in the judgment of Krämer, the historian of the Egyptian Jews, the Brotherhood has to bear what she calls "at least the moral responsibility for much of this violence." Al-Banna himself was arrested yet again, in connection to the bombings in Cairo.

And, all the while, al-Banna kept up his solidarity campaign for the Grand Mufti, who was under arrest in France. Will anyone be surprised to learn that, in the atmosphere of rioting, bombings and assassinations in Egypt, a political leader who commanded a million disciplined followers and a gigantic secret military apparatus and who was presiding over a good deal of violence might prove to be influential? Al-Banna was by then a major player in Arab politics. Anyway, his was the popular position. The Egyptian government yielded to the pressure. The Arab League was a new organization. In 1944, one of the conferences that led to the forming of the League expressed official grief over the sufferings of the European Jews, though the full scale of those sufferings had not yet been learned.

Nonetheless by 1946 the Arab League called for the mufti's release. Saudi Arabia and the League lob-

bied Yugoslavia to drop the demand for a trial. The
British grew thoughtful on the topic of their own imperial interests. Should Britain seek justice in the case
of a notorious war criminal like Amin al-Husseini?
Or should Britain seek to avoid irritating the notorious criminal's armed and organized mass support?
This turned out to be a simple question. A Jewish
clamor insisted on going ahead with a war-crimes
trial. Nobody in power had any reason to attend to
the Jewish clamor. (There was not even a Jewish
state.) And, under those circumstances, with fragile
Yugoslavia buckling under the Arab pressure and the
powerful British and the Americans looking to their
own interests, the French authorities quietly permitted the mufti to slip away.

After the war a number of Nazi criminals made
their way to Argentina along what were called
"ratlines"—underground escape routes organized
by ultra-right-wing networks within the Catholic
Church. The mufti's escape from Europe was en-
abled, instead, by his supporters in the Arab world.
Instead of a Catholic ratline, here was an Islamic
ratline. The Islamic ratline took the mufti to Cairo.
The Nazis who made their way to Argentina after
the war found it advisable, in the next years, to keep
a low profile. The mufti of Jerusalem, on the other
hand, returned to the Arab world in triumph, greeted
as a hero—if not by everybody, then certainly by
Hassan al-Banna (though not just by al-Banna). Jeffrey Herf, in going through the American archives
for his *Nazi Propaganda in the Arab World*, has come
up with still another extraordinary document bearing on these events. It is a report by the Office of
Strategic Services containing a statement by al-Banna from 1946, which Herf describes as "the most
remarkable statement to accompany Husseini's ar-

rival." Al-Banna in the statement addresses the Arab
League in a tone of booming grandiloquence. The
statement is a speech celebrating the mufti's success
in escaping his enemies in Europe. It is al-Banna's
trumpet blast of victory—a fanfare to the success of
his own solidarity campaign for the mufti. Al-Banna
calls on the Arab League to welcome the mufti—to
take the steps that will allow the mufti to resume a
position of power within the Arab world. Herf has
quoted the statement at length. I will repeat most of
the quotation here. In Arabic, the Muslim Brotherhood is *al-Ikhwan al-Muslimin*.

Hassan al-Banna declared in 1946, in the name
of that organization:

*It is that Al-Sayed Amin Al-Husseini has left France
and arrived in an Arab country.*

*Al-Ikhwan al-Muslimin and all Arabs request the
Arab League on which Arab hopes are pinned, to declare that the Mufti is welcome to stay in any Arab
country he may choose and that great welcome should
be extended to him wherever he goes, as a sign of appreciation for his great services for the glory of Islam
and the Arabs.*

*The hearts of the Arabs palpitated with joy at
hearing that the Mufti has succeeded in reaching an
Arab country. The news sounded like thunder to the
ears of some American, British and Jewish tyrants.*

*The lion is at last free and he will roam the Ara-
bian jungle to clear it of the wolves.*

*The great leader is back after many years of suf-
fering in exile. Some Zionist papers in Egypt printed
by La Société du Publicité shout and cry because the
Mufti is back. We cannot blame them for they realize
the importance of the role played by the Mufti in the
Arab struggle against the crime about to be committed*

by the Americans and the English...

The Mufti is worth the people of a whole nation put together. The Mufti is Palestine and Palestine is the Mufti. Oh Amin! What a great, stubborn, terrific, wonderful man you are! All these years of exile did not affect your fighting spirit.

Hitler's and Mussolini's defeat did not frighten you. Your hair did not turn grey of fright and you are still full of life and fight.

What a hero, what a miracle of a man. We wish to know what the Arab youth, Cabinet Ministers, rich men, and princes of Palestine, Syria, Iraq, Tunis, Morocco and Tripoli are going to do to be worthy of this hero. Yes, this hero who challenged an empire and fought Zionism, with the help of Hitler and Germany. Germany and Hitler are gone, but Amin Al-Husseini will continue the struggle.

He is but one man, but Mohammed was also one man, and so was Christ, and they achieved great results. Amin has a divine spark in his heart which makes him above human beings. God entrusted him with a mission and he must succeed. The armies of colonization occupied Germany and hoped to catch Amin, but he was too clever for them. He managed to escape to France and now he returns to his people to resume the struggle against the criminal British and against Zionism. The battle has begun and it is easy to foresee the result. The Lord Almighty did not preserve Amin for nothing. There must be a divine purpose behind the preservation of the life of this man, namely the defeat of Zionism.

Amin! March on! God is with you! We are behind you! We are willing to sacrifice our necks for the cause. To death! Forward March...

...America traded on the San Francisco and At-

*lantic Charter but she has now been unveiled and we
know her for what she really is. She used to talk about
freedom when she herself was fighting a wild beast.
Now she attempts to throttle the Arabs, and adopts
the Nazi methods!*

Al-Banna's reference in the last paragraph to "Nazi
methods" shows that, given the reports about the
extermination camps in the Arab press, even the Supreme Guide had to acknowledge that something in
the Nazi cause had begun to look less than admirable—though his statement also implies that, whatever the "Nazi methods" may have been, they were
no crueler than America's policy in the Middle East.
But I am struck mostly by how frankly al-Banna acknowledges the mufti's alliance with Hitler. In the
immediate period after the war, even some of the
mufti's most ardent supporters hesitated to acknowledge the role he had played. The supporters, some
of them, tended to insist that, in collaborating with
the Nazis, the mufti had merely gambled on Germany's victory in the war, or had responded to harsh
necessity, but, in either case, he deserved none of
the opprobrium that was retrospectively falling upon
the Nazis. The mufti himself, in later years, tried to
minimize the Nazi episode in his career. But that was
not al-Banna's impulse.

Al-Banna in 1946 was not the slightest bit reluc-
tant to invoke the names of Hitler and Mussolini as
Husseini's allies. Al-Banna's phrase about the mufti,
"this hero who challenged an empire and fought Zionism, with the help of Hitler and Germany," expresses a sentiment toward Hitler that can only be
described as gratitude. The speech was not an apology, nor an obfuscation. It was a cry of defiance.

The description of the mufti as a lion, roaming free in the Arabian jungle to clear it of wolves, lends itself to no other interpretation. "Germany and Hitler are gone, but Amin al-Husseini will continue the struggle" is a sentence that is meant to stir an enthusiastic audience to applause. Which struggle does al-Banna have in mind? The struggle against the British and French imperialists, of course. But also the struggle to achieve, in al-Banna's words, "the defeat of Zionism." And what do those two nouns signify—*Zionism* and *defeat*—in the context of al-Banna's speech? The meaning is inescapable. The whole thrust of the speech was to endorse the mufti, and the mufti himself had spent the previous several years broadcasting over the radio exactly what he meant by Zionism and its defeat.

Zionism, in the mufti's oratory, was the Jewish conspiracy to destroy the entire Arab world and Islam—the diabolical plotting that got its start in the seventh century in Medina and had never come to an end. And the struggle against this demonic evil? In the mufti's oratory, the struggle against Zionism was never merely a campaign to achieve political rights for Arabs in Palestine. The struggle against Zionism, in the mufti's version, was a struggle that could end only when, as a sacred hadith proclaims, "The Last Hour would not come until the Muslims fight against the Jews and the Muslims would kill them...."—the hadith that came to be quoted in the Hamas charter many years later. Or, as the mufti plainly said, in the single best-known of his many wartime speeches (forgive me for harping on these words, but al-Banna's triumphant celebration of the mufti in 1946 and his acknowledgment of "the help of Hitler and Germany" adds a chilly resonance to these dreadful italicized phrases): *"Kill the Jews wherever you find them. This pleases God, history and religion."*

One last glance at al-Banna's speech. Does the speech contain perhaps some halting phrase to acknowledge that al-Banna himself might have made a mistake in speaking admiringly of Hitler in the past? Is there a phrase suggesting that Amin al-Husseini may have ended up on the wrong side of the war? Is there a suggestion perhaps that the mufti was merely a man, prone to the weaknesses and faulty decision-making or even the criminality of mere humans—a suggestion, therefore, that Hassan al-Banna might have made a terrible error in declaring his reverence and support for the mufti? A suggestion that al-Banna might have felt ever so slightly betrayed or even discomfited by the mufti's wartime activity? There is nothing of the sort. On the contrary: "*Amin has a divine spark in his heart which makes him above human beings*"—like Christ (whom Muslims regard as a prophet of God) and Muhammad. The notion that Amin al-Husseini, in allying with Hitler and calling for the extermination of the Jews, might have committed a crime against Islam was certainly not Hassan al-Banna's notion. If there was a choice to be made between one Islam and another, the Supreme Guide of the Muslim Brotherhood knew which choice was his own.

Al-Banna's decision to stand by the mufti in his time of troubles surely contributed, arguably in a major way, to one of the great peculiarities of modern Middle Eastern history. In other regions of the world, the champions of the Axis and especially of Nazi policies went down to defeat in the aftermath of the Second World War—a flat-out military defeat in some places, a political defeat elsewhere. An intellectual defeat, too. In any case, a moral defeat. Movements of the extreme right in most of Europe went underground or semi-underground after the war, sometimes in fear and almost always in disgrace. The

Catholic Church, which could have chosen to regard itself merely as a victim of the Nazis and the war (and the Church was certainly a victim, on a vast scale), eventually chose to plunge, instead, into a period of sophisticated introspection—the self-examination that led to large theological reforms in the 1960s: an epochal development in the history of Catholicism.

In the Spanish-speaking world, the reaction to the war was smaller. Franco's dictatorship in Spain wavered not at all, even after the defeat of the Axis. Franco's troops had fought side by side with the Nazis, and Franco saw no reason to apologize. Still, Spanish fascism lost something of its glamor. In Latin America, quite a few stalwart admirers of the Axis remained powerful and popular after the war, which is why the Nazi refugees could find new homes in one Latin American country after another. And yet, in Latin America, the old-school philo-fascists tended to downplay their fascist themes in the post-bellum years. Not in every case, but sometimes. The notion of a big-scale right-wing revolution, the fascist dream of a new world order, faded away—in favor of a smaller-scale ideal of piously Catholic military dictatorships. Some of the outright fascist intellectuals in Latin America abandoned their old views altogether—in some cases, in favor of liberal democracy, in other cases in favor of Marxism.

The Arab world, too, might have taken the occasion to rethink the war. There could have been a moment of reckoning—a moment to consider what had happened, and to reflect on who had acted nobly during the war, and who had acted otherwise. A moment to honor the many Arabs and Muslims who had fought in the Allied armies or had contributed to the anti-fascist cause. A moment to condemn the people who, for one reason or another, had lent their own energies to the fascists. A moment to re-examine the old ideas and to renounce what ought to be renounced. The victorious Allies in Europe and the United States might have made themselves help-ful in this regard.

Only, the Allies did nothing of the sort. The Arab and African war veterans were treated with scandalous condescension. The Allies never lost an occasion to betray their friends. During the war it-self, the British had kept an eye on al-Banna, when they weren't keeping him under lock and key, and, after the war, they catered to al-Banna's demands; and, in both cases, they acted in their own inter-est, narrowly conceived, which had nothing to do with the interests of Egypt. A war-crimes trial of Amin al-Husseini might have afforded an occasion to examine the mishmash ideology that the mufti and his Arab and Nazi colleagues had concocted dur-ing the war—might have permitted an open discus-sion of the supernatural theory of Jewish power and of Jewish evil. An occasion to advance civilization, as happened in Europe. Maybe a trial would have sparked a little self-reflection about the confusions and self-contradictions within Islam, too, something like the self-reflection that began to take place within the Catholic Church in the decades to come. But there was no trial. Nor was there any other effort on the part of the victorious Western powers to coun-ter the fascist propaganda. In the United States, the entire matter was discussed at length by the State Department and other agencies, as Herf has discov-ered. But the American officials worried about the cost to American popularity in promoting unpopular ideas. America's short-term interests required saying nothing at all about anti-Semitism and the fascist propaganda; and America said nothing. Or, at least, hardly anything.

And so, the Arab zone ended up as the only region in the entire planet in which a criminal on the fascist side of the war, and a major ideologue to boot, returned home in glory, instead of in disgrace. In that one region of the world, the old categories of supernatural phantasmagory about Jews and conspiracies continued to reign over the political imagination of huge and powerful political movements like the Muslim Brotherhood, and other movements, as well. And the supernatural beliefs and the obscurantist doctrines went on to produce in the Middle East what they had already produced in Europe in the 1930s and '40s: an era of totalitarian movements, of ranting dictatorships, and of war.

Or will someone argue that, in my presentation of these developments in the Middle East, I am making too much of the Nazi contribution? I do not wish to succumb to the allures of single-cause explanations, and least of all to explanations that emphasize factors outside of the region. Anyway, it is not my intention to provide a grand analysis of Middle Eastern history. I wish to make only a simple and modest point—a straightforward observation that, when the word *fascism* is uttered in connection to the political heritage of Hassan al-Banna and the modern Middle East, there is good reason why some people respond today with an agitated rush of memory, reaching back into the 1930s and '40s. And good reason why some people fall into worried contemplation of our own age of indiscriminate massacres and mad ideas. I offer a sub-observation. I note how oddly upset some other people seem to become, how quickly they clamp their hands to their ears, whenever the topic of fascist influences on the Islamist movement comes under discussion. The mere mention of the topic arouses a red-faced consternation. The consternation is interesting in itself—a topic for investigation.

I have cited a number of writers from Middle Eastern and Muslim backgrounds, and I will cite one more, who has published just now a telling fable precisely on my sub-observation—on the peculiar reluctance among some people to engage in any discussion at all of the Second World War and the fascist influence on the Islamist cause. This person is the novelist Boualem Sansal, one of the best-known of the Algerian writers. In 2008 Boualem Sansal brought out an angry and fascinating novel called, in the original French, *Le Village de l'Allemand: ou le Journal des Frères Schiller*, which attracted a lot of attention in the French press. The book was translated in 2009 into English under the title *The German Mujahid*. In English it failed to attract as much attention. But this is a book that cries out for attention.

Sansal has explained, in an interview with the French weekly *Le Nouvel Observateur*, the origin of his novel. One day in the 1980s he was traveling through the Sétif region of Algeria, and he stumbled on a strangely European-looking village. He stopped to ask about the village, and he heard a story about an old German soldier from the Second World War. An officer of the SS. After the war, the officer made his escape to Egypt, and then was sent to Algeria by Nasser to offer his military expertise to the Algerians in their war of independence against the French. The officer decided to settle down. He, too, converted to Islam. His contribution to the war won the admiration of his new Algerian neighbors. Then again, the neighbors admired him also because of his past. Nazism was well regarded in Algeria. And the German officer ended up influencing the look of his own adopted village.

Sansal, the novelist, never met the real-life German. The story set him to thinking, though. Sansal imagined an SS man escaping from Germany after the war and making his way through Turkey and Egypt to Algeria. He imagined the SS man embracing Islam, changing his name from Helmut to Hassan, marrying an Algerian woman, and having Algerian sons. Sansal imagined the sons, two of them. Sansal imagined the boys growing up in an Algerian village without the slightest knowledge of their father's past, apart from the simple fact that he had come from Germany. Sansal imagined the brothers making their way to France to live with relatives and enjoy the benefits of a French education. He imagined the brothers, grown up now and living in France in the 1990s, observing the Islamist movement beginning to prosper in their own world of the French immigrant suburbs. The spread of Islamist ideas in stairwell discussions in the French projects. The enforcing of dress codes by the Islamist imam. The murder of a young woman on the imam's orders. The preparation of jihadi groups for Afghanistan.

Sansal imagined the brothers learning that, back in the humble village of their childhood in Algeria, Islamist radicals have staged a massacre. Their own mom and dad have been killed, their throats slit—which, to be sure, was an entirely common event in Algeria in the 1990s. Sansal imagined the young men discovering only then, in the aftermath of the Algerian massacre, the truth about their father—his life before he made his way to Algeria and became a Muslim. His career as a Nazi. And Sansal imagined the young men's reaction to the revelations about their father. Their response is moral shock: the novel's deepest theme. And political shock: the alarming recognition that Nazism and Islamism have something in common, which is a passion for irrational and ideological hatreds of the sort that lead sooner or later to massacres. A personal shock, too: a horror at discovering something dreadful about their own father. And a still more intimate shock: a feeling of horror at not having known. The shock of discovering their own ignorance. Sansal's novel is powerful because he has found a way to speak about the fascism of the past and the Islamism of the present, and to make comparisons and linkages. But the novel is powerful mostly because Sansal, in recounting his imaginary tale, has come to grips with a moral peculiarity of the modern age.

This is the lure of avoidance—the multi-motivated disinclination to discuss or even think about the very largest of crimes. The urge to look somewhere else—to look anywhere at all, except at the main thing. Sansal insists on looking at the main thing. And so, at the climax of his novel he goes all the way, and—risky though it is for any novelist to do— he sends the elder of the Algerian sons on a tour in search of his lost father and his father's unknown career in the SS. The tour leads to where it has to lead. This is to Auschwitz-Birkenau. The biggest of the death camps. The camp where the father had faithfully toiled for the SS—Auschwitz, where, incidentally, according to the testimony of one of the Nazis convicted at the Nuremberg trials in 1946, the mufti of Jerusalem once accompanied Adolf Eichmann to inspect the gas chambers. Which may or may not be true: the testimony is regarded as dubious.

But in Boualem Sansal's novel, yes, the elder of the Algerian sons comes to inspect. The young man takes his place among the visiting tourists. He wants to know and acknowledge every last wretched detail about his father. He wants to be done with concealment. He wants to give himself the freedom to despise his own father. And more: he wants to assume moral responsibility for his father's actions, which cannot be done. The young man insists on assuming responsibility anyway. He is distraught. And even then, at a moment when the young man has entered a kind of delirium over his father's guilt, the lure of avoidance proves to be irresistible.

The young man notices an old lady entering the camp. He takes her to be a returning survivor, and not merely a tourist like everyone else. He strikes up a conservation. He inquires about her past and the camp. The conversation between these two people turns out to be the most brilliant scene in Sansal's book—almost a humorous scene, except that it is piercingly painful. The old lady responds warmly and soberly to the young man. She explains that, no, she was never at Auschwitz-Birkenau. She was at Buchenwald, with her parents. Her sister was at Auschwitz-Birkenau, and was killed.

In a kindly and courteous way, the old lady says to the young man (in the translation by Frank Wynne), "What about you?"

"Me? I... well, I..."

The old lady prompts him: "One of your parents?"

The young man responds: "Yes... My father... My father was at Birkenau and at other camps... miraculously he survived. I never knew, he never said anything... I only found out recently, by accident, after he died."

The young man's statements are true, narrowly speaking. But they are, of course, wholly misleading, given the unbearable reality that his father was indeed at Auschwitz-Birkenau, and at other camps. Only, not as a victim.

"I understand," the old lady tells him. "You mustn't feel bitter... these are things you cannot speak of to your children."

But she has not understood. The young man has misled the old lady, and he has done so because, although he does know the truth by now, he cannot get himself to say it aloud—not in that one conversation, anyway. Not to the face of one of his father's innumerable victims.

But I have gone on now for a long time about all kinds of writers and scholars and their reflections on fascism and its relation to the Islamists of past and present. The moment has come to turn back to Tariq Ramadan and see how, in his own writings, he has coped with these same difficult issues: the question of fascism and Islamism and their relation. The question of his own grandfather, and his grandfather's solidarity campaign for the mufti of Jerusalem, and the grandfather's steadfast commitment to his campaign, and the grandfather's success at rescuing the mufti from the Allies and returning him in glory to the Arab world. The question of the grandfather's religious reverence for the mufti. The question of the grandfather's admiration for Hitler. The question of the grandfather's continuing influence on the modern Middle East and on the religious and political beliefs of our own moment and on the doctrines of Tariq Ramadan.

Ramadan does address these issues. He takes them up in the course of the intellectual biography of al-Banna in *The Roots of the Muslim Renewal*. So far as I can judge, Ramadan's discussion is entirely accurate, in the narrow sense. The discussion is amazingly brief, though. Ramadan devotes two sentences of the main text of *The Roots of the Muslim Renewal*, plus two footnotes, to al-Banna's alliance

with the mufti. In the first of those references, in a
footnote on page 203, Ramadan writes: "Al-Banna
wished to establish connections with all of the active
Islamic movements in the world. In Palestine connections were established with the mufti Amin al-
Husseini, which would be the beginning of a support
after 1936. See *infra*."

The *infra* appears three pages later, in the main
text. Ramadan writes, describing events of 1936:
"The Muslim Brotherhood had already established, a
year before, relations with Palestine and in particular
with the grand mufti al-Haj Amin al-Husseini (Hassan al-Banna had written to him for the first time in
August 1935 assuring him of his respect and his support)." On the next page, describing money raised
by al-Banna: "This money was principally disbursed
to the association led by Amin al-Husseini, the Arab
Higher Committee, who wrote to him to thank him
for the support." Another footnote, on the previous
page, referring to the mufti: "Hassan al-Banna would
later on prepare and organize his political exile in
Egypt in 1946." And, unless I have missed something,
not another word.

Anyone who relied on Tariq Ramadan's book
for insight into these matters would have no way
to judge this handful of remarks—no way to know
why the mufti needed to go into political exile in
1946, or why al-Banna would have taken it upon
himself to "prepare and organize" the exile. A reader
of Ramadan's book could only assume that Amin al-
Husseini was one more stout-hearted anti-imperialist
firebrand, like al-Banna himself. On the topics of
the SS, the Holocaust, Hitler, and the Nuremberg
trials, someone reading Ramadan's account of the
mufti and the mufti's debt to al-Banna would learn
nothing at all. Nor does Ramadan comment on the

German government's support for the secret military apparatus of the Muslim Brotherhood, and a dozen other related themes—the lines of influence and support that ran from the Axis to al-Banna's movement in Egypt.

I have mentioned Caroline Fourest, the author of *Brother Tariq* back in 2004—the earliest and most influential of the criticisms of Ramadan published in France. In *Brother Tariq*, Fourest argues that, on the topic of al-Banna and his connection to fascism, Ramadan has misled his followers in a conscious and intentional manner. She points to Ramadan's discussion, in *The Roots of the Muslim Renewal* and in his audio recordings, of al-Banna's religious and political program. In his *Epistle to the Young*, al-Banna proclaimed the clauses of the Muslim Brotherhood's motto: "God is our goal; the Prophet is our guide; the Koran is our constitution; struggle is our way; death on the path of god is our ultimate desire" (which is usually followed by the cry, "God is great, God is great"). And then al-Banna went on to describe the stages of his program: the creation of a properly Muslim individual person, in thought and belief; of a properly Muslim family; of a properly Muslim people or community; of an Islamic state; and finally the resurrection of the Caliphate.

Only, as Fourest points out, Ramadan's account of these stages in al-Banna's *Epistle* (which appears on page 281 of *The Roots*) omits some striking remarks. A passage where al-Banna invokes Mussolini's vision of resurrecting the Roman Empire as a model to follow and an admiring invocation of the "German Reich"—these are omitted. Is Fourest right about these omissions? I'm afraid she is. In al-Banna's *Epistle*, the lines about Mussolini and the German Reich appear almost immediately after the passages that Ramadan does quote. Omission is commission, here. Someone could argue in Ramadan's defense that, in excising a couple of fascistic flourishes from his grandfather's *Epistle*, Ramadan merely meant to act as a benign editor, polishing an old text by means of an occasional tasteful deletion.

But I wonder what sort of defense could be made of the truncated discussion in *The Roots of the Muslim Renewal* of the alliance between al-Banna and the mufti. You could argue that Ramadan, in writing about al-Banna, was unaware of al-Banna's 1946 address to the Arab League—the particular speech dug up by Jeffrey Herf from the OSS files. That one speech, though, merely lays out the logic of al-Banna's larger political position. The speech displays al-Banna's loyalties and enthusiasm and his grandiloquent fanatic's tone, which makes it interesting to read today. But nobody has needed to pore over al-Banna's address to the Arab League to know that Amin al-Husseini was Adolf Hitler's most prolix and prominent champion in the Arab world, and that Hassan al-Banna was, in turn, the mufti's most powerful supporter. Al-Banna's speech merely repeated what al-Banna's organization, the Muslim Brotherhood, had already proclaimed in its own press. Nor can any of this be news to Tariq Ramadan. I have already quoted al-Banna's tract "To What Do We Summon Mankind?", which al-Banna's grandson has certainly read—the tract where al-Banna points to Hitler and King Ibn Saud of Saudi Arabia as his two examples of inspiring heroes from modern times, models of audacity and success for his own Muslim Brotherhood to emulate.

The remarkable omissions in Ramadan's book about his grandfather, then—the discreet shrinking of al-Banna's alliance with the mufti to a mere two sentences and a couple of footnotes, the silence on the mufti's calls for genocide and his wartime role, the silence on al-Banna's admiration for Hitler, the silence on the impact that Amin al-Husseini's oratory has evidently left on such people as Yusuf al-Qaradawi, al-Banna's keenest supporters—how to account for these omissions? Meir Litvak and Esther Webman, in their *From Empathy to Denial: Arab Responses to the Holocaust*, shed light on this question. Litvak and Webman describe the very unusual intellectual atmosphere that came to dominate the Arab lands after the Second World War.

In other parts of the world, the educated public took in the revelations about Hitler and the Nazis, and a great many people saw in those revelations a serious argument, surely the weightiest argument of all, in favor of Zionism. It was the argument to the effect that, in the modern world, Jews did need a homeland of their own, just as the Zionists had always said. The Jews could not rely on the rest of the world to protect them. And the world needed a Jewish state, if only in order to solve a practical exigency of the immediate post-bellum period—namely, the question of where to put masses of homeless inmates of the Nazi camps, the surviving remnant, who, having been rescued at last, were languishing miserably in a further set of camps, the DP camps (for "displaced persons"), which were sometimes the same old camps. The people in those camps had no place to go. It was an unsustainable predicament. A Jewish state, however, would be able to absorb the all-too-displaced camp inmates, and this would make for a practical and just solution to a difficult problem—so long as the Palestinian Arabs likewise ended up with a state of their own. And so, there needed to be two states, side by side. The partition that had been proposed in 1937, which then was re-proposed in 1947 and 1948.

And yet, all of this, which seemed logical to a good many people in other parts of the world, posed a vexing problem to the journalists and political think-ers of the Arab countries. In principle, the readers of newspapers like *al-Ahram*, who knew exactly what had happened in Europe, ought to have been able to conceive a similar sympathy for Zionism—maybe a begrudging sympathy, tempered or even overwhelmed by a greater and warmer concern for the Palestinian Arabs and the proposed new Palestinian state. The Arab newspaper readers appear to have conceived no such sympathy, though. Or scarcely any. In the Arab world, where the old wartime superstitions about the invisible and demonic power of evil Jews never did come under challenge, even the best-educated of readers, a great many of them, appear to have re-acted to the news from Europe in a spirit of wary suspiciousness. They asked questions. What if the Zionists, with their mysterious capabilities and dia-bolical intentions, had grotesquely distorted the war reports from Europe in order to deceive the world into supposing that Jews needed a state? What if Jewish suffering in Europe was not what it was re-ported to be? What if the news from Europe, far from being news, was merely clever propaganda dis-seminated by international Jewry for conspiratorial purposes? Journalists and intellectuals fretted over those possibilities from the start, and the skeptics set about constructing alternative interpretations of everything that was being reported from Europe.

Litvak and Webman have compiled a catalogue of the alternative explanations—arguments about the

Nazi slaughter of the Jews that began to appear in the Arab press as early as the mid-1940s and went on being elaborated in the following decades, in constantly updated versions. The arguments followed a variety of paths. Thus: the Nazis slaughtered the Jews, but did so in self-defense, and were right to have done so. Or, the Nazis slaughtered the Jews, which was wrong, but the Zionists exaggerated the numbers, and Jewish suffering was not really especially terrible. Or, the Nazis slaughtered the Jews, but the Zionist movement was secretly complicit with the Nazis, and Nazism and Zionism were equally criminal. Or, whatever the Nazis may have done to the European Jews, the Zionists were doing the same to the Palestinian Arabs, and the Nazis and Zionists ought again to be seen as brothers in crime. Or, the whole story of genocide in Europe was a lie invented by the Zionists, and the Nazis never did slaughter the Jews. Holocaust justification was the most horrific of those several arguments, and Holocaust denial was the weirdest. Holocaust denial, apart from being the weirdest, ultimately became the most popular of those arguments, too—the single "most pervasive theme" in the Arab press on the topic of Nazism, according to Litvak and Webman's study.

But all of those arguments pointed to the same conclusion. This was the belief that, whatever may have happened in Europe, the Arab world had no reason to give the matter any thought. This conclusion appears to have enjoyed an overwhelming triumph in the Arab press. It was not so much a question of Holocaust denial, nor of Holocaust justification, nor of Holocaust belittlement, but of Holocaust avoidance. It was the belief that Nazism's deeds had no bearing on their own part of the world, therefore a belief that Arab journalists and intellectuals had no reason to reflect on the meaning of Nazi doctrines and their implications for modern life.

In *The Roots of the Muslim Renewal* Ramadan cites a number of French and other Western scholars, but I suspect that, in writing his book, he drew mostly on the assumptions about modern history and the Second World War that Litvak and Webman have documented in the Arab press. Al-Banna's alliance with the Grand Mufti of Jerusalem played a major role in the rise of the Islamist movement in Egypt and other places, including Palestine, and the ideas that al-Banna shared with the mufti played an even larger role in condemning the Islamist movement to its endless and hugely self-destructive war against the Jewish state—the war that has brought so much devastation upon, most of all, the Palestinian Arabs. Ramadan could hardly avoid commenting on the matter. But his comments were designed to avoid commentary. He mentioned a few minimal facts about al-Banna and the mufti. But he left out the principal facts. The French reporter Aziz Zemouri, in his book *Should Tariq Ramadan Be Silenced?*, questioned Ramadan on this matter. Ramadan went so far as to say, in responding, "Hassan al-Banna resisted colonization, founded schools, but he also used slogans that could be badly understood..." Only, he said nothing about the nature of those slogans, nor of the understandings that arose from them. Zemouri gave him every opportunity to correct or clarify what he had written in the past. Ramadan preferred to be cryptic. And defensive. Sometimes he has adopted a silence that is not even cryptic. The question of al-Banna's alliance with the mufti was raised by Caroline Fourest in 2004 and by Paul Landau in 2005, and then I raised the issue myself in *The New Republic* in 2007. But Ramadan takes the view that none of this is any concern of his. He declines to respond. He published *What I Believe* in 2009. The book came out at roughly the same moment as Herf's *Nazi Propaganda in the Arab World*. Ramadan said, "I will not waste my time here trying to defend myself." This is the kind of evasion that Boualem Sansal has so cleverly and furiously denounced in his novel *The German Mujahid*. A matter of Holocaust avoidance.

I am struck, though, by how systematically Ramadan's avoidances are themselves avoided in the friendly publicity that comes his way. I glance back at my prime American example, the profile of Ramadan in *The New York Times Magazine* from 2007. Ian Buruma commands a genuine expertise on the vexed topic of European fascism and its influences and echoes in other parts of the world. Buruma has tilled this particular field in depth, in the past. He has been, on this topic, the best of journalists—which makes his reticences in this one instance all the more striking. In his profile of the grandson of Hassan al-Banna, after all, the best of journalists managed to arch his eyebrow skeptically over Ramadan's phrase about his grandfather as a champion of a British-style parliamentary system. But Buruma offered not the slightest hint to indicate why his eyebrow might have arched. The omissions were omitted. Such was the coverage in the *Times Magazine*.

And in the universities? I wonder about Notre Dame. At Notre Dame, that most venerable of American Catholic universities, the topic of Catholic collaboration with the Nazi "ratlines" after the war has surely occupied its share of anguished attention over the years. I wonder how quickly the University of Notre Dame would offer a professorship to a certain kind of right-wing Catholic philosopher—a Lefebvrite sympathizer, let us say—whose scholarly work treated Catholic collaboration in a spirit even remotely similar to Ramadan's treatment of Muslim collaboration in *The Roots of the Muslim Renewal*. I wonder what kind of controversy would break out—how noisy the controversy would be within the Catholic Church itself—if Notre Dame ever did offer a professorship to such a person. Noisy enough, I like to think. A noisy protest did break out when Pope Benedict XVI made the mistake, in 2009, of rehabilitating Bishop Williamson, the excommunicated Lefebvrite schismatic—and the noise and dissension were surely a sign of health and vigor and modernity in the Catholic Church.

But I won't dwell any longer over the mythology that Tariq Ramadan has constructed of his grandfather and the Islamist movement in its early period—a question of history, of which it can be said, as the Koran says more than once (Surah 4, verses 22 and 23), "What is past is past." Anyway, Ramadan is not his grandfather, and Rommel was defeated, and what are we to think of Ramadan and the meaning of his doctrines and historical interpretations for our own time?

Chapter Five
UNIVERSAL VALUES

"What does he stand for?" The journalists inquire. The correspondent for *The New York Times Magazine* put the question directly. Ramadan replied. He spoke about philosophical principles.

He stands, he explained, for "universal values" in line with the European Enlightenment. He stands for a rationalism seeded by doubt. Only, he prefers to invoke these concepts and beliefs by citing the wisdom of Islamic philosophers, instead of their European counterparts.

"Doubt did not begin with Descartes," Ramadan instructed the *Times Magazine*. "We have this construction today that the West and Islam are entirely separate worlds. This is wrong. Everything I am doing now, speaking of connections, intersections, universal values we have in common, this was already there in history."

So he stands for the commonalities linking the West and Islam—for the values that everyone ought to share, except that, in his version, he prefers to give these values an Islamic inflection.

Ramadan's responses were philosophically reasonable, and certainly they were historically defensible, given the medieval sages and the influences of

Plato and Aristotle this way and that. On the other hand, it is worth asking why anyone should care what was "already there in history," in Ramadan's phrase. Why bother with historical chronologies or with the question of whether Descartes came first? These are not trick questions. There might be simple answers: to remind the hubristic Western publics of Muslim contributions to world civilization. Or to hearten the many publics of the Muslim world, who may feel a little discouraged and beset nowadays. Or merely to draw an accurate timeline of the history of ideas, which would be valuable in itself.

Then again, if Ramadan, in pointing to Islamic philosophers of the Middle Ages, meant to suggest that ancient roots are everything; or that science and rationality come in different versions depending on people's cultural origins, a version for Muslims and another for non-Muslims; or that universalism itself comes in different versions, and truth varies from place to place—if that was his idea, a troubling question arises. The notion that science and rationality come in different versions is, after all, an old notion, and not a reassuring one. It is the idea that, taken to a logical conclusion, led the Nazis to suppose that physics came in an Aryan version and in a Jewish version, which were not identical, even if Jewish physics and Aryan physics appeared to be identical; and led the Stalinists to suppose that proletarian science was one thing, and bourgeois science a different thing, in spite of every superficial resemblance; and so forth. The same argument crops up fairly often in the Islamist literature: the notion that science comes in a Western version and also in an Islamic version.

Ramadan's position, then, his grounds for dwelling over the history of universal values and rational doubt—what are those grounds? The interviewer for

the *Times Magazine* did not push his inquiry any
further. Ian Hamel, the author of *The Truth About
Tariq Ramadan*, has pursued the question, though.
Hamel serves up a number of quotations suggesting
that Ramadan draws a suitably careful line between
religious outlooks and scientific outlooks; and Ramadan does know that medicine is medicine, regardless
of its origins; and Ramadan's notion of universality
is genuinely universal. But it is hard to judge the
significance of Hamel's set of quotations outside of
their original context. I see that, in *The Roots of
the Muslim Renewal*, Ramadan describes al-Banna
himself as a man with lucid views on natural science, and this would be good to learn, if true. But
then again, in *Islam, the West and the Challenges of
Modernity*, Ramadan makes plain that, from his own
standpoint, Muslim universalism is not, in fact, the
same as Western universalism; and Muslim reasoning,
with its acknowledgment of doubt, is not the same
as Western reasoning, with its own acknowledgment
of doubt. Ramadan's beliefs on this matter might
explain why he regards a conventional biology education as something that ought to be supplemented
by a bit of Islamic biology. (The Islamist argument
against Darwin has been proposed, I might add, by
Qutb, who invokes the authority of Alexis Carrel, an
ultra-right Catholic scientist in France with a Vichy
affiliation and a Nazi-like doctrine about eugenics
and gas chambers—which suggests that even anti-
Western biology draws on Western roots.) In any
case, in *Islam, the West and the Challenges of Modernity*, Ramadan does seem to regard Islam and the
West as cosmically different, philosophically speaking. "We are indeed dealing with two different universes of reference," he writes, "two civilizations and
two cultures."

He invokes his grandfather's favorite medieval sage, Abu Hamid al-Ghazali, the Persian philosopher. Al-Ghazali, in Ramadan's interpretation, proposed arguments that anticipated Descartes by several hundred years. Ramadan must have been thinking of al-Ghazali when he pointed out to *The New York Times Magazine* that "doubt did not begin with Descartes." In *Islam, the West and the Challenges of Modernity*, however, he goes into more detail, and the details suggest that al-Ghazali's philosophical notion of doubt leans in one direction, and Descartes', in another. About al-Ghazali, Ramadan writes, "At first, we can find innumerable correspondences between his thought and that of Descartes. Such correspondences certainly exist, but the frame of reference which gives the solution to going beyond doubt is fundamentally different."

That is because, in Ramadan's version of Islam (and here he invokes another medieval philosopher, Ibn Taymiyya), the zone of the sacred contains only a single concept. The single concept is *tawhid*, or the oneness of God. *Tawhid* leaves no room for tension between the sacred and the non-sacred, such as you see in Western thought. Nor does *tawhid* allow for a Promethean spirit of rebellion. Nor does *tawhid* permit a sense of the tragic. A deep and tragic sense of doubt is not even a conceptual possibility. Tensions, rebellions, tragic doubts—these are Western concepts. There is no room for anything of the sort in the version of Muslim civilization that Ramadan draws from al-Ghazali and Ibn Taymiyya. Buruma in the *Times Magazine* pursued this question sufficiently to ask if Ramadan has, in Buruma's phrase, "ever experienced any doubts himself."

Ramadan replied, "Doubts about God, no."

And Buruma seemed not to realize that, in responding with this easy certainty, Ramadan was surely offering more than a self-confident autobiographical observation. Doubt, in Ramadan's interpretation, can exist only within the limits allowed by *tawhid*—meaning that, for a proper Muslim, doubts about God are literally inconceivable. A Muslim, in Ramadan's formulation, may forget, but a Muslim cannot doubt.

Ramadan's harsher critics would argue that in speaking to Buruma the way he did on these abstract and historical questions, not to mention on his grandfather's ideals, Ramadan was cagily employing a "double discourse"—a language intended to deceive Western liberals about the grain of his own thought. An accusation of "double discourse" has dogged Ramadan for many years in France. It is a big source of anxiety among his critics. Caroline Fourest, in *Brother Tariq*, documents what appears to be rather a lot of "double discourse"—instances in which Ramadan appears to have said one thing to the general public and something else to his Muslim audiences. One of Ramadan's other critics, Paul Landau, in *The Saber and the Koran*, offers his own documentation. On the other hand, Ian Hamel in his *Truth About Tariq Ramadan* will have none of this. Hamel is a Swiss journalist from a Moroccan background, and he does seem to have listened to a great many speeches and audio recordings by Ramadan, and to have conducted many interviews, and generally to be more at ease in Ramadan's European Muslim environment than Fourest and Landau appear to be; and Hamel earnestly believes that Fourest and Landau, in their animosity, have wrongly allowed themselves to think the worst.

And yet, what are we to do with the expansive puddle of footnoted documentation that lies at the bottom of Fourest's pages, and the additional puddle at the bottom of Landau's? I have no way to resolve this quandary, except to hazard a guess that all of these commentators, friend and foe alike, may have found their way to a reality. Islam, in Ramadan's view of it, is a comprehensive system that takes in the universe. The comprehensive system allows him—requires him—to view each new thing in an Islamic light, as if from on high. I think that, from his lofty Islamic perch, he ends up speaking in a naturally dialectical language, secular (in a style descending from both Descartes and al-Ghazali) and at the same time Islamic (in a style descending from al-Ghazali alone). Ramadan's outlook allows him to speak on a level that is true, and on a level that is truer; and sometimes the two levels are the same. Is there something deliberately deceptive in this way of speaking about the world? Some people are bound to think so. Still, someone else, more willing to grant the presuppositions, might conclude that Ramadan has stayed reasonably consistent all the while, and, if some people cannot make sense of him, that is the fault of his undialectical listeners.

I would suppose that, in the case of *The New York Times Magazine*, Ramadan must have figured that, if the inquiring journalist required on-the-spot instruction into the deeper meanings of words such as *doubt* in their al-Ghazalian and Cartesian contexts, this was not up to Tariq Ramadan. Nor was it Ramadan's obligation to explain how Grandfather al-Banna's intention to abolish the multi-party system was compatible with British-style parliamentarism. I would imagine that, from Ramadan's perspective, with his notion of "two different universes of reference, two civilizations and two cultures," there was not much point in spelling out every last nuance to an inquiring journalist, especially since, in his books, Ramadan has already done so. Some things may be ambiguous, but nothing is secret.

How to define Ramadan's version of Islam, then—his own "universe of reference," the interpretation of Islam that, via his grandfather, he traces back to the medieval philosophers? What name to assign to it? In his books, Ramadan has identified several modern currents and subcurrents of Islamic thought, even apart from the ancient denominations that have transfixed everyone's attention right now. In the *Times Magazine*, Buruma very properly asked Ramadan to specify which of those currents is his own. Ramadan replied. His own current of Islamic thought goes under the paradoxical-sounding label of "salafi reformism."

Which means? Buruma came up with a definition by plucking a sentence out of Ramadan's book *Western Muslims and the Future of Islam*. A "salafi reformist," Buruma explained, quoting Ramadan's book, is someone who aims at the following goals: "to protect the Muslim identity and religious practice, to recognize the Western constitutional structure, to become involved as a citizen at the social level, and to live with true loyalty to the country to which one belongs." The quotation is accurate, in the narrow sense—I have located it on page 27 of Ramadan's book, as well as in a slightly different setting in another of his books, *To Be a European Muslim*. But Buruma has severed the quoted words from some other remarks on the same page and on the previous one—and those other remarks plainly change the meaning.

Taken in isolation, the quoted words make salafi reformism sound like an earnest effort to update Islam for life in a modern democracy—to reform the ancient tenets and interpretations in accord with the principles of liberal society. But that is a mistake. It is an old mistake, too, which journalists persist in making, as both Caroline Fourest and Paul Landau point out with a lot of exasperation in their respective books. In a passage on the topic of "reformism" in *The Roots of the Muslim Renewal*, Ramadan himself acknowledges the potential for misunderstanding in his choice of words—though he thinks his vocabulary is justified, even so. Salafi reformism, in any case, signifies something precise in Ramadan's usage, and the precise meaning has nothing to do with liberal reformism in the conventional sense.

Buruma asked Ramadan to list his two favorite Muslim philosophers for the readers of the *Times Magazine*. Ramadan responded by mentioning Jamal al-Din al-Afghani and Muhammad Abduh. Those were al-Banna's nineteenth-century forebears. Among the readers of *The New York Times*, not too many people were likely to recognize those names, however. And yet, if Buruma had asked Ramadan to cite a few more recent thinkers in the salafi reformist vein, Ramadan could have extended the list into the twentieth century, and some of the additional names might have turned out to be fairly recognizable. Ramadan has already listed some of those names in *Western Muslims and the Future of Islam*—and he has done this, as it happens, in the paragraph directly preceding the one from which Buruma has plucked his misleading definition about protecting the Muslim identity and being a good citizen.

Here, on page 26, is al-Banna himself, the greatest figure of all in the history of salafi reformism. Here is Mawdudi from the Indian subcontinent, whose activities Ramadan's father, Said Ramadan, coordinated with the Muslim Brotherhood back in

Egypt. Here is Ali Shariati, the grand theoretician of Ayatollah Khomeini's Islamic Revolution in Iran—the man who took al-Banna's Sunni and Arab political legacy and adapted it for a Shiite and Persian population. Here, too, is Sayyid Qutb, listed without comment. Salafi reformism turns out to be, in short, the philosophical underpinning for what is generally described as political Islamism, in its various and sometimes quarreling subcurrents. Ramadan identifies some of those subcurrents in *Western Muslims and the Future of Islam*, though in order to appreciate the gist of his commentary, you have to inspect his remarks rather closely, unto the fine print, meaning the footnotes. This is worth doing.

His own subcurrent of salafi reformism is outspokenly Western—a variant whose particularities he defines with the attractive language of religious fidelity and civic responsibility that Buruma has mistakenly applied to the entire movement. But Ramadan's subcurrent merely represents a tendency within the original idea, which has been adapted to the circumstances of the Muslim immigration. Salafi reformism in its principal variant flourishes only in the Muslim-majority countries (and, in Ramadan's book, only in the footnotes)—though my word, *flourishes*, may give the wrong impression. Salafi reformism in its mainstream version, as Ramadan observes with a touch of bitterness, is "almost everywhere, though in different degrees, subjected to imprisonment, torture and persecution." Ramadan is evidently speaking here about the Muslim Brotherhood, together with (I suppose) the Brotherhood's several national and sectarian variations and offshoots in the Muslim countries themselves. The goal of this mainstream variant is to create what the salafi reformists regard as a fullscale Islamic society—a revolutionary goal, though different factions may go at the revolutionary goal with different tactics.

And then, in his honesty, Ramadan ruefully cites still another subcurrent that flows from the salafi reformist source—though, in his view, this final tendency has wandered fatefully far from the original impulse. This final tendency, he tells us, has gone over to what he calls "strictly political activism," joined to "a literalist reading" of the sacred texts, leading to "radical revolutionary action." Ramadan calls this tendency "political literalist Salafism"— which Buruma in the *Times Magazine* mentioned by name, though without identifying the tendency as an offshoot of the reformist idea. Ramadan in his book explains that political literalist salafism has attracted "a lot of public attention"—though the tendency is represented in the Western countries only "by structures and factional networks." This last phrase is incomprehensible to me. Still, the phrase communicates an impression that, in spite of the public attention, political literalist salafism does not count for much, at least in the Western countries.

Ramadan disapproves of political literalist salafism, owing to its textual literalism and some unspecified departures from salafi reformist principles—though he also rushes to ascribe the tendency's errors not to any elements intrinsic to its salafi reformist origins but, instead, to the ghastly way that dictatorial governments have suppressed the salafi reformist mainstream. As to why the political literalist salafists should have attracted "a lot of public attention," Ramadan says nothing at all in the main text of *Western Muslims and the Future of Islam*— although in a footnote he does mention "violent and spectacular actions." Not even there does he remark on any sort of departure from simple morality. Nor does he define any relation that might exist between the "violent and spectacular actions" and sundry traditions of the Muslim Brotherhood in the time of al-Banna. A veil of euphemism hangs over the entire discussion in *Western Muslims and the Future of Islam*, both in the main text and in the footnotes, and the veil could lead a sleepy reader to miss Ramadan's meaning altogether.

Still, the reader who pinches himself awake ought to be able to recognize what Ramadan is talking about. Political literalist salafism is one of the doctrines (Ramadan seems to argue that it is the only such doctrine) underlying the myriad waves of terrorism that have flowed out of salafi reformism—the terrorist campaigns that have swept across so many regions of the Muslim world and beyond. By "violent and spectacular actions" he means terrorist atrocities. He does refer somewhat cautiously in a footnote to "a section" of the Islamic Salvation Front of Algeria. These are the people whom Boualem Sansal has described in a fictional version in his *German Mujahid*—the dreadful terrorists who, in Sansal's novel, massacre the Algerian village and have begun to infiltrate the immigrant apartment-house projects outside of Paris: the people whom Sansal likens to Nazis. Naturally Ramadan says nothing even remotely similar. From Ramadan's coded remarks you would have no way even to guess that, in Algeria, the violence unleashed by the radical wing of the Islamist movement has killed as many as one hundred thousand people. Ramadan's footnote about "violent and spectacular actions" nonetheless strikes the eye. At least he does note a link between this sort of violence and the larger salafi reformist movement—which is more than can be said about the discussion of salafi reformism that ran in *The New York Times Magazine*.

Ramadan has omitted a few pertinent details, though, and some of those details bear on Sayyid Qutb and Ramadan's family. I have already mentioned that, in his interview with the *Times Magazine*, Ramadan remarked that al-Banna and Qutb "didn't even know each other." Al-Banna and Qutb were the same age, but, while al-Banna was a salafi reformist from the earliest moments of his career, Qutb began his own career as a secular intellectual. Qutb wrote poetry and literary criticism. He took up socialism. He was a modern person. He and al-Banna, from their separate corners of the Egyptian intellectual universe, could only have disapproved of one another. Certainly they had no reason to meet. Still, each of those men seems to have vibrated to the same tone, each man in his own fashion.

Qutb, as I learn from a biography by Adnan A. Musallam called *From Secularism to Jihad: Sayyid Qutb and the Foundations of Radical Islamism*, adhered to a school of Romantic poetry in Egypt, influenced by the likes of Hazlitt and Coleridge. His ideas about poetry led him to seek truth by plumbing the depths of his own heart—instead of by relying on the established conventions of classical verse. Qutb yearned, in the Romantic style, for death. His poetry took an apocalyptic turn. Musallam, the biographer, has rendered a few of Qutb's lines into English:

> My brother, the armies of darkness will be an-
>   nihilated,
> And a new dawn will arise in the universe;
> So set the radiance of your soul free.
> You will see the dawn gazing at us from afar.

This is the sort of fantasy, in a cliché version, that Rimbaud used to conjure in a non-cliché version back in the 1870s ("the holy Redemption!/—Splendid, radiant, in the heart of the great seas"). Or Rubén Darío, the finest of the Latin American Symbolists, in the years around 1900:

> The magic hope announces a day
> on which, on the rock of harmony,
> the perfidious siren will expire.
> Hope! Let us hope!

Or Yeats in the 1920s ("The blood-dimmed tide is loosed... Surely some revelation is at hand," etc.). The poetry avant garde in one language after another was awash with ideas like those, for a few decades.

But it wasn't just the poets. Al-Banna's salafi reformism, after all—what was this doctrine, deep in its agitated soul? Salafi reformism was the belief that truth could be obtained by gazing directly back at the Koran and the seventh century—instead of by relying, in a conventional fashion, on the calcified schools of Islamic jurisprudence. And what was al-Banna's phrase about "the art of death" and "death as art"? Here was an Islamic variation on Qutb's Romantic yearning for the eternity of the tomb. As for the apocalyptic yearnings that quite a few people in the poetry avant garde seemed to share—well! here was Islamism itself, in its Mussolinian, Third Reich-style yearning for the final jihad and the impending resurrection of the Caliphate and its global triumph.

And then Sayyid Qutb's literary career turned a corner. All kinds of people in Egypt began to drift in Islamist directions in the course of the 1940s. Qutb, the socialist literary dreamer, solemnly chose to drift along with everyone else. Al-Banna was anything but displeased. Qutb and Naguib Mahfouz made up a mutual admiration society in those days. Qutb, in his capacity as literary critic, played an important role in bringing public recognition to Mahfouz's talent. Qutb and Mahfouz and a few colleagues launched a magazine. Qutb assumed the editorship. And al-Banna saw an opportunity. He tried to woo Qutb's magazine for the Muslim Brotherhood. Qutb resisted. His resistance appears to have been less than total.

At the moment when al-Banna was assassinated, in 1949, Qutb happened to be in Washington, DC, in a hospital having his tonsils removed. In one of the weirder passages of his own report on the visit, he remarks that Americans on the street outside the hospital window were jubilant over al-Banna's death—which has got to be a fantasy, given that hardly anyone in the United States would have heard of al-Banna. Even people who knew al-Banna's name would hardly have regarded him as a terrible menace to America. Qutb entertained the fantasy nonetheless, and this may suggest that, just as Hassan al-Banna had lately conceived a sympathetic interest in Sayyid Qutb's literary endeavors, Qutb had begun to look on al-Banna as a world-historical figure—a titan whose death would reverberate on the other side of the earth.

Qutb returned to Egypt. He found his way to al-Banna's son-in-law, "the little Hassan al-Banna"—Said Ramadan, the editor of *al-Muslimun*. Said Ramadan's magazine launched a campaign to present the ideas of Mawdudi to the Arabic-speaking world and especially to the Islamist movement. Mawdudi's brilliant idea was the notion of excommunicating other Muslims in the name of the proposed Koranic revolution. And Mawdudi borrowed a few principles from the communists. Qutb appears to have studied those ideas closely in the pages of *al-Muslimun*. And

Qutb began contributing articles of his own. Some of his articles were eventually gathered together in a book called *Toward an Islamic Society*. Qutb began a monthly series of commentaries on the Koran.

His commentaries turned out to be strikingly original—scriptural exegeses written in the spirit of Romantic literary criticism, drawn from the heart and not from the traditional Islamic scholarship. The commentaries proved to be popular, too. Qutb signed up at last with the Muslim Brotherhood. A publisher signed up Qutb. And the commentaries in *al-Muslimun* eventually blossomed into his gigantic prison masterwork, *In the Shade of the Qur'an*—this mega-exegesis which, having emerged from the Muslim Brotherhood, has gone on to influence Islamist movements around the world, not just organizations like the Palestinian Hamas and Islamic Jihad and the mainstream Muslim Brotherhood but the Iranian revolution (in a Persian translation by Ayatollah Ali Khamenei, the Supreme Leader of the Islamic Republic) and the Afghani Islamists (in a Dari translation by Burhanuddin Rabbani, the former president of Afghanistan), even apart from al Qaeda.

Tariq Ramadan has every right to insist that Qutb and al-Banna "didn't even know each other"—but only because the assassination in 1949 interrupted a developing mutual interest. It stands to reason that, but for the assassination, Qutb and al-Banna would have ended up comrades and, at least, acquaintances. In any case, Qutb and Tariq Ramadan's father, "the little Hassan al-Banna," came to know each other well—something you would never suspect from Ramadan's interview with the *Times Magazine* or, for that matter, from his history of Islamist ideas in *The Roots of the Muslim Renewal*. Said Ramadan served at the crucial moment as Qutb's most important supporter in the world of the Egyptian intellectuals.

It was Said Ramadan who launched Qutb on his life's work—certainly a highpoint of the elder Ramadan's editorial career. We can suppose that Qutb's contributions to *al-Muslimun* magazine marked a high point of his own career, as well—the moment when Qutb, in his mid-40s, discovered his own vocation. As for the low point in Qutb's life (which Qutb himself, who loved martyrdom, described as a moment of joy), this came about in 1965 and 1966, when he was accused one last time of plotting an Islamist revolution in Egypt. He was returned to the dreadful Egyptian jails. The gallows approached. And during those final painful months, Qutb's path through life and Said Ramadan's intersected yet again, if only because Said Ramadan was accused of participating in Qutb's revolutionary plot—though Said Ramadan remained in Switzerland all the while, safely removed from arrest and execution, presiding over his Islamic Center and his family and his four-year-old son, Tariq.

Ian Hamel in *The Truth About Tariq Ramadan* insists that Said Ramadan, during his last years, put some distance between himself and Qutb's legacy. But that is a late-life detail. The biographies of Said Ramadan and Sayyid Qutb are otherwise intertwined—and, in this instance, what is past is not, in fact, past. Tariq Ramadan's career has likewise entwined itself around the Qutb legacy. Said Ramadan worked long ago with Mawdudi, and Mawdudi's British followers established their Islamic Foundation to promulgate his ideas. The Islamic Foundation has been slowly bringing out an edition of Mawdudi's own multi-volume Koranic commentary, *Towards Understanding the Qur'an*, translated from the Urdu into English. But the Islamic Foundation's most ambitious project, at least in regard to book publishing, has consisted of bringing out a full English-language edition of Qutb's *In the Shade of the Qur'an*—some ten handsomely-designed volumes of which, out of a projected eighteen, now sit upon my own bookshelves. The Islamic Foundation reveres al-Banna, too, as could be supposed. An Al-Banna Hall occupies the English campus. And here, at the Islamic Foundation, al-Banna's grandson spent his year of study, and here he published his first two English-language books—all of which may seem a little surprising to anyone whose knowledge of Tariq Ramadan depended on the *Times Magazine* profile, with its easy dismissal of any sort of connection between Ramadan's grandfather and Sayyid Qutb, not to mention between Ramadan himself and the Qutb legacy. And yet, the connections between these various people are perfectly natural. Al-Banna, Mawdudi, Qutb, Ramadan senior and Ramadan junior—these are, all of them, stars in a single constellation, to which Tariq Ramadan himself has assigned the name of salafi reformism.

The institutional and family ties between Tariq Ramadan and Sayyid Qutb offer an analytic opportunity. It can be difficult to make sense of Ramadan's ideas, given his reputation for less-than-frankness and the lurking possibility of an esoteric meaning. Still, there is a way to put his ideas into some kind of perspective, and this is to stand the younger Ramadan next to Qutb and draw comparisons—Said Ramadan's son next to Said Ramadan's magazine contributor, the Islamic Foundation's book-writer next to the Islamic Foundation's book-writer. Tariq Ramadan himself devotes a chapter of *The Roots of the Muslim Renewal* to Qutb, which suggests that nothing is inappropriate in making such a comparison. And, with one thinker posed next to the other, it ought to be possible to return to the question: what does Ramadan stand for, in the end? Salafi reformism—what does it amount to, finally?

Judging from Qutb and Ramadan, it amounts to a Rousseauism, Islamized. There is a pure and authentic way of living. This is the Muslim way. And yet, the Muslims, who were born free, are everywhere in chains. The Muslims are oppressed by what Ramadan calls "a Western cultural invasion"—which is the kind of language that Qutb liked to use half a century ago (and al-Banna before him). A very great danger arises from the Western "colonization of minds," in Ramadan's phrase, by which he means the influence of television. Qutb nursed the same worry, even in the pre-television age—the fear he expressed with a phrase about "the cultural influences which had penetrated my mind." And so, the road back to the pure and authentic way of living must be found.

The road is textual, and it leads to the seventh-century founding documents of Islam, which record the pure and the authentic from well before the days of Western cultural aggression and the colonization of minds. And yet, neither of these men, Qutb and Ramadan, wants to reconstruct the seventh century brick by brick. Both of them are convinced that, in its comprehensiveness, the Koranic revelation is larger than the modern world and can swallow it whole. They are convinced that, instead of reconstructing the seventh century, they can reconstruct the modern age, and do so along salafist lines. They can fill each element of modern life with a proper Islamic meaning. Therefore they need to read the ancient texts with an eye to the modern world. They need to come up with Islamic responses, point by point, to the challenge from the West, which conventional Islam has failed to do. That is why they are "reformists"—unlike the scholastic traditionalists (to use Ramadan's phrase) who merely go on rehearsing the ancient Islamic jurisprudence, and unlike the starker fundamentalists, who do want to rebuild the seventh century.

It has to be said that, in regard to reading the ancient texts with an eye to the modern world, Qutb is more absorbed by the ancient texts, and Ramadan, by the modern world. The principle remains intact either way, though. And then, since both men are seeking practical results—the reconstruction of a proper Muslim community, as defined by the ancient texts in a modern interpretation—they have no alternative but to put a political face on their religious project. And so, both of these salafi reformists grab hold of modern political vocabularies, which they treat as empty glasses, and they fill the modern vocabularies with Koranic meanings. Do modern political thinkers speak about such-and-such? Qutb and Ramadan will rush to do the same, using a properly modern language—which, if you examine the meanings closely, turns out to be faithful to the Koran. Qutb, following this procedure, sometimes sounds like a revolutionary anarchist from the 1910s. He thunders about freedom and injustice. Then again, in one of his early books he sounds like a New Dealer from the 1930s. "Social security" figures among his ideals. An occasional communist turn of phrase turns up in his work.

Ramadan, being a man of the post-modern era, prefers to sound like a liberation theologian from Latin America in the 1970s. Or he sounds like one of his anti-globalist allies of our own moment, railing against the World Bank and the International Monetary Fund. He cites the philosopher Cornelius Castoriadis, the theoretician of left-wing "autonomy," which is Ramadan's way of indulging in his own anarchist-like flights of fancy, 1968-style. Or Ramadan makes a point of sounding like a moderate reformer in the conventional civic sense—someone with a few practical and well-intentioned proposals, offered in a liberal or left-wing spirit on behalf of needy and marginalized populations.

Yet the modern rhetorics invariably turn out to be translations, in one fashion or another, of Koranic concepts. They are worldly exteriors with Islamic interiors. Qutb, in launching his anarchistic odes to freedom, means to say that, under his proposed resurrected Islamic Caliphate, human beings will no longer be tyrannously ruled by other human beings, but only by God, as interpreted by God's representatives. The libertarian rhetoric turns out to be a theocratic argument against democracy. Instead of Kropotkin's *Conquest of Bread*, he is thinking of ancient Medina. By "social security," Qutb means the solemn and sacred Islamic obligation to pay a charity tax. When he speaks, Lenin-like, of a "vanguard," he is thinking of the Companions of the Prophet Muhammad, the original salafis. Ramadan, for his part, invokes civil libertarian arguments in order to defend the autonomy of his reconstructed Muslim community. Ramadan invokes the anti-globalist rhetoric of his left-wing allies in order to defend the mainstream Islamist movements in the Muslim world. And so forth, through the gamut of modern political concerns.

None of this is meant to deceive anyone. These people are trying to conduct a thorough "reform" of Islam, and only secondarily the world—a campaign to ensure that Islamic thinking will expand to match each new innovation of modern life, without losing touch with the original revelation. So they look for modern concepts and Koranic equivalents (or other scriptural equivalents from early Islam), and they fill the modern with the scriptural. And, having figured out how to speak about Islam and the modern world in a properly integrated fashion, they set about posing their challenges to the unreformed Muslims and to everyone else, as well.

The challenges they pose turn out to be different, however. Qutb wrote his Islamist commentaries and analyses in the years between the mid-1940s and 1966, and, like the fascists in those years, or the Marxists, he pictured the entire world hurtling toward a catastrophic crisis, which he interpreted along paranoid and apocalyptic lines. His vision of the impending collapse of both the capitalist West and the East Bloc world of Soviet Communism, his vision of an Islamic vanguard establishing a revolutionary Islamic state somewhere on earth and using that one lonely outpost to export Islamic revolution to the rest of the Muslim world and then to everywhere else, his vision of the Koranic utopia to come, the resurrected Caliphate, and his dedication, meanwhile, to martyrdom—all of this was visibly extreme. His whole instinct was to take al-Banna's already pop-eyed Mussolinian idea about resurrecting the Islamic Empire and give it a desperado extra twist. Qutb's revolutionary ideas enjoyed, to be sure, one great advantage over fascism and communism, and this was Islam, an exceptionally sturdy base on which to rest a radical new program—a sturdier base than German philosophy has ever offered, either in its right-wing fascist versions or its left-wing Marxist versions. Still, Qutb's revolutionary theory conformed to the mid-twentieth-century mode.

Tariq Ramadan and his own ideas bear no relation to any of this. Ramadan is post-paranoid and
post-apocalyptic. He thinks that Western-dominated
globalization produces the poverty of the underdevel-
oped "south," which includes the Muslim world. He
thinks that globalization ought to be resisted. He is
furious about Western assaults on the Muslim world,
which to his eyes seem to be taking place no matter what the big Western powers happen to be doing or not doing—failing for such a long time in the
1990s to intervene in Bosnia on behalf of the Muslims
there, or choosing to intervene in Afghanistan, which
strikes Ramadan as an American "retaliation against
the people of Afghanistan." In the 1990s he swelled
with indignation at the sanctions imposed by America
and its allies on Saddam Hussein's Iraq, and a few
years later he swelled with still more indignation at
the invasion that overthrew Saddam. Everything the
United States does strikes him as something of a plot;
but this is not unusual. He does not seem obsessed
by an impending world catastrophe. He has no intention of launching revolutionary wars. He adheres to
the preaching, or *dawa*, school of salafi reformism
(which, to be sure, is most prominently articulated
by Yusuf al-Qaradawi, just to show that, among *dawa*'s leaders, preaching has its limits). But Ramadan's
chief idea is to construct an Islamic counter-culture
within the West—a counter-culture that, instead of
withdrawing behind ghetto walls, will take its place
within the larger, modern, non-Muslim society.

He wants a share of the public space, not just
a share of the private sphere. Or more than wants:
he demands a share of the public space. A properly Muslim life is physical and communal and not
just spiritual and internal, and it must be lived in
physical space, and this will require modifications in

the strictly secular system that dominates Europe to-day. Therefore he needs to stick a few sharp elbows into the larger society, demanding his extra space. Or does he harbor still other dreams—clandestine extravaganzas of the imagination, hidden from the public? Maybe he does, on some theological level, as his critics have suggested. This would not be un-usual. Great religions dream great dreams; and great dreams are bound to be dangerous. His harshest crit-ics worry about something more worldly, though. They suspect that, in secret, Ramadan nurses the larger pop-eyed and more-than-theological Islamist aspiration—the Islamic conquest of the world, pic-tured as a practical campaign. The critics suspect that Ramadan intends to deploy his proposed new European Muslim counter-culture as a fifth column for the Muslim Brotherhood and its own resurrec-tion of the Caliphate.

Exactly why Ramadan's critics in Europe would entertain these panicky thoughts ought not to puzzle us. The Muslim emigration to Western Europe dur-ing the last three or four decades has turned out to be one of history's huger events—vast, unexpected, and headed toward a future that no one can pre-dict. In scattered places across Western Europe, old-stock populations wake up today to discover that newly-arrived immigrants from distant corners of the Muslim world have suddenly come to dominate whole neighborhoods, and Arabic and Turkish have begun to outpace some of the smaller European lan-guages, and wild-eyed Islamist groups are demanding censorship of one thing or another, or are insisting on less health care (e.g., forbidding women to see male doctors) or on gender-segregated beaches, or are making their peculiar curricular demands about Voltaire, Darwin and the history of Nazism. One or another exotically costumed Islamist scholar is always delivering fantastical sermons about the impending Muslim conquest of the world, which can be cited as evidence of a giant conspiracy. And it is true that, in Europe, the Muslim Brotherhood and similar groups are prospering among the immigrant populations, not to mention Qutb's radical fringe groups, who are thoroughly terrifying, not to mention some non-Qutbian groups. And it is true that, at times, the Muslim Brotherhood, even in modern times, does seem to cultivate a taste for deception and conspiracy. And it is true that Tariq Ramadan has worked up some ideas regarding the Muslim advance, and he wants his Muslim counter-culture to prosper and grow, and wants his counter-culture to defend and strengthen the mainstream Islamist organizations of the Muslim world, which can only mean the Muslim Brotherhood.

Still, my own reading of Ramadan has never led me to suppose that he is engaged in some kind of elaborate conspiracy or is acting on a secret plan. He does entertain a worldwide ambition, but the ambition, so far as I can judge, is what he says it is. He wants his Muslim counter-culture in the West to assume a shape of its own, under the name of "Western Islam"—though, to be sure, by this phrase he does not mean what someone like Bassam Tibi, the liberal, means by "Euro-Islam." Ramadan means a salafi reformism, and not a Westernized Islam—a salafi reformism that has taken into account the conditions and vocabulary of the Western countries, and yet has remained faithful to the seventh century. He would like his salafi counter-culture to become a main center, instead of a faraway outpost, of the larger Muslim world. The ambition is large. It is not a millenarian eschatology, though.

Judged on strictly literary grounds, there is no comparison between Qutb and Ramadan. Even in translation, Qutb commands a prose style of his own, serene, discursive and grand, punctuated with an occasional note of hysteria, just to keep you on the edge of your chair. Qutb's background in literary criticism allows him to comment easily on the Koran and its own style and mood. His writing enjoys the advantage of the Koran itself, which is the center of his attention. His commentaries betray no embarrassment in noting the seventh-century barbarities, whenever the barbarities seem apropos—the cruel amputations and other punishments ordained by *huddud*, the penal code, which Qutb carefully discusses ("In case of a third or fourth theft, scholars have different views as to what is cut off," and so forth). Amputation, considered as a sacred obligation, adds a peculiar thrill to his writings, a *frisson* of the weird and the forbidden that seems all the more powerful because, at those moments especially, the sonority of his voice remains preternaturally calm and tranquil: the tone of a man speaking with confidence about things that are cosmically true.

Qutb rains mighty blows upon the Jews, and yet he is not the Grand Mufti of Jerusalem, and he generally refrains from screaming. He scrupulously acknowledges that, in certain of its verses, the Koran shows compassion or kindliness to this or that individual Jew. Still, Qutb does not draw from the generous and tolerant passages anything resembling the compassionate and kindly Islam that H. Graetz evoked long ago in his *History of the Jews*. Qutb prefers the *other* passages: the Koran's angry descriptions of Jewish treachery and enmity during the Prophet Muhammad's years in Medina, the descriptions that, in Qutb's estimation, represent the eternal

Jewish traits. From time to time in his Koranic commentaries, Qutb invokes *The Protocols of the Elders
of Zion*, in a simple display of the Nazis' success,
over the long haul, at grafting the European superstitions onto their own preferred version of Islam. And
yet, from Qutb's point of view, his references to the
Protocols merely illustrate how sincere and practical
is the salafi reformist desire to stay abreast of the
modern world and its latest ideas. Nazism, after all,
was a modern movement, and a classic text of Nazi
propaganda could only be a modern text.

Tariq Ramadan, by contrast, who has never lan-
guished in an Egyptian jail, has never managed to
work up a reliable prose style, either. Sometimes Ramadan writes in a heated and emotional tone, personal, slightly archaic, grim and tight-lipped. The very
first sentences of Ramadan's *Islam, the West and the
Challenges of Modernity* offer a breathless description
of an unnamed person who turns out to be the author's father: "I still have the intimate memory of his
presence and of his silences. Sometimes, long silences
sunk in memory and thoughts and, often, in bitterness. He had a keen eye and penetrating look that
now carried his warmth, kindness and tears, and now
armed his determination, commitment and anger."

At other moments Ramadan lapses into a faux
esoteric and ecumenical guru tone, suitable for all
denominations. The first sentence of his biography
of Muhammad, *In the Footsteps of the Prophet*: "In
the hours of dawn when this book was written, there
was silence, meditative solitude, and the experience
of a journey, beyond time and space, toward the
heart, the essence of spiritual quest, and initiation
into meaning."

But mostly Ramadan produces a solid, professorial expository prose, unremarkable, orderly and

clear, even if some of the clarity turns a bit cloudy in the course of translation from the French. He never even toys with the idea that pulses so insistently within Qutb's Koranic commentaries—the idea that, merely by flipping through the pages, you are engaged in a brave and pious action, like a soldier embarking on a dangerous mission. Ramadan does not inspire, but neither does he incite. He is not a hater. Sulfurous odors do not seep upward from the page. Nor any other odors. Ramadan, considered as a prose writer, tends to be indifferent to smell, color, melody and rhythm. His philosophical heroes from the Middle Ages, al-Ghazali and Ibn Taymiyya, wrote their tracts in exalted tones of mysterious grandeur. But when Ramadan comments on these people, the medieval intensities discreetly fade away, and exaltation flattens into a spirit of level-headed calm, until, like the Koranic Jews who are supernaturally transmogrified into apes and pigs, the medieval sages appear to have been transmogrified into law-school professors, emotionless and dry.

Ramadan's biography of the Prophet appears to have fallen under a steamroller. "Life went on in Medina." "The situation had become difficult for the Muslim community in Medina." "The Muslims returned to Medina and daily life had resumed its course, in a far less tense atmosphere than before." The Prophet himself is presented as a nice person. Muhammad adores his first wife: "He loved her so much." Also his other wives. The vexing contradictions that pop up in the Koran, which Qutb enjoys disentangling, pretty much disappear from Ramadan's account. On the topic of the Jews—to stick with the controversies in Medina—Ramadan presents Muhammad as thoughtful and just. The Jews behave badly. And yet, as Ramadan puts it, "those developments by no means affected the principles underlying the relationship between Muslims and Jews: mutual recognition and respect, as well as justice before the law or in the settlement of disputes between individuals and/or groups." Muhammad orders the massacre of all the males of a Jewish tribe. But Ramadan makes clear that, in issuing his order, Muhammad has acted out of a need to impose a stern lesson on his enemies, Jewish and otherwise. The lesson takes hold, too, and no further massacres are required—thus demonstrating Muhammad's wisdom and even his restraint.

From the standpoint of ethics instruction, Ramadan's presentation of these several matters is altogether commendable. It is very nearly Graetzian. Certain of the passages could lead you to suspect that, if Islamic scholars ever wanted to spell out a scriptural basis for Muslim recognition of a modest Jewish state, the prophetic revelations might prove to be, upon examination, more elastically flexible than previously imagined. On the other hand, the tone of civic virtue and multicultural piety can begin to seem overdone after a while. You find yourself wondering if some crucial element hasn't been deleted or suppressed in Ramadan's account of seventh-century affairs, just as in his interview with the *Times Magazine* or in his discussion of Hassan al-Banna in *The Roots of the Muslim Renewal*.

His books, not just the one about his grandfather, do seem a little bowdlerized. Sometimes he strikes a peculiar chord, which appears to consist of three parts harmony, and two parts rancor. His book *What I Believe*, from 2009, presents a program for a revitalized Islam in a version so bland and uncontroversial that no reasonable and open-minded person could possibly object. And yet, Ramadan introduces his program by fulminating for several pages against his critics and detractors, whom he regards as odious; and he concludes the discussion by fulminating for another several pages, and now and then he sprinkles still more embittered complaints into the middle of the text, as well. He refers darkly to an unnamed "ideology and/or interests" that appears to animate his enemies. And the combination of these several tones, the affectless and the furious, makes you wonder yet again—makes me, at least, wonder—if some quirk in his thinking hasn't been conveniently hidden from sight. A theory about conspiratorial Jews, maybe? A few ideas concerning terrorism? Women's rights? I do not bring up these three particulars to be provocative. Ramadan's polemics during the last few years have touched on these questions exactly: Jews, violence and women. And the history of his polemics pulls me back into one last tour through my larger theme: the double ambiguity of Tariq Ramadan's Genevan opinions and their shimmery Lake Léman reflections in the general press.

Chapter Six
THE PEOPLE ON THE LEFT

As for the People on the Left: how miserable will be the People on the Left!
   —The Koran, Surah 56, verse 41

Tariq Ramadan and the Jews, then—the Jews of our own time, and not of seventh-century Medina, nor even of the 1940s.

Buruma's *New York Times Magazine* profile of Ramadan looked into this matter. Buruma recounted the history of one of Ramadan's principle polemics from the last several years—an argument that Ramadan launched in 2003, whose reverberations, in the years since then, have never entirely faded away. Ramadan wrote a brief and angry essay called "Critique of the (New) Communitarian Intellectuals," which he sent to *Le Monde* and a series of other journals. The various editors declined to publish it. Therefore he published it himself online—where the essay attracted quite as much attention as would have happened on paper.

The essay named six well-known writers in France whom Ramadan designated as Jews. These people were Pierre-André Taguieff, Alexandre Adler,

André Glucksmann, Bernard-Henri Lévy, Alain Finkielkraut and Bernard Kouchner. And Ramadan leveled an accusation. In his judgment, those six distinguished people had abandoned a commitment to the universal principles of truth and justice that ought to animate anyone with a claim on the lofty office of *intellectual*. And, having abandoned their high principles, they had sunk to the lowly status of being mere—but I will quote Buruma's summary from the *Times Magazine*—"knee-jerk defenders of Israel."

Was this accusation reasonable or fair on Ramadan's part? The *Magazine* summary concluded otherwise. The six intellectuals under accusation, in Buruma's judgment, "had all championed many causes other than Israel, including putting a stop to the mass murder of Muslims in Bosnia." Still, Buruma, in his even-handed way, left an impression that something about those six intellectuals might, in fact, be open to criticism. He likened the intellectuals to "many early neoconservatives" in the United States— and this comparison, which might have struck five or six readers of the *Times Magazine* as an objective and judicious evaluation, was bound to strike the magazine's other million readers as a withering condemnation. The readers might even have surmised that Ramadan's selected group of erring intellectuals could, in all fairness, be described as knee-jerk defenders of Israel. What does anyone mean, after all, by this terrible epithet, *neoconservative*, if not, among others things, tub-thumping for Israel? And Buruma went on.

He observed that, after Ramadan had launched his original "Critique," two of the writers under accusation, Glucksmann and Lévy, came out with counter-critiques of their own, which boiled down to accusing Ramadan of anti-Semitism. This seemed to Buruma outrageous—"shrill" responses, "vastly over-blown." And harmful. Accusations of this sort, Buruma observed, "have a way of sticking to their target." And yet Ramadan, in his estimation, "is in fact one of the few Muslim intellectuals to speak out against anti-Semitism."

Such was the account in the *Times Magazine*. There were reasons to wonder about it, strictly on journalistic grounds. In his "Critique of the (New) Communitarian Intellectuals," back in 2003, Ramadan's chief complaint about the people whom he described as Jews did not add up to calling them, in Buruma's phrase, "knee-jerk defenders of Israel." Ramadan accused the intellectuals, more subtly, of having abandoned the universal principles of reason and fairness in favor of militating for the narrow interest of their own ethnic or religious group, the Jews. He accused his six intellectuals, in short, of committing the crime that every educated reader in France would remember at least dimly from a classic pamphlet of the 1920s, *The Treason of the Intellectuals*, by Julien Benda: the crime of promoting one's own little community over everyone else. The crime of bathing ethnic self-promotion in a light of universal rationality. The worst of all crimes, for an intellectual. A perversion of reason. Nor did this have to do merely with Israel.

Ramadan accused his six intellectuals primarily of having made a false issue of anti-Semitism in present-day France—a false or misleading contention that, in France, a new kind of pernicious bigotry against the Jews has lately arisen and blossomed into something of a problem. The writer who has chiefly advanced this notion is the historian Pierre-André Taguieff, the author of a book called *La Nouvelle Judéophobie*, or *The New Judeophobia* (which has been published in the United States under the baffling title, *Rising from the Muck: The New Anti-Semitism in Europe*). Taguieff made the argument that Europe and the Muslim countries have lately been seeing, in his words, "a wave of Judeophobia unprecedented in scale or intensity in the post-Nazi period." This was precisely what Ramadan wished to complain about. Ramadan duly placed Taguieff at the head of his list of ethnically-motivated, unethical intellectuals, which, from Ramadan's perspective, was a logical thing to do, given the main thrust and large influence of Taguieff's argument. But it was also a blunder, given that, despite the Eastern European sound of Taguieff's name, the man does not happen to be Jewish. Buruma duly noted Ramadan's error in the *Times Magazine*.

The accusation against Taguieff nonetheless raised a question, which remains a question regardless of ancestry or religious affiliation. To wit, does Taguieff's argument about a "new Judeophobia" reflect some kind of communal loyalty to the Jews on his part, perhaps a loyalty that he has freely chosen for one reason or another, which has distorted his scholarly research and reasoning? Has Taguieff for some reason decided to devote his scholarly work to the service of Jewish interests instead of to the disinterested quest for truth? The obnoxiousness of these questions ought to be obvious. The only reasonable question to ask about Pierre-André Taguieff ought to be: is he a good historian? Do his research and conclusions merit respect and attention?

These questions are, at least, answerable. Ramadan concentrated his criticism on France, and in that country, at least, a new kind of phobia about the Jews does seem to have cropped up during the last several years—a phobia that has emerged not so much from the zones of the true-blue French far right (the traditional right-wing loathing of the Jews is the *old* Judeophobia), but in a newer corner of French life, amid the immigrant working-class suburbs. The evidence for this proposition has the misfortune of being overwhelming. There has been, during the last ten years, a much-reported harassing of Jewish students in some of the suburban schools; the much-discussed difficulty or inability of schoolteachers in those same suburbs to instruct their students in the history of German policy in the Second World War, out of fear of arousing the neighborhood bigots; a series of ghastly and sensational violent crimes and even murders of Jews; and finally a Jewish flight from some of the suburban neighborhoods. It is true that, when a few public complaints about a "new Judeophobia" first began to be aired, in 2000 or 2001, the national government in France and the mainstream press, both of them, reacted skeptically.

But the problem failed to go away, and, after a while, the government organized an advisory commission. The commission arrived at the conclusion—reported in *The New York Times* in March 2005—that 62 per cent of the hate crimes committed in France during the previous year had been directed at Jewish targets. This kind of pseudo-precise statistic always seems dubious. Still, the figure did suggest a trend, especially when you consider that Jews in France amount to less than one per cent of the total French population. The government report, some two years after Ramadan had launched his attack, made Pierre-André Taguieff look prescient. And what has been the source of the "new Judeophobia"? There are several. But the biggest of those sources has plainly been the Islamist movement, newly active and powerful in the immigrant neighborhoods—the legacy of North

Africa's Muslim Brotherhood and its splinter groups
and related tendencies, transported into the dreary
French housing projects. Islamism: an "ideological
corruption of Islam," in Taguieff's formulation, with
its influences from—he mentioned these sources—al-
Banna, Qutb, and the European ultra-right. Taguieff
noted the extraordinary success of *The Protocols of
the Elders of Zion*. And yet he emphasized that, for all
the connections to the traditional ultra-right, something in the new Judeophobia was identifiably *new*.

As to how dangerous the new Judeophobia has
turned out to be, on the scale of possible threats
right now menacing France and other places in
Western Europe—well, that is a separate question.
Jumpiness is a modern French condition, and it is
a Jewish perennial, and, in the years around 2005,
some of the jumpier commentators left an impression
that France's Jews were undergoing a horrific wave
of hatred and ought to flee for their lives to Israel.
The prime minister of Israel during the height of
the scare was Ariel Sharon, and Sharon advised the
French Jews to pack their bags and make *aliyah*—
only to be rebuked by André Glucksmann, as could
never have been predicted by anyone relying on Ramadan's denunciation of him or, for that matter, on
the description of Glucksmann in the *Times Magazine*. The point of Ramadan's accusation from 2003,
in any case, was to challenge the very idea of a new
Judeophobia and to accuse Taguieff and his fellow-
thinkers of engaging in a campaign to advance Jewish interests. The denunciation of Taguieff as a man
with an ethnic or religious axe to grind strikes me,
I have to say, as still another element, in the zone
of intellectual debate, of what Taguieff himself has
done so much to identify.

Ramadan's "Critique of the (New) Communitarian Intellectuals" offered a second indictment, too, which touched on the Iraq war and its accompanying disputes—and, on this issue, yes, he brought up the matter of Israel and its national interests. Ramadan looked on Israel as central to the Iraq war. In setting out to overthrow Saddam, the United States, in his interpretation, "certainly acted in the name of its own interests, but we know that Israel supported the intervention and that its military advisers were engaged among the troops." More: "We also know that the architect of this operation in the heart of the Bush administration is Paul Wolfowitz, a notorious Zionist, who has never concealed that the fall of Saddam Hussein would guarantee a better security for Israel with its economic advantages assured." I cringe at having to point out that Paul Wolfowitz, whatever his other sins, has never been known for his Zionism (though I realize that, given the confluences of z's, hardly anyone will believe me). But these little details may not matter much, from Ramadan's perspective.

In the course of his *Western Muslims and the Future of Islam*, he dwells on the American Jews for a moment, and his comments suggest that American Jews, taken as a whole, constitute a "lobby" (the word has been internationalized) to advocate Jewish and Israeli interests, in lieu of standing for the higher principles of "right, justice and ethics"—and this argument could lead you to suppose that, in the Bush administration, pretty much any Jew at all would have pushed for Israel's interests, instead of for right, justice and ethics. Even someone not notorious for Zionism must be notorious for Zionism. In his "Critique of the (New) Communitarian Intellectuals,"

Ramadan delivered a roughly similar judgment on the French intellectuals, as well—the ones whom he designated as Jews.

He wrote, "Intellectuals as different as Bernard Kouchner, André Glucksmann or Bernard-Henri Lévy, who had taken courageous positions on Bosnia or Chechnya, have curiously supported the Anglo-American intervention in Iraq." Another error turned up in this sentence. Lévy, back in 2002 and '03, when the Iraq war was under debate, declined to endorse the invasion. (This error on Ramadan's part was compounded, by the way, in the account of the same affair published in *The New York Times Book Review* in 2007, where Stéphanie Giry, the reviewer, erroneously listed Alain Finkielkraut as yet another French Jewish supporter of the invasion. A peculiar interchangeability of Jewish names has turned out to be a minor quirk of our time.) Still, it is true that two of the people on Ramadan's list, Kouchner and Glucksmann, did, in fact, support the American intervention—Kouchner in a highly modulated version. (He supported the overthrow of Saddam, though he opposed Bush's way of going about it. And should I add that Kouchner is only half-Jewish? No, it would be absurd to get into this sort of thing. But there is no concealing that André Glucksmann is entirely Jewish, and he entirely supported the invasion of Iraq!) Only, why would Ramadan suppose that, in taking these positions, Kouchner and Glucksmann had acted, in Ramadan's word, "curiously"? And why see in those positions a tribal Jewish retreat from universalist principles of the past?

Kouchner has spent a lifetime campaigning for humanitarian action and human rights around the world. If anyone is notorious for his agitations, surely it is Kouchner, the man who got himself

photographed carrying a sack of rice up a Somali
beach. Kouchner's agitations for the overthrow of
the Baathist dictatorship in Iraq got started as long
ago as 1988, not because his Jewish roots (on his
father's side) had led him into conspiratorial loyalties
to Zionism, but because he had labored in person to
bring medical aid to the most wretched of Saddam's
victims, the Iraqi Kurds. Saddam's terrorist network
had even done its best to blow up Kouchner's auto-
mobile. In the months before the 2003 war, the Kurds
themselves, by all accounts, tended to favor a foreign
invasion. Anyone paying attention to Kouchner over
the years should have been able to predict that, in
2003, he, too, like his Kurdish friends, would see a
virtue in overthrowing the dictator. Glucksmann has
likewise drawn interventionist conclusions from the
humanitarian logic, and he has done so more than
once. Nor have either of these people, Kouchner or
Glucksmann, kept the public uninformed about his
reasoning. These are voluble men, at book length.
They have even acknowledged, both of them, an influence from their Jewish backgrounds on their recent
thinking—though, in both instances, the influence has
nothing to do with Israel. These men were shaped by
their experiences as toddlers during the years when
Nazis occupied France—experiences that, recollected
in adulthood, has led each of them to conclude that
powerful countries have a solemn duty to protect vulnerable populations in other countries from murderous governments. The Kurds, for instance.

Still, Ramadan denounced Kouchner, Glucksmann and Lévy for taking public positions that, in
his view, concealed a Jewish agenda. Glucksmann,
for one, was happy to reply. He unloaded in *Le Nouvel Observateur*. His response began, "Mr. Ramadan
says, in short: Glucksmann doesn't think with his

head, he thinks with his race" (though Buruma, in his *Times Magazine* summary of the affair, skipped over this opening line, which contains the nub of the argument, and which incidentally became famous because Nicolas Sarkozy went on to borrow it. Instead, Buruma merely quoted Glucksmann's insult: "What is surprising is not that Mr. Ramadan is anti-Semitic, but that he dares to proclaim it openly.") Lévy, too, responded. Lévy saw in Ramadan's accusations a conspiracy theory about the Jews. He was not too shy to bring up *The Protocols of the Elders of Zion*.

Those were angry responses. But were they also, in Buruma's words, "shrill" and "overblown"? To some people in France, Ramadan's polemic conjured the atmosphere of an ultra-right-wing rally, with a demagogue at the microphone calling out the names of Jewish journalists to the jeers of a racist crowd—the atmosphere of the old Judeophobia, scarcely updated. I think that, outside of France, the right-wing and racist echo may have been hard to hear, though it ought not to be hard to imagine. It was audible in France, though. Ramadan's polemic put in a good word for the left-wing French anti-globalists, and the grateful comrades responded by posting his essay on their Social Forum website. Still, in France even the anti-globalists seem to have fretted over the racist echo, and, after a while, once Glucksmann and Lévy had replied, the anti-globalists took Ramadan's polemic down again.

But never mind the Jews, and the half-Jews, and the non-Jews with potentially Jewish-sounding names. The most striking comment in the *Times Magazine* account of this affair was something else entirely—Buruma's indignant plea, in Ramadan's defense, that "Ramadan is in fact one of the few Muslim intellectuals to speak out against anti-Semitism." Here was genuinely a curious note. It is true that, even apart from his benign interpretation of the Jews at Medina, Ramadan has said and written, on the topic of racism and hatred of the Jews, a number of commendable denunciations, even if not in his essay on Taguieff, Glucksmann, Kouchner et al. Ian Hamel quotes Ramadan having observed about Israel, "Criticism is legitimate, but racism, never. Anti-Semitism is never justified"—which is an admirable thing to say, even if Ramadan has never taken the inconvenient step of discussing in any detail the nature of anti-Semitism, or the further step of applying his condemnation to the Muslim Brotherhood and the sundry other mass movements that invoke the legacy of Hassan al-Banna. Still, I am confident that, if a group of mischievous kids or ranting hooligans were to run around toppling tombstones in a Jewish cemetery or painting swastikas on French synagogues, Ramadan could be counted on to say the right thing. He is vandalism's enemy. Hassan al-Banna did not wish to be the leader of a mob in 1945, and neither does Ramadan. On the other hand, is this so remarkable?

Buruma's comment about Ramadan as "one of the few Muslim intellectuals to speak out against anti-Semitism" could lead you to suppose that, in the universe of Muslim intellectuals, people who stand up to issue even the easiest or most formulaic denunciations of prejudice and superstition are, in fact, a rare and remarkable breed. But you have only to glance at your own bookshelves to see otherwise— your shelves full of books by this or that erudite or imaginative person from a Muslim background, one book after another demonstrating that liberal culture in our modern age has come to be animated by no small number of people who, in childhood, set about memorizing whole chunks of the Koran.

Why look on Ramadan, then, as "one of the few"? I will speculate. Could it be that Buruma, in describing Ramadan in this fashion, was thinking only of Muslim intellectuals in the Francophone world? But, no, that is impossible. French, the language of Tariq Ramadan, is one of the principal languages of Muslim liberalism.

Or could it be that, in saluting Ramadan as "one of the few Muslim intellectuals to speak out," Buruma meant to distinguish between two kinds of Muslim intellectuals—the authentic and the inauthentic, with Ramadan figuring as an authentic? This is possible. But the logic is curious. Why should a Swiss-born professor like Ramadan count as authentic—and not, say, a Tunisian-born writer like Abedewahab Meddeb? Why Ramadan, in preference to, say, Tahar Ben Jelloun, the novelist—Moroccan-born and educated, the winner of the Prix Goncourt, not to mention the Impac Dublin literary prize? Ramadan intended his book *In the Footsteps of the Prophet* to be something of a primer of Islam, but Ben Jelloun has also written a primer, called *Islam Explained*, which likewise presents Islam in a mild and sagacious light. In his own primer, though, Ben Jelloun takes the occasion to distinguish between a good and noble Islam, and the alternative, which seems to him a perversion. *Islam Explained* by Ben Jelloun blames the perversion of Islam on Hassan al-Banna. Does Ben Jelloun's rejection of al-Banna somehow disqualify him as a Muslim intellectual? I apologize to Meddeb and Ben Jelloun for invoking their names in this context. There is something grotesque about being cited as a good citizen, just as something is grotesque in tabulating the ancestry of French intellectuals with Jewish-sounding names. But that is what happens when an argument is reduced to matters of ethnic or religious authenticity.

Or could it be that, in describing Ramadan as "one of the few Muslim intellectuals to speak out against anti-Semitism," Buruma had something else in mind? Perhaps Buruma was thinking of Ramadan's audience, and not of Ramadan himself. Writers like Meddeb and Ben Jelloun speak mostly to the literary and intellectual world—though both of them have addressed a mass audience as well, Meddeb through his radio work, Ben Jelloun as the first staff writer from an Arab background to be hired at *Le Monde*. But maybe Buruma was thinking of a different kind of audience entirely—not the sophisticated book-buyers, and not the mainstream radio audience, and not the readers of a top-flight newspaper like *Le Monde*, no matter how many of those people might be Muslims, but, instead, the kind of religiously pious audience that might file into a lecture hall through separate doors for men and women. Maybe Buruma was picturing the kinds of intellectuals who, like populist politicians, seek out their followings among the fist-wavers at militant meetings in the immigrant neighborhoods. And, to be sure, in regard to pulpit-pounding Muslim preachers with fist-waving audiences, Buruma may be on to something. The number of Islamist firebrands who speak out against anti-Semitism is less than large.

Still, let us not fall into the easy belief that, in modern Europe, the immigrant neighborhoods are, by definition, dominated by the Islamist legacies that descend from al-Banna. Taguieff's "new Judeophobia" is all too real; but, as his coinage suggests, the phenomenon does happen to be new—something that dates roughly from the 1980s, when the Islamists began to have their moment. The immigrant neighborhoods are old, though. In some of those neighborhoods, the anti-Islamists, too, have now and then had moments of their own. The immigrant zones of Lyon, in eastern France—to pluck a pertinent example from the life and career of Tariq Ramadan—used to be famous, not so long ago, for a generous political spirit that owed nothing at all to the Islamist legacy. I will explain.

The immigrants in Lyon are largely people from North Africa who, in some cases, came to France to escape political persecution, but, more often, in search of personal opportunity. And they did escape persecution, though only in its crudest version. But opportunity was hard to find. In 1983 a tiny group of young immigrants in Lyon, unhappy at their own circumstances, organized a political protest called the "March for Equality" to denounce their own social condition and those of people like themselves, and to call on democratic France to live up to its egalitarian ideals. The tiny group set out for Paris, on foot. The simplicity of their protest captured the public imagination. By the time the marchers had arrived in the capital, their numbers had swollen to a hundred thousand, and the protest had become known as the "March of the Beurs." *Beurs* is a slang word in French for young Arabs—a friendly and affectionate word, not at all pejorative or even ironic.

Here was a genuinely mass movement. The March of the Beurs gave rise, a year later, to an organization called SOS Racism. The organization likewise proved to be popular. SOS Racism called a rally in the Place de la Concorde in Paris in 1985. Hundreds of thousands of young people attended, Arabs and everyone else, glorying in their multi-hued splendor—which SOS Racism made a point of rendering fashionable. I happened to be staying in Paris at the time, and I participated myself. It was an excellent event. The people at the Place de la Concorde were the avatars of anti-racism and social equality. They were young people determined to shout down the anti-Arab and anti-Muslim bigotries of Jean-Marie Le Pen and the French extreme right. SOS Racism defined its principles broadly and nobly, though, and therefore it was the enemy of anti-Semitism, as well. Explicitly, I mean. In the working-class suburbs, SOS Racism organized Arabs and Jews conjointly. SOS Racism's slogan was *"Touches pas à mon pote!"*— "Don't touch my buddy!"—and this was an affecting and popular slogan for a trendy movement of the anti-racist young. Masses of people, the indignant buddies, wore a cheerful-looking button bearing that slogan. In some neighborhoods the button itself came into fashion, pinned to every lapel.

A number of media-savvy writers stood behind the movement and orchestrated the press and offered a bit of intellectual guidance. Marek Halter, the popular novelist, was one of those helpful writers—Halter, who has entertained enormous reading publics with his multi-generational sagas on Jewish themes. At Halter's side stood Bernard-Henri Lévy, an even better-known writer—someone whom the readers of Ramadan's polemic in 2003 could only regard as an agent of the Zionist network, and whom the readers of Buruma's piece in the *Times Magazine* would take to be an incipient neocon. SOS Racism was not a Zionist project, though, nor a neocon project. It was a left-wing project. SOS Racism expressed a left-wing spirit of generosity and liberal values that, in the 1980s, seemed to have replaced the surly old-fashioned Marxist left—a liberal leftism that applauded with enthusiasm for Amnesty International, and ap-

plauded the East Bloc dissidents, and approved any
number of relief efforts to combat famine in Africa,
and felt rather good about itself for taking those several stands, quite as if anti-racism, human rights, immigrant rights, women's rights, anti-totalitarianism
and humanitarian action had somehow merged, in a
tizzy of stylishness, with the natural rebelliousness of
the young and a passion for World Beat boom-box
music and the cult of the motorcycle.

But that was 1985. A good moment for those
of us who identify with the liberal left. Then came
some less-good moments. And the liberal left went
down to defeat—gradually, undetectably, but certainly. That is the big story lurking behind these
several current debates about Tariq Ramadan and
salafi reformism. SOS Racism was defeated partly by
its own missteps—by a series of foolish maneuvers
and political errors, none of which were especially
dreadful. But the stumbles and errors left a cumulative impression that, regardless of its proletarian origins in the streets of Lyon, the movement had ended
up as a feel-good exercise for soft-heads, secretly
manipulated by crafty back-room politicians in the
Socialist Party—a fatal image for any left-wing rebellion to acquire. But mostly the new movement
was defeated by a newer movement, which com-
peted for support in the immigrant neighborhoods.
The newer movement (as I learn from the various
French biographies of Ramadan) likewise sprung up
in the streets of Lyon.

The newer movement was led by an organization called the Union of Young Muslims. The Union
of Young Muslims got started in 1987, four years
after the March of the Beurs, and it got started precisely in order to combat everything that had come
out of the March of the Beurs. The Union of Young

Muslims was a movement for social justice, and, in that one respect, you could imagine that it resembled SOS Racism. Only, instead of vibrating to the trendy tones of 1980s left-liberalism, the new movement defined its idea of social justice by invoking the principles of seventh-century Arabia. Instead of "Don't touch my buddy!", the legacy of al-Banna. The two movements, the left-wing liberals and the brand-new Islamists, went head-to-head. SOS Racism campaigned to prevent nightclubs in France from discriminating against young Arabs and blacks. The Islamists campaigned to prevent young Muslims from going to nightclubs.

What did those Islamist agitations look like? Boualem Sansal offers a fictional portrait in *The German Mujahid*—the sheikh arriving from North Africa to assert his influence over the young immigrant men loafing around in the French streets. The young men getting drawn to the sheikh as they would to a gang leader. The gradual imposing of Islamist demands on the neighborhood—the demands about clothing, the demands about gender relations. *The German Mujahid* is fiction, though. In real-life Lyon, a similar progression seems to have taken place. By 1992 the Union of Young Muslims was five years old, and it was flourishing. Already it could boast of a publishing house and bookstore, called Tawhid. According to Paul Landau in *The Saber and the Koran*, the Tawhid bookstore was filled with anti-Semitic tracts and ranting tape cassettes.

Tariq Ramadan arrived from Switzerland in that same year and was bound to be useful to a movement of that sort—even if, being a Geneva bourgeois, he could never make himself entirely at home in the working-class streets. Ramadan commanded the kind of polish and sophistication that were in short supply in a movement of that sort. He knew how to speak to the non-immigrant rest of the world, a rare talent. He knew how to argue with the liberal intellectuals, a still rarer talent. The movement in Lyon would have prospered even without Ramadan. But he helped. And so, in the immigrant zones of Lyon, the fiery hard-headed Islamists outcompeted the politician-ridden soft-headed liberal leftists. To be sure, this was more than a local story. Islamists defeated leftists all over the world.

There is another half to this story, though, which is what happened on the left in the wake of those defeats. The rise of Islamism around the world in the 1980s and '90s created a tremendous crisis on the European and even the American left—even if, for a lot of people, the crisis went unnamed and undiscussed. The crisis was huge, even so. What does it mean to be on the left, after all? I mean the broad left, the left that includes everybody marked by even the faintest and most attenuated of left-wing impulses—the outright ultra-leftists in their sectarian varieties, but also the vaguer progressives and even the people who, with maximum sophistication, shudder with savvy distaste at any ideological label at all, yet whose hearts beat, even so, on the left. To be on the left, for those many people: doesn't this mean a feeling of solidarity with the poor and the downtrodden? That has got to be the minimum definition.

The March of the Beurs excited a lot of French people in 1983 because, for the first time on a national scale, the sincere young anti-racists of old-stock France discovered a way to manifest their own solidarity with France's oppressed new immigrants. The old-stock anti-racists were thrilled at the opportunity, and they rushed into the street to march with

the Beurs. At the Place de la Concorde the demonstrators loved themselves, and they loved the Other.
But once SOS Racism had lost its altruistic sheen,
everybody who identified even marginally with the
left had to pause and consider what new attitude
to adopt. In Lyon and other towns, the Islamists
were shouldering aside the liberal left, and shouldering aside the dowdy mainline Muslim organizations,
too—the Islamists, claiming to be, at last, the true
and authentic tribune of the poor and the downtrodden. The Islamists—in spite of a thousand principles
anathema to the left. In spite of the seventh century!
The Islamists—who, by every normal reckoning,
ought to have been regarded as a movement of the
extreme ultra-right, in some perplexing new style.
This development required a left-wing response.

In France—and in Britain and other countries,
too—the first people on the left to recognize that
something big was afoot proved to be the tiny and
ridiculous-looking Trotskyist sects. The non-liberal
left. Trotskyists saw an opening. The Trotskyists
knew very well that, from a conventionally Marxist
perspective, Islamism was less than congenial. Back
in the 1940s, the Trotskyists generated a literature
of their own on the topic of Islamism and fascism—
namely, an essay on the fascist nature of the Muslim
Brotherhood by Tony Cliff, the founder of the British
Socialist Workers Party. But that was long ago. And
Trotskyists pride themselves on not being finicky.
And Comrade Cliff was not the only authority from
the past. The Trotskyists of the 1980s and '90s were
perfectly capable of recalling that Trotskyism began
as a splinter from Soviet Communism—capable of
recalling that, in the early years of the Soviet revolution, the communists in Central Asia and South Asia

used to pursue their own, crafty and friendly policy toward Islamic revolutionaries (which, by the way, left an influence on the Islamist doctrine).

The Trotskyists of the 1980s and '90s abominated the newly trendy liberal left. SOS Racism, Bernard-Henri Lévy and his New Philosophers, anti-totalitarianism, humanitarian do-good-ism, feel-good soft-head appeals to civic virtue, dippy-looking lapel pins—every one of those bourgeois and liberal excrescences was bound to drive a red-blooded Trotskyist deeper into his leather jacket. And so, the Trotskyists eyed the newly visible streetcorner Islamists, and, by squinting, they found a sympathetic new way of viewing the entire development. This was sociological, instead of ideological. A focus on social class, instead of a focus on ideas. Islamism may have been appalling, from any kind of normal left-wing standpoint. Looked at sociologically, though, the Islamists appeared to be a proletarian rebellion. A movement from below. A poor people's righteous agitation, astir in the immigrant streets. The Trotskyists were impressed. And, in a spirit of Marxist solidarity, the Trotskyists reached out.

Nor were the Trotskyists the only people on the Marxist left to think along those lines. Ayatollah Khomeini's Islamist revolution in Iran came to power in 1979 by striking up an alliance with the pro-Soviet Marxist factions of Iran, and the communist leaders in Moscow duly directed their fraternal parties around the world to look on Iran's Islamists as a progressive development. The Islamic revolution: a blow against imperialism and a blow for social justice, even if, from an ideological standpoint, something about Khomeini's doctrine might have seemed a little troubling. The French Communist Party followed the Soviet line more ardently than any of the other large communist parties in the Western countries, and the French communists took to marching through Paris in their May Day parade together with, as Ladan Boroumand has pointed out, an Iranian delegation called Hezbollah. "The Party of God"—an unusual organization to see at a communist parade.

You might suppose that, by the 1980s, this kind of development on the old-school Marxist left would have counted for nothing at all in the larger political world. Communist parties in the past used to command the support of a huge percentage of the Western European population—a quarter of the electorate in France as recently as the 1970s, an even larger percentage in Italy. The 1980s were rough on communism, though. As for Trotskyism, it was, almost by definition, a microscopic cause. Still, no one should be counted out. In the first round of the French presidential election of 2002, a lot of high-minded progressives wanted to register an anti-bourgeois protest vote, and Trotskyist candidates were on the ballot, and a full ten per cent of the electorate ended up voting Trotskyist (which is how, back in 2002, Le Pen edged past the Socialist candidate in the opening round of the elections and ended up in second place). Trotskyism in France remained a tiny movement, but the tiny movement knew how to shape events.

Nor was Trotskyism's ability to mobilize masses of people merely an idiosyncrasy of the present-day French. Gigantic demonstrations against the impending invasion of Iraq took place in February 2003 in Paris and London, not to mention in New York, Washington, San Francisco and other places. *The New York Times* published a breathless editorial describing the demonstrations as a thrilling new development in world events—the arrival of a brand new force in world history, which was public opinion. And yet, tiny Marxist groupuscules with the most peculiar of ideologies played an outsized role in organizing most of those big anti war marches, which they did either behind the scenes, as in the United States (where the groupuscules were exceptionally tiny), or front and center, as in Europe. And the Marxist organizers, with their new analysis of the Islamic ultra-right and their new and peculiar alliances, introduced into those gigantic marches a fresh and novel tone, audibly distinct from any left-wing tone of the remembered past.

The most striking example turned up at the march in Paris, not just because a contingent of Baathists took their place in the parade carrying placards in favor of Saddam Hussein. A group of peace demonstrators broke away from the march and beat up some yarmulke-wearing Jews standing on the sidelines (who, needless to say, turned out to be anti-war protesters themselves, in continuing demonstration of the interchangeability of one Jew for another). The attack on the Jews was a minor event, and it was universally condemned. Still, violence at the peace parade hinted at something new. Nothing even faintly resembling a mob attack on random yarmulke-wearers could possibly have taken place at any previous left-wing mass demonstration in Paris during the last many decades—Paris, where "Don't touch my buddy!" had once been a left-wing slogan; Paris, where, back in 1968, masses of left-wingers trembled with emotion as they marched through the boulevards chanting, "We are all German Jews!"

At the big 2003 march in London, nothing shameful or embarrassing took place. Everyone was well behaved. Public decorum only made the situation easier to identify, though. A coalition called

Stop the War organized the march and a good many subsequent demonstrations—and the Stop the War coalition was visibly dominated by the tiny Socialist Workers Party, in alliance with Britain's version of the Muslim Brotherhood, the Muslim Association of Britain. Trotskyists and Islamists: "an odd marriage," as *The Economist* put it. Millions of non-Trotskyists and non-Islamists nonetheless took their place in the coalition's march, quite as if everyone felt confident that, no matter what might come of the big demonstration, the Socialist Workers Party could reasonably be ignored (a safe assumption) or even regarded with irritable fondness; and quite as if Britain's Islamists, whom nobody could ignore, authentically represented the oppressed and the downtrodden, and therefore lent majesty to the march. Such was the implication. Nothing like a Trotsko-Islamist alliance could possibly have mobilized millions of Britons in the past.

And among the progressive intellectuals in various countries, the people who sound off in the magazines and write their books? Here, too, a shift got underway. I have selected Ian Buruma's journalism as my chosen example of the intellectual atmosphere of our moment—the atmosphere at its most refined and sophisticated, its most admirably engaged. And I will go on pointing in Buruma's direction—in this instance, to his book from 2004, *Occidentalism*, the one he wrote with Avishai Margalit. *Occidentalism* took the position that, all over the world in the modern age, radical and extreme ideologies of different sorts have weighed heavily on events, and the nature and components and history of those ideologies ought to be spelled out and examined. And so, Buruma and Margalit spoke about the allure of fascist and Nazi ideas, and about European fascism's influence on various thinkers around the world. *Occidentalism* analyzed Islamism. Back in 2004, Buruma was nothing loath to call a spade a spade, in the field of ideas. *Occidentalism* is a brilliant book.

In the next couple of years, though, Buruma's emphasis evolved. The book he published in 2006, his account of Theo van Gogh's murder by an Islamist fanatic, *Murder in Amsterdam*, examined some of those same doctrinal issues. The murderer was a Moroccan immigrant to Holland named Muhammed Bouyeri, who, judging from Buruma's description, decided to kill van Gogh on the basis of a fairly distinct set of jihadi and salafi ideas—doctrines of the sort that, via Sayyid Qutb's schismatic factions, have descended from the Muslim Brotherhood. By the time he wrote *Murder in Amsterdam*, though, Buruma no longer seemed especially interested in the history of ideas and their influence. He glanced in passing at the murderer's ideology and concepts, and then he lavished his true attention on the sociological landscape of immigrant life in modern Holland and the miseries of Amsterdam life.

The social texture of Dutch immigrant life is a big theme, and, in *Murder in Amsterdam*, Buruma did a good job of examining it. His artistry, his investigative energy, his ability to bring people to life on the page—these are genuine talents, and he put his talents on display. You can learn a lot about the Europe of our time from *Murder in Amsterdam*, and doubly so if you were to set the book side by side with Boualem Sansal's *The German Mujahid*—a journalist's account of Moroccan immigration to Holland, and a novelist's account of Algerian immigration to France: different books that end up illuminating similar landscapes. But there is no mistaking that Buruma, in turning from *Occiden-*

talism's examination of extremist doctrines to *Murder in Amsterdam*'s portrait of social conditions, has changed his focus. Instead of an attention to ideas, an attention to social class. In this one particular, *Murder in Amsterdam* departs rather sharply from Sansal's *The German Mujahid*. Then Buruma went further still, and, a year after publishing *Murder in Amsterdam*, he wrote his portrait of Ramadan for the *Times Magazine*, and his interest in ideas and doctrines seemed to dissipate almost entirely, as if he were no longer concerned in spelling things out with any precision or concern for accuracy.

Buruma lobbed his questions about doctrines and the history of ideas in Ramadan's direction, and the grandson of Hassan al-Banna swatted the questions back with his misleading remarks about salafi reformism and Sayyid Qutb and his grandfather's political theories. And the sophisticated journalist seemed unperturbed. Anti-Semitism? Ramadan was "one of the few Muslim intellectuals to speak out." It was as if, without realizing what had happened, the journalist had quietly come to accept Ramadan's picture of himself as a man in touch with the Muslim masses, sociologically authentic, therefore politically progressive. And Buruma had come to accept the notion that liberals from Muslim backgrounds are of no significance at all, or may even be the immigrants' worst enemy. And there no longer seemed any purpose at all in looking closely into what Ramadan has actually said over the years.

But then, if journalists like Buruma have ended up showing very little interest in the texture and details of Ramadan's thinking, how much confidence should we put in the additional argument, affirmed in the *Times Magazine* and echoed in a dozen other places, that Ramadan, the benign salafi, has offered, in Buruma's phrase, "an alternative to violence"? I have some thoughts on this issue.

It is true and it is wonderful that Ramadan has, on more than one occasion, condemned terrorist violence. Better still, his condemnations seem consistent with his larger program for the Muslim community in the West, which ought to require many agitations and protests, but nothing even remotely resembling a violent campaign. Anyway, the entire shape of Ramadan's career would make no sense at all if ultimately he wanted to mold his followers into some sort of violent force. He has spent too much energy projecting his image and ideas onto the public stage in Western Europe and beyond, and too little energy organizing his Muslim followers into proper phalanxes, if his purpose were to lead a militant charge. Ramadan is said to have been influenced by the example of Malcolm X in the United States, or at least by Spike Lee's Malcolm X—Malcolm, whose last letter in real life, unsent at his death, was addressed, or so it is claimed, to Said Ramadan at the Geneva Islamic Center. But Tariq Ramadan, who has something of Malcolm's air of touchy dignity, has nothing of Malcolm's demeanor of unstated threats.

Still, what does anyone mean by words like *violence* and *terrorism*? A necessary question, unfortunately. Bomb attacks on random crowds in the mass transit systems of Madrid or London are the very definition of terrorist acts, and I think that everyone would agree on the label, except for people who themselves might like to blow up a mass transit system. But what about bomb attacks on random bus-riders in Tel Aviv or Jerusalem? Ramadan's position on this particular matter can only be described as

layered. If Ramadan has put in a sympathetic word
for the Israelis somewhere, I am not aware of it. He
regards Israel as a colonizing entity. He applauds
the Palestinian resistance. In keeping with his general condemnation of violence, he has been careful
to specify, however, that not every action performed
in the name of Palestinian resistance merits approval,
and this is a crucial distinction to affirm. Then again,
one of the passages in the introduction to his book
Islam, the West and the Challenges of Modernity introduces a troubling nuance into his own distinction.
The remark appears in the course of the breathless
and emotional tribute to his recently-deceased father,
and to his father's selfless devotion to the principles
of al-Banna.

About Said Ramadan, Tariq Ramadan writes,
in a passage that has been translated less than grace-
fully: "Often, he spoke of the determination in his
commitment, at all moments, against colonialism
and injustice and for the sake of Islam. This determination was though never a sanction for violence, for
he rejected violence just as he rejected the idea of an
'Islamic revolution.'"

An "Islamic revolution" in this context means, I
think, an armed uprising or coup d'état, which Said
Ramadan rejected in favor of the slower, cannier and
more cautious proceedings of the Muslim Brotherhood. But the passage continues. The time frame is
evidently the late 1940s:

"The only exception was Palestine. On this, the
message of al-Banna was clear. Armed resistance was
incumbent so that the plans of the terrorists of Irgun
and of all Zionist colonizers would be faced up to.
He had learnt from Hassan al-Banna, as he said it
one day: 'to put one's forehead on the ground.' The

real meaning of prayer being giving strength, in humility, to the meaning of an entire life."

So there is an exception. Violence is wrong. Even against colonialism. Violence against Zionism, however, is right—violence against the Zionist right-wing extremists, the Irgun (who were in fact terrorists, just as al-Banna says). But also violence against "all Zionist colonizers." This phrase can only mean the Zionist population as a whole. You do have to wonder why, if violence against colonialism is wrong, violence against the Zionist variant of colonialism is right. Why call for restraint against the gigantic British Empire, and non-restraint against the tiny Zionist enterprise? I cannot answer this question, except to suppose that al-Banna's notion of Zionism conforms to the general Islamist theory of Zionism—the notion that Zionism represents an assault on the whole of Islam and on the whole of the Arab people, a diabolical undertaking, precisely as described by the mufti of Jerusalem. Not a tiny enterprise at all—a supernatural enterprise. Cosmically larger than the British Empire. Tariq Ramadan in his portrait of his father leaves this matter undiscussed—as he always does. To my ears, though, the truly peculiar note in the passage about Said Ramadan in *Islam, the West and the Challenges of Modernity* arises from a single word, and this is *incumbent*, describing the duty to oppose the Zionists with violence. "Armed resistance was incumbent..." *Incumbent* suggests that armed action against the Zionists ought to be regarded, on religious grounds, as obligatory. A principle, not a tactic. A duty, as Tariq Ramadan goes on to say (paraphrasing his father's summary of his grandfather's view), linked with prayer, forehead on the ground. A duty that gives meaning to an entire life. A sacred duty.

That is a heartbreaking passage. The entire tragedy of the Palestinian Arabs can be found in statements of this sort—the ideological dogma that, beginning with Amin al-Husseini and the Muslim Brotherhood, has led so many Palestinians to look upon the
entire struggle with Zionism as a religious affair, and
to look upon violence as a sacred principle, therefore
as something that can never be abandoned. If only
the Palestinian national movement had been able to
see in violence merely a tactic, the movement's leaders might have noticed after several decades that,
realistically speaking, violent tactics were advancing
the struggle not one whit, and counterproductive tactics ought to be jettisoned in favor of actions better
calculated to succeed at building a Palestinian state,
side by side with Israel, if need be—as could prob-
ably have been achieved at various moments over the
years, beginning in 1947.

If violence is obligatory, though, *incumbent* on
the partisans of the Islamic renewal movement, if
violence is a duty that, as al-Banna suggests, distin-
guishes anti-Zionist struggles from all other struggles
of the era—well, there can be no question of sur-
rendering a principle, regardless of the practical cost.
And, during the long history of the Palestinian struggle, the principle has not, in fact, been surrendered,
and the cost has been terrible. The cost to the Palestinians, above all, whose tragedy has only grown
deeper. The alliance of Amin al-Husseini and Hassan
al-Banna bears, I would think, a huge responsibility
for bringing about this disastrous result—al-Banna
with his demand, quoted at the beginning of the
Hamas charter, that Israel be *nullified*, or, in the
alternative translation, *obliterated*.

Something else about that word, *incumbent*.
Tactics speak to a given circumstance, but religious

obligations speak to the eternal. The notion of a religiously mandated violence opens a door, and it is hard to see what could prevent ever wilder, yet equally pious obligations from ultimately pushing their way through the open space. Al-Banna introduced the idea of the "art of death" and "death as art" to the Islamist movement, and Qutb and his followers extended the idea by coming up with the opinion that Muslim "hypocrites," quite as much as Zionists or any other enemy of God, merited a violent resistance. In this fashion, Qutb and his followers opened the way to mass slaughters not just of non-Muslims, but of Muslims, as well, to be committed ritualistically in the name of Islam. It goes without saying that Tariq Ramadan himself would never tolerate any such elaboration of al-Banna's idea. Qutb, as Ramadan has put it, "radicalized" the doctrines of al-Banna, and radicalization distorted the original notion. Al-Banna's idea remains the true idea, as Ramadan would have it. Such is the argument in *The Roots of the Muslim Renewal*.

Still, I do not think it entirely fair to lay the onus for the terrorist developments solely on Qutb. Among Qutb's admirers in the past has been Yusuf al-Qaradawi, who employs an epigraph from Qutb in one of the books about al-Banna that Ramadan so greatly esteems, *Islamic Education and Hassan al-Banna*. The epigraph calls for enforcement of the Islamic idea of divinity—an enforcement, that is, of the Islamist movement's theological concept: the basic principle of an Islamic state. But Sheikh Qaradawi did not have to look to Sayyid Qutb to find such an epigraph. He could have drawn any number of similar remarks from al-Banna himself. In more recent years, Qaradawi has pulled away from Qutb's legacy and has deplored it, and his objections to

Qutb have earned him a reputation as a moderate—a centrist, in his own term. But none of this has made Qaradawi a more peaceful man than in the past. Qaradawi remains a faithful disciple of al-Banna, the most faithful disciple of all, so far as I can judge— and the faithful disciple still boasts of having seen, as a young man, al-Banna orate on the agreeable nature of death in the service of God.

The September 11, 2001 attacks were carried out by people who regarded themselves as Qutb's followers. Qaradawi duly condemned the act. But what Qaradawi disliked was the target. He also disapproved of terrorists appropriating the lives of their fellow passengers in the airplanes. And he disapproved of killing Muslims randomly. But he did not disapprove of suicide terror per se. Two years after the 9/11 attacks he issued a fatwa authorizing suicide terrorism by Palestinians. The fatwa proved to be a tremendous boon to the terrorist organizations. At least, Hamas looked on it as a tremendous boon. The leader of Hamas, Khaled Mashal, thanked Qaradawi in person in a speech broadcast on Al Jazeera TV in 2007. (During which the Hamas leader also took the occasion, by the way, to let loose a rant about the Jews and Nazism. From the MEMRI transcript of Khaled Mashal's speech: "I want to make it clear to the West and to the German people, which is still being blackmailed because of what Nazism did to the Zionists, or to the Jews. I say that what Israel did to the Palestinian people is many times worse than what Nazism did to the Jews, and there is exaggeration, which has become obsolete, regarding the issue of the Holocaust. We do not deny the facts, but we will not give in to extortion by exaggeration. As for the Zionist holocaust against the Palestinian people, and against the peoples of the Arab and Islamic nation—this is a holocaust that is being perpetrated in broad daylight, with the coverage of the media of globalization.")

Mashal, in his appearance with Qaradawi, pointed out that, in the world of Islam, various religious scholars had expressed what he called "dissenting views" on suicide terror. This was unfortunate for Hamas. In Mashal's phrase, the dissenting views "caused us great embarrassment." But Qaradawi and his fatwa eased the embarrassment. Mashal: "That was unparalleled support for the people of Palestine, because, brothers and sisters, you cannot imagine how difficult it is psychologically for a young Palestinian man or woman to sacrifice themselves or what is most dear to them, only to encounter a conflict in their minds and hearts as to whether they are on the path of righteousness, or whether they are committing a religious violation."

Qaradawi replied, "I support Hamas, the Islamic Jihad, and Hezbollah. I oppose the peace that Israel and America wish to dictate. This peace is an illusion. I support martyrdom operations."

Qaradawi issued still another fatwa, permitting women to commit acts of suicide terror and dispensing the women terrorists from the normal obligation to conceal their hair beneath a *hijab*—a bizarre touch on his part, underlining the ritualistic nature of this kind of violence. Or not so bizarre, given that Qaradawi's area of special expertise concerns the everyday concerns of women—the rules for what women are permitted to do and are not permitted. Qaradawi endorsed insurgent attacks on American and British troops in Iraq. And, all the while, he managed to strike an oddly giddy tone. In 2007, as part of his endorsement of suicide terror by Palestinians, he joked about standing next to the Hamas leader. Qaradawi said, in a mocking humor, "What am I supposed to do? This great terrorist next to me will get me into trouble... He gave me a picture of Jerusalem and of the Al-Aqsa Mosque, and showed me respect—that's it, my guilt has been proven."

Qaradawi seems to have worried that some skeptical person might pointedly observe that he himself has never committed suicide. He said, "The only thing I hope for is that as my life approaches its end, Allah will give me an opportunity to go to the land of Jihad and resistance, even if in a wheelchair. I will shoot Allah's enemies, the Jews, and they will throw a bomb at me, and thus, I will seal my life with martyrdom. Praise be to Allah." The Iranian news agency *Muhr* accused Qaradawi of being an agent of the Jews and even of rabbis (an unconvincing accusation, if ever there was one), and Qaradawi responded on his website, in 2008, by boasting in a jaunty spirit about his own fatwa: "I am an enemy of Israel and the Mufti of martyrdom operations." Which indeed he is.

Among the religious authorities who have promoted the vogue for suicide terror, Qaradawi appears to stand in the very first rank—someone who has outdone everyone else in rendering the concept of ritual suicide and terrorism acceptable and even admirable and even, as I say, *moderate* in the eyes of people who are not, in fact, the wild-eyed followers of Sayyid Qutb. We might wonder, how can this be? How could a man who speaks the way that Qaradawi does about suicide, mass extermination, God's plan for Hitler, and all the rest—how could a man of this sort have ended up commanding a moral and religious prestige in the respectable mainstream?

Here is a mystery. But it is an old mystery, and we have always known how to penetrate its secrets.

Charismatic people with grotesque ideas end up wielding prestige and authority because they know how to deploy the symbols of even greater authority, and this Qaradawi has done by invoking the prestige of al-Banna and the grand tradition of the Muslim Brotherhood—invoking these things all too plausibly. And charismatic people with grotesque ideas end up wielding prestige and authority because other people, the ones who appear to be sober and sensible, offer public displays of deference and homage. The people with sane and mild demeanors attest to the moral authority of the people with giddy demeanors and grotesque ideas. This has been Tariq Ramadan's role.

I have said that Ramadan admires Qaradawi, but, when I run my eyes across my shelf of Ramadan's writings, it occurs to me that *admiration* understates the case. Ramadan reveres Qaradawi. The veneration is unmistakable. Ramadan appears to hold Qaradawi in higher regard than any other present-day Islamic scholar. Ramadan has sprinkled the signs of personal homage throughout his books, and not just in *The Roots of the Muslim Renewal*—one reference after another, always expressed in a tone of humble respect and deference, always designed to induce a feeling of respect and veneration among the readers, as if Qaradawi were an entirely reputable scholar, and nothing controversial or objectionable attached to his name.

Ramadan's *To Be a European Muslim*, from 1999: "Yusuf al-Qaradawi aptly notes that..." "Yusuf al-Qaradawi reminds us aptly, following the statements of al-Ghazali, Ibn al-Qayyim and ash-Shatibi that all that is in the Qur'an and the *Sunna* is..." "Al-Qaradawi says..." "For details, see Yusuf al-Qaradawi..." And so forth, culminating in a section of *To Be a European Muslim* that begins, "Yusuf al-Qaradawi, who attends many meetings dealing with the problems of our modern life and the formulation of appropriate Islamic solutions, has tried to fix some of the rules..."—and then proceeds to a four-page analysis, entirely admiring, of Qaradawi's work.

Ramadan's *Islam, the West and the Challenges of Modernity*, in 2001: "In this sense, Yusuf al-Qaradawi is right in clarifying that..." "See on this subject the excellent introduction to these questions in the text of Yusuf al-Qaradawi, *The Lawful and the Prohibited in Islam*..." "Following the example presented by Yusuf al-Qaradawi in his book on the problem of poverty, we should reflect on the sources and on the reality of our societies nowadays..." "This study is of prime importance and its usefulness is incomparable as the two shaykhs Muhammad al-Ghazali and Yusuf al-Qaradawi, remind us in their respective prefaces..." "Yusuf al-Qaradawi goes as far as admitting the possibility of payment of *zakat* by non-Muslims if this is done by their own free-will." "For more details, see the excellent work of Dr. Yusuf Qaradawi..." Ramadan's *Western Muslims and the Future of Islam*, from 2004: "Yusuf al-Qaradawi rightly recalls...." "For details, see Yusuf al-Qaradawi..." And Ramadan has contributed prefaces to two collections of Qaradawi's fatwas in French editions.

To be sure, Ramadan has now and then broached, in a humble tone, a mild and friendly criticism, too, generally to the effect that Qaradawi, for all his wisdom, has not kept up with the times—a young man's respectful criticism of his venerable elder. Sometimes Ramadan has hinted that Qaradawi, who lives in Qatar, may not be up-to-date with the latest of Western trends. In *Western Muslims and the Future of Islam*: "In his book *On Law and the Juris-*

prudence of Muslim Minorities, Yusuf al-Qaradawi adds a telling subtitle: *The Life of Muslims in Other Societies*. In his mind, Western societies are 'other societies' because the societies normal for Muslims are Muslim-majority societies. But this is no longer the case..."—followed by an apologetic footnote explaining that Qaradawi's failure to appreciate the growth of the Muslim immigration in Europe is, in Ramadan's phrase, "entirely understandable since he does not live in the West." And so, Ramadan, for all his veneration, does seem capable of expressing his own views, sometimes even at variance with Qaradawi's, if he is of a mind to do so. But, as I judge it, this merely makes Ramadan's veneration of Sheikh Qaradawi appear more impressive still.

Back to the question of sacred violence, then, and especially the kind of violence that Ramadan's father and grandfather regarded as an *incumbent* duty—the violence that Qaradawi in our own time has promoted among women as well as men and has extended into the zone of suicide. On this darkest of topics, then, what else does Ramadan choose to say? His own views, apart from his genuflections to Qaradawi—what have they been?

One of Ramadan's pamphlets is called *Jihad, Violence, Guerre et Paix en Islam*, which Tawhid, the Islamist bookstore and publishing house in Lyon, brought out in 2002, and then reprinted in 2004—though the pamphlet has not been translated into English, to my knowledge. *Jihad, Violence, War and Peace in Islam* appears, on first inspection, to contain a straightforward, frank and commendable discussion of jihad and Islam. In his opening sentence, Ramadan poses the question, "Is the world of Islam intrinsically violent?" He acknowledges reasons why some people might think so. He notes passages of the

Koran that convey a warrior attitude. He acknowledges that some people in the Muslim world—the
unnamed foolish militants who embrace a "literalist" interpretation, as he describes it—call for violence. He acknowledges that, in a foolish spirit, some
people have even argued that, because of American
oppression or because of the Zionists, everything is
permitted—which, in Islam, can never be the case.

He acknowledges that, in the Muslim world,
some people have tried to evade discussing these
troubling matters by saying that, in regard to the
September 11, 2001 attacks, there is no proof of Bin
Laden's responsibility. To which Ramadan responds
by tying himself into a pretzel: "That definitive proofs
are lacking is a fact, but that Muslims, including Bin
Laden himself (who has said so and written so), exist
who think that one can spread violence and kill the
non-Muslims and the deniers, the *kuffar*, no matter
who they are without any other consideration than
that they exist—this is no less a proven fact. And it
is necessary to say and to repeat that these ideas do
not respect the principles of Islam, and they betray
its general teaching." In short, Ramadan takes no
position on whether Bin Laden bears the responsibility for September 11. But Ramadan condemns him,
anyway—if only for his opinions. And Ramadan
does say and repeat that, in Islam, it is forbidden to
kill Jews, Christians or atheists merely because they
are Jews, Christians or atheists. Nor is it right to attack synagogues and churches.

He recalls a prophetic tradition according to
which a man who rescues a dog dying of thirst is
promised Paradise, whereas the woman who beats
her cat to death will receive the worst of punishments.
He adds, "The message of Islam is this message of
love." Muslims, he says, would do well to speak of

this message more often than they do. As for jihad, properly understood, it should be regarded, above all, as the struggle *against* violence—the struggle for mastery of oneself. Then again, jihad, as Ramadan presents it, is a struggle for political and social justice—a struggle against poverty, illiteracy, delinquency, social exclusion and other injustices. This, too, ought to be a nonviolent affair—even if not in every instance. "Islam encourages us to seek out peace; but not peace without justice. Peace without justice is not peace." And so, under expressly circumscribed conditions, war can, in fact, be accepted, if only as a last resort. Under the circumstance of foreign occupation, for instance. Ramadan cites examples. One of those examples is the unhappy situation of the Afghan people, who, having been subjected to foreign attacks, have a right—a religious duty, I would imagine, if I follow Ramadan's argument—to put up a violent resistance. The passages on Afghanistan in Ramadan's *Jihad, Violence, War and Peace in Islam* would seem, in sum, to endorse the Taliban—though Ramadan never mentions the Taliban by name.

Anyway, the greatest violence of all, as he sees it, is created by injustice, and not by the struggle against injustice. An old argument. He writes: "Every day that passes, entire peoples undergo repression, the abuse of power, and the most inhuman violation of their rights. Until when is it necessary that they keep quiet, or else be judged as 'dangerous' by the West if they dare express their refusal?

"It is not a matter of justifying violence, but of understanding under what circumstances it arises: the North-South disequilibriums, the exploitation of men and of primary materials...," and so forth. At the very end of the book he concludes, in his wind-up analysis: "It is necessary to struggle against the causes of violence and war." What are those causes? His final, climactic declaration: "The world needs other poles to be created against the American hyper-power: Europe should awaken itself and all the forces of resistance throughout the world, for the citizens of the world, their liberty and justice." The struggle against American power, then—this would appear to be jihad's ultimate goal, though he presents the argument somewhat elliptically, as if he were the champion of an independent foreign policy for France.

He is clear and forceful on the right and wrong ways to engage in violence. "It is necessary to denounce the political violence that expresses itself by assassinations of tourists, priests, women and children, and by blind bombs and bloody carnage. These actions are not defensible and they do not respect the Koranic message." Here he has the Qutbists in mind. And yet, what about the exception—the religious duty to commit violence against Zionists, as argued by his father and grandfather? In his writings on his father and grandfather, Ramadan leaves an impression that his own path in life has been set by them, and he is their faithful follower, and he has not one word of criticism to propose. Even so, in certain passages, he does seem to veer away from the family line. In Ramadan's judgment, attacks on civilians would appear to be indefensible, even in the case of the Palestinians.

And yet, with Ramadan there is always another "and yet." About the Palestinians, he says that, given the Israeli oppression, "their last recourse was operations against civilians"—which may suggest a degree of flexibility in his condemnation. He is careful about apportioning the blame, too: "One cannot place all the blame for these acts on the women and men,

denied and oppressed, whose only recourse is to sacrifice their lives in attacking the civilian targets they
can reach (recognizing the incredible Israeli military
arsenal), and forget to condemn the Israeli policy
that has been the prime producer of this violence."
This would appear to suggest that, when Palestinian terrorists set out to murder random crowds of
Israelis, the prime responsibility belongs to the Israelis. Or more than prime responsibility. If I follow
Ramadan's logic correctly, the entire responsibility
would seem to fall upon the Israelis—given that, in
his estimation, the Palestinians have no other alternative. Suicide attacks on civilian targets are their
"only recourse."

Israeli state terrorism, he says again, "pushes the
Palestinians to the ultimate recourse of attentats solely in order to be heard." *Attentat* is an old-fashioned
word for terrorist acts—the old anarchist word. Attentats, then: who could blame an oppressed person
for resorting to such things, given that people do
need to be heard, and attentats are their last resort?
Surely an oppressed person is right to make himself
heard. And so, attentats are bad, but something in
them can only be regarded as good.

None of this alters the fact that, on one level,
Tariq Ramadan has said more than once that he disapproves of terrorism. But there is a cost in structur-
ing an argument on more than one level—in noisily
affirming his own place in the salafi reformist tradition, while pretending that terrorist components of
the movement belong only to a distant offshoot; or
in affirming his own disapproval of violent action,
while exalting his grandfather's memory and even his
grandfather's vision of anti-Zionist violence as a religious duty; or in condemning the terrorist aspect of
the Palestinian movement, while leaving an impres-

sion that ultimately the Palestinian terrorists have no alternative but to be terrorists; or in denouncing the people who preach in favor of suicide terrorism, even while genuflecting in one book after another to Sheikh Qaradawi, the world's most authoritative champion of suicide terrorism in its Sunni Islamic version.

The cost to Ramadan in all of this is a dark smudge of ambiguity, and the smudge runs across everything he writes on the topic of terror and violence. The ambiguity makes the various police and legal allegations against the Ramadan family in Geneva (in connection with the distinctly shady Al-Taqwa Islamic bank in Switzerland, continually suspected and sometimes accused of terrorist financing, though never convicted of it; in connection with a Qaeda financier who was jailed in Spain in 2002; in connection with a Qaeda militant who came from the Lyon region; and so forth) look no more convincing than before. Yet neither do the accusations look outlandish.

The ambiguity touches on Ramadan's visa case in the United States—the case that began in 2004, when he wanted to make his way to Indiana to assume his professorship at Notre Dame. The Bush administration, in denying him a visa, invoked a law aimed at people who "endorse or espouse terrorist activity." No one pointed to any particular endorsement or espousal, though, which made the ruling seem a tad capricious. The American Civil Liberties Union and its allies in the Ramadan case— PEN, the American Academy of Religion, and the American Association of University Professors—filed their protest. And, after a while, the administration came up with a more solid-looking charge. Ramadan was accused of having donated money to a couple of charities that support Hamas—a French organization (with an office that happens to have been located in the same Lyon building as the Tawhid bookstore and publishing house), together with the organization's Swiss chapter. In the United States, Hamas has been legally designated as a terrorist organization, which means that sending money in Hamas's direction runs contrary to American law.

Even so, the new, more specific accusation seemed a little flimsy, from a legal point of view. Ramadan freely acknowledged donating the money. But he protested that, in sending in his contributions, he did not know where his money was ultimately going. Besides, the United States government put those two charities on its blacklist only in 2003 -- and, by then, Ramadan had already made his contribution. Officially speaking, the blacklist was retroactive. But retoactive blacklists are bound to seem unfair. And so, the ACLU kept hammering. In 2009, a United States federal court reversed the original ruling against Ramadan. In January 2010, Hillary Clinton signed a document lifting the ban against him. She did the right thing, in my opinion. Certainly her decision represented a grand victory for the ACLU and its allies—a victory for the free circulation of ideas. I have never thought that any good purpose was served in keeping Ramadan out of the United States. The freer the debate, the better for everyone. Will somebody try to ban or censor Ramadan's books, someday?—his book on jihad, for instance, with its uncertainty about Bin Laden's role in 9/11 and its implicit defense, on religious grounds, of the Taliban? I would protest any such ban, without a moment's hesitation.

Still, something in the Bush administration's accusation against Ramadan, the part about donating to Hamas, does catch the eye. It could well be true that Ramadan never inquired into exactly where his money was going. Even so, would anyone really be surprised to learn that Ramadan has wished to shower favors on Hamas and its cause? The philosopher who reveres Yusuf al-Qaradawi is not in a strong position to turn away requests for donations from Qaradawi's favorite organizations. And Hamas openly declares its debt to Hassan al-Banna. And why would Ramadan agree to look upon Hamas as a terrorist organization, anyway? In an op-ed for the *Washington Post* back in 2006, he described Hamas's fundraising arms in France and Switzerland as "humanitarian organizations," dedicated to "serving the Palestinian people," which is pretty much how Hamas would describe itself: a benign institution, with the most commendable of purposes. And there is the matter of ultimate goals.

Ramadan has explained in *Islam, the West and the Challenges of Modernity* that he favors an Islamic state in the Muslim-majority world. An Islamic state is precisely what Hamas intends to construct in Palestine some day, perhaps even before achieving its other goals, which are to "negate" Israel and kill the Jews. Why wouldn't Ramadan send a few euros to Hamas's European fund-raising campaigns, then? In any case, he sent the euros. And the United States government blacklisted the charities, and there was reason to do so. On August 19, 2003, a suicide bomber blew up a bus in Jerusalem. The explosion killed twenty-three people and wounded more than 130 others. Hamas claimed the attack. The Israeli police likewise attributed the attack to Hamas— though Islamic Jihad also claimed the credit. Four days later, the U.S. Treasury Department blacklisted the charities. According to the Treasury statement, the two organizations were "primary fundraisers for Hamas in France and Switzerland."

You could wonder why, if Ramadan were sincere in his condemnations of terrorist violence, he doesn't make his own positions more consistent. Why not condemn the terrorist organizations, as well as the terrorist deeds? Why not condemn the pro-terrorist theologians, the people with mainstream influence and not just the champions of what he calls the "literalist" deviation? Why not denounce some main tenets of the Muslim Brotherhood itself, and not just its schismatic offshoots—the tenets that have led to organizations like Hamas? Why not make a few critical remarks about the Islamist past, as well, in his effort to clarify the issue? A few sober reflections on al-Banna's theories about death and art might be apropos. To reform the reformists—wouldn't that be a good idea?

But Tariq Ramadan cannot take any of those steps. The whole problem lies in the terrible fact that his personal milieu—his grandfather and his father, his family contacts, his intellectual tradition—is precisely the milieu that bears the principal responsibility for generating the modern theory of religious suicide-terror. What can Ramadan do about any of this? He is hardly going to turn against his family. He is the family's prince. He has timidly offered opinions contrary to certain of Qaradawi's, on gender relations, for instance; but Ramadan, unlike Qaradawi, is a university philosopher, a secular figure (in spite of everything), and not an authoritative theologian. Ramadan's opinions are op-eds; Qaradawi's are fatwas. And Ramadan worships Qaradawi. And Qaradawi led the prayer at Said Ramadan's funeral. And Qaradawi represents a living link to al-Banna. What is

Tariq Ramadan to do about any of this? To reject Qaradawi's authority would mean challenging the system of authority as a whole, which would take him well beyond the salafi reformist idea. And would be personally wrenching. And so, Ramadan comes up with nice-sounding slogans. And he devotes his life to singing the praises of his father and grandfather and their works and their comrades, which means Sheikh Qaradawi. He promotes the cause of salafi reformism as whole. And Ramadan is a pious man, and he fulfills his religious duty by contributing to pious charities, which behave the way that leaders like Sheikh Qaradawi solemnly advise, which is to provide sufficient funds to care for the families of Palestinians who blow themselves up in the course of murdering as many other people as possible—a humanitarian sort of funding, from one point of view, which is also crucial to the terrorist campaign, from another point of view.

Ramadan's final message, therefore, ends up calling for—but what is Ramadan's final message, with regard to terrorism? It is a message in four parts. To wit: 1) Ramadan condemns terrorism. 2) He wants to understand terrorism, though not to justify it. 3) He understands terrorism so tenderly that he ends up justifying it. 4) He justifies it so thoroughly that he ends up defending it. And perhaps his message contains yet another element, which is not hard to detect in some of his writings, to the effect that: 5) who are you to question Tariq Ramadan about terrorism? Are you a racist? A notorious Zionist? An enemy of Islam? And Hassan al-Banna was the greatest figure of the last one hundred fifty years, and Said Ramadan was a pious and heroic Muslim, and long live Sheikh Qaradawi, the mufti of martyrdom operations!

I don't mean to be cynical, but it is worth adding that Ramadan's ambiguous stance on sacred violence does seem to advance his own career. To the world of people around Sheikh Qaradawi and the Muslim Brotherhood, where Ramadan's criticism of terror tactics might raise doubts about his piety, he can always defend his reputation by pointing to the nuances and subtleties in his position. And he can be confident that other people won't mind the nuances and subtleties, or may not even notice them. The ACLU, as part of its law suit, confidently affirmed, "Tariq Ramadan is a consistent and vocal opponent of terrorism and extremism"—which, after all, is what quite a few journalists have insisted on saying, though the statement is true only if you agree to accept Ramadan's own preferred definitions of words like *opponent*, *terrorism*, and *extremism*. The ACLU lawsuit came to be known as American Academy of Religion v. Napolitano. The American Academy of Religion is an association of some ten thousand religious scholars, according to the association itself. In November 2009, during the period when Ramadan was still prohibited from visiting the United States, the organization held its annual conference in Montreal, which meant that Ramadan could attend. He attended. He addressed a couple of plenary sessions. Naturally a number of Muslim liberals took the occasion to denounce him. Ramadan's greatest enemies have always been the Muslim liberals. But at the American Academy of Religion conference, the audience as a whole was thrilled to see him. According to Allan Nadler's report in the New York Jewish *Forward*, Ramadan received a hero's welcome—which suggests that his contributions to Hamas and the other little incongruities in his stand on violence and terrorism have damaged his reputation not at all.

Now, someone could argue that Ramadan's ambiguities on these questions do not amount to much, and his many admirable statements cancel out the various lamentable statements and contributions, and nothing dangerous or deadly will ever come of any of this, especially now that he knows not to send any more money to the blacklisted organizations. Caroline Fourest, in her book *Brother Tariq*, makes a different argument, though. She pictures Ramadan delivering a lecture somewhere in Europe, and an impressionable young North African immigrant deciding to attend. And Fourest wonders what notions and impulses such a person might take away. Which half of Ramadan's thinking might prove to be the persuasive to such a person—the commendable half? Or the other half? The answer does not seem to her obvious. Ian Hamel, in his *The Truth About Tariq Ramadan*, scoffs at Fourest and her argument. Hamel points out that, for all the talk about Ramadan and terrorism, not even the slightest connection to any sort of terrorist deed has ever been proved. Hamel observes that, out of the many thousands of people who have, in fact, attended lectures by Ramadan, only a single person, somebody from the Lyon region, is known to have ended up in Al Qaeda's Afghan training camps.

Who is right in this dispute? Hamel, the scoffer, would carry the day in a court of law. Even the contributions to Hamas's fundraising campaign were legal, at the time. Still, it is easy to imagine that Fourest is on to something. Salafi reformism, after all— this is a movement without any kind of natural barrier between its pro-terrorists and its anti-terrorists. What is Ian Buruma's position on the Fourest-Hamel debate? The author of *Murder in Amsterdam* seems to have missed this particular controversy, which is too bad. The assassin of Theo van Gogh is precisely the kind of bewildered young man whom Fourest has asked us to imagine: a second-generation North African immigrant who has had to sort through the doctrines coming his way, looking for the signs of prestige and glamor, trying to estimate which of those many ideas ought to be regarded as honorable, dignified and pious. Even incumbent. Fourest published her worries about Ramadan's influence in October 2004. Muhammed Bouyeri, the fanatic, murdered van Gogh one month later. Buruma published his book about Bouyeri's crime in 2006, and his portrait of Ramadan, a year later. His response to Fourest, in the *Times Magazine*, was dismissive. But Caroline Fourest had raised a good point.

Buruma's *Times Magazine* profile of Ramadan did not miss one other issue, however, and this is surely the biggest issue of all, odd though it may be to say so, given how much we hear about anti-Semitism and terrorist violence. This is the question of women's rights. It is here that Ramadan's dialectical language has proved to be exceptionally flexible, a language capable of striking tones that are modern and ancient at the same time, as if in octaves—the treble tones of an Islamic renewal for the modern age, which are also the basso tones of the ancient salafi past. And on this topic, too, the journalistic response, some of it, has proved to be no less remarkable—a response from the twenty-first century that somehow keeps finding a soft spot in its heart for the seventh century.

Chapter Seven
THE REALM CELESTIAL

Ramadan told the *Times Magazine*: "The body must not be forgotten. Men and women are not the same. In Islamic tradition, women are seen in terms of being mothers, wives, or daughters. Now woman exists as woman." This is a traditionalist's remark. The traditions he has in mind, however, are not the same as folk customs and peasant gowns. Islamic tradition, for Ramadan, means Islamic law, in his version of it. A religious matter, not a folk habit. A question of sacred and inviolable texts. But then, since religious law bespeaks the eternal, nothing prevents Ramadan from seeking to express the ancient textual traditions in a cheerful and progressive-sounding modern language.

And so, Ramadan considers himself to be—it goes without saying—a feminist. Better: an "Islamic feminist," which is an old claim among the Islamists. The Muslim Brotherhood used to affirm an "Islamic feminism" long ago in Egypt. The "Islamic feminist" argument makes the case that Islam itself, in its pure salafi version, should be regarded as a force for women's rights. In the period before the Koranic revelation, people in the Arabian peninsula acted on relatively primitive cultural assumptions about women and their role in society. But Islam improved upon the assumptions, and then moved from Mecca (where cultural customs regarding women were less advanced) to Medina (where customs were more advanced), and, in that fashion, improved upon the improvements. Islam came to stand for the general principle of improvement. Islam, as Ramadan interprets it, requires women to wear headscarves or veils in order to advance the cause of women's autonomy. The scarves and the veils, the separate entranceways and seating sections, the general ban on intermingling the sexes and other such traditional Islamic rules and customs—these things are not at all intended to repress women or push them into a lower status than men. The purpose is to uphold a spirit of sexual modesty and, by doing so, to remove women from the oppression of male considerations.

Modesty is liberation, from this perspective. Separate makes equal. And Ramadan's argument merges finally into a larger argument, which appears to be, at first glance, the modern argument for rights—the argument for the right to choose one's own path, regardless of the tyrannous opinions of an oppressive majority. It is the argument that might almost be called, using the English-language political vocabulary, liberalism—though Ramadan, with his French vocabulary, is more likely to speak of progressivism. It is an argument for individual rights, which is also an argument for cultural rights—an argument for the right of each separate culture to go on wending its disparate and traditional way. And the whole of Ramadan's presentation of these points, his talk of Islamic feminism, his modern-style but Islamically-inflected talk of rights in general, together with his enthusiasm for cultural diversity—the whole of this vocabulary has, like so many other aspects of his thinking, pushed its way into the public debate, not just in France. But first of all in France.

This was because, in 2004, the French government adopted a law mandating a dress code in the public schools, and the law ignited a fractious debate. The law banned the display of showy religious symbols in the schools. By the provisions of the law, Christian students could no longer wear large crucifixes to school, and Sikh boys could no longer wear their turbans, and Jewish boys could no longer wear their yarmulkes. But everyone knew that, in the end, the law was aimed at Islamic headscarves or veils. Nothing in the French law forbade the wearing of discrete and unobtrusive religious symbols in the schools—a small Christian medallion, for instance, or an Islamic amulet displaying a Koranic verse. And nothing prevented students from donning the showiest of religious clothes as soon as they had exited the schoolhouse doors. The streets remained dress-code-free. But the schools were regulated. The law became known as the headscarf law, or sometimes as the law of the veil (with headscarves and veils being regarded, from the point of view of this particular law, as the same: ostentatious displays of religious identity). And, all over the world, people argued over the new French law.

Naturally Ramadan objected to the law, and he posed his opposition precisely as a kind of liberal advocacy. "Rights are rights," he said. "And to demand them is a right." Such was his argument to Buruma at the *Times Magazine*. He meant that Muslims have the right to observe the requirements of their own religion and have the right to protest against people who deny them the right. This way of presenting the debate evidently struck Buruma as persuasive. Ramadan, Buruma wrote, "promoted the right of Muslim women to wear the veil at French schools"—which was pretty much how Ramadan himself likes to put it. *The New York Times Book Review* followed suit, under Stéphanie Giry's byline. Ramadan, in Giry's presentation (reviewing the Muhammad biography), opposed the headscarf law on what she described as "classic libertarian grounds—the right of Muslim girls to choose for themselves whether to cover up."

And yet, these descriptions were remarkably one-sided, simply from a news-reporting standpoint. You could easily have imagined, from reading about Ramadan and the headscarf law in the *Times*, that French arguments over the law broke down into two distinct camps—a civil libertarian argument favoring rights for Muslims, nobly upheld by Ramadan and his fellow-thinkers, and an argument opposed to rights for Muslims, upheld by the enemies of Islam and by people indifferent to individual freedom. Other sides of that debate nonetheless existed. In France the government organized a commission to look into the merits of the law, and the commission held hearings, and any number of arguments emerged. Some of the arguments were silly. Some of the arguments reflected antique Christian or European prejudices against Islam. Still other arguments drew on anti-Christian instincts from the French Revolution and resentful memories of Catholic domination of the schools. The stately theme of French republican tradition sailed into view. Some people cried, "*Écrasez l'infâme!*" But the most telling of the arguments over the headscarf law rested on a social issue of our own time, and not the past. It was invoked by one witness after another at the hearings—though you would hardly know any of this from the reporting on Ramadan and his own position.

This last, narrow argument touched on the history of the Muslim immigration and its motivations. The millions of people who have made their way from their original homelands in the Muslim world to a chilly new life in Western Europe, across the Mediterranean—what have those people been looking for? A bit of schooling, among other things. Grown-ups looked for jobs, and maybe some of the grown-ups looked for welfare; but everyone, or nearly everyone, meanwhile sent the children to school. They sent the boys, but they also sent, the girls, which was sometimes a novel thing to do. And the immigrant girls, as they made their way to the schoolhouse, what did they wear? During the first twenty or thirty years of the mass immigration in France, they wore the same kinds of clothes that other girls, their non-Muslim schoolmates, wore.

The Islamist movement has always emphasized dress-codes, however. And the Islamists began to prosper, and 1989 was their moment. The very first headscarves that caused any kind of big stir appeared in the French schools in that year—a sign of the new political development. And, as headscarves became more common, a small controversy began to unfold, which became a large controversy. The Islamists, as they grew stronger in France, made their curricular demands about Voltaire, Darwin, and the history of German war crimes, and these demands attracted most of the attention in the French press, if only because of how simple and cranky the demands seemed to be. But the truly important demands bore on the question of female education. The Islamists launched a campaign to limit the education of girls and women, and to limit their access to health care, too. In the schools, Muslim girls under the Islamist influence—a handful at first—refused to participate

in gym class. It was because of the immodest clothes
that sports require. The girls under an Islamist influence refused to be alone with male teachers. In the
hospitals and clinics, girls and women refused to be
examined or treated by male doctors. At the national hearings, a number of witnesses described those
developments. And one other large and extremely
disturbing fact emerged.

Quite a few Muslim girls and women in France
honestly had no desire to see their educational and
health care opportunities demurely shrink into something less than the maximum. The girls and women
refused to take gym class and engage in other activities for one reason only: they were under pressure to conform to the Islamist demands. Sometimes
the pressure came from their families at home, and
sometimes from other people in the Muslim community, in opposition to their families. Either way, the
pressure came, in the end, from the Islamist movement, which had become a neighborhood power.
Islamists demanded headscarves. Schoolgirls did as
they were told. Headscarves became a symbol of Islamist power. Headscarves were also a mechanism of
Islamist enforcement. Headscarves guaranteed that
any erring Muslim schoolgirl who dared to venture
into the wrong classroom or into a forbidden gym-
nasium was going to be instantly visible to every
disapproving eye.

The headscarf for those schoolgirls was not a
sign of Muslim piety, nor of religious humility, nor
of sexual modesty. Nor was the headscarf an admirable gesture of immigrant defiance against the tyrannical demands of the rest of society. Nor were
those headscarves a teenage rebellion (though some
people figured they were, and applauded). The headscarf, for those particular girls, was a sign of their

own intimidation. Some of the frightened schoolgirls explained the reality in closed sessions at the hearings, under a promise of anonymity.

And so, the debate over the headscarf law took on a new dimension, once the French public had heard this other and unexpected side of the story. Why ban Islamic headscarves from the schools? A good many people came to think that ultimately the issue was not whether Muslim girls had a right to wear headscarves in the schools, but whether Muslim girls had the right *not* to wear headscarves. The purpose in proposing a law was not to crush Islam. The purpose was to transform the public schools into a zone beyond the control of an authoritarian political movement. And a larger purpose: to preserve and enforce one of the major achievements of modern society, not yet entirely realized, which is the extension of full rights and benefits to the half of society that is not male.

The battle for education and health care for women has been going on for long enough that, by now, you might have figured that no one could fail to recognize it—a battle that, for two hundred years, has always taken the same form, in one version or another. It is a battle against obscurantist clerics, reactionary patriarchs, and the entrenched prejudices of a conservative society. The nineteenth-century novelists sketched those battles at length. And yet, to judge from the reporting on Ramadan and his opinions in the American press, the entire question of women's rights, virtually every aspect of it, appears to have disappeared from the journalistic imagination. Ramadan and his fellow-thinkers on the headscarf law presented the issue straightfaced as one of rights for Muslims. And the journalists never thought to ask: which Muslims? The Islamists, or the non-

Islamists? Rights for the salafi reformists, or rights for the immigrant strivers, who want to get out from under the salafi reformist thumb? Boualem Sansal has described the streetcorner struggles of Islamists and non-Islamists in his novel, but the journalists reported no such thing.

Then again, the truly fundamental issue in regard to women, more portentous even than classroom opportunities and medical services, has always been a matter of violence and brutality—the violence of husbands against their wives. The genital mutilations of Muslim women from certain regions of Africa, which are said by now to affect some thirty thousand women in France alone. The problem of group rapes, a sinister fad in the French immigrant suburbs in recent years, which has prompted feminists from immigrant Muslim backgrounds, the genuine feminists, to organize a movement called *Ni Putes Ni Soumises*, or Neither Whores Nor Submissives (it sounds better in French)—though Ramadan has denounced the immigrant organization as an anti-immigrant organization. The lurking potential, finally, of outright murders: the so-called honor killings of women by their fathers or brothers in punishment for transgressions of the sexual code. The Norwegian anthropologist Unni Wikan brought out a thorough study of this problem in 2008, called *In Honor of Fadime: Murder and Shame*, and she explained that, in Pakistan, as many as a thousand honor killings take place every year. This is not a minor problem. And, as she explained, the problem is not confined to the Muslim countries. She cited multiple examples from Holland and other countries in Western Europe.

And on this question, too, on the matter of violence against women and especially on the fraught question of religiously-sanctioned murder, Ramadan has taken a remarkable public stand—though it may be that he adopted his stand without much forethought, as something blurted out inadvertently. His position emerged during the course of a television debate in 2003, on the French program "One Hundred Minutes to Convince." His debate opponent was Nicolas Sarkozy, a man of the political right. In those days, Sarkozy was France's hyperactive minister of the interior. The hyperactive minister showed up at the television studio with a debater's trick up his sleeve. He awaited his moment.

The moment turned out to be a question about Ramadan's family—in this case, about Tariq's older brother Hani, who has always taken harder-line positions than Tariq. The two brothers, Tariq and Hani, have cooperated over the years. Both of them have published their writings at the Tawhid house in Lyon. Still, the brothers have been known to get along less than well, sometimes. The question, then, at the television debate: how large was the gap between Hani and Tariq? Sarkozy brought up Hani's view on the proper punishment for women who commit adultery. Hani Ramadan has favored stoning the women to death. The Islamist movement, in its mainstream version, has always dreamed of reviving the corporal punishments of the Koranic past, and the call to stone adulterers to death has been an insistent one.

And Sarkozy pounced. He wanted to know where Tariq Ramadan stood. His own position on the practice of stoning women to death—what was it? Ian Hamel, in *The Truth About Tariq Ramadan*, argues that Ramadan's response to Sarkozy proves at last that Ramadan does not, in fact, practice a "double discourse." He says what he thinks. Candor is his principle. And maybe so, though you could just as plausibly argue that Sarkozy caught Ramadan off guard, and he had no time to drape a discrete and modern curtain across his salafi convictions, and his thoughts came tumbling out undisguised and naked, for all to see. In any event, Tariq Ramadan, as Buruma correctly reported in the *Times Magazine*, "replied that he favored a 'moratorium' on such practices but refused to condemn the law outright."

Aziz Zemouri provides a transcript in his book *Should Tariq Ramadan Be Silenced?*. The transcript offers a fine display of the French fondness for the ellipsis as an expressive punctuation:

> Mr. Sarkozy: A moratorium... Mr. Ramadan, are you serious?
>
> Mr. Ramadan: Wait, let me finish.
>
> Mr. Sarkozy: A moratorium, that is to say, we should, for a while, hold back from stoning women?
>
> Mr. Ramadan: No, no, wait... What does a moratorium mean? A moratorium would mean that we absolutely end the application of all of those penalties, in order to have a true debate. And my position is that if we arrive at a consensus among Muslims, it will necessarily end. But you cannot, you know, when you are in a community... Today on television, I can please the French people who are watching by saying, 'Me, my own position.' But my own position doesn't count. What matters is to bring about an evolution in Muslim mentalities, Mr. Sarkozy. It's necessary that you understand...
>
> Mr. Sarkozy: But, Mr. Ramadan...
>
> Mr. Ramadan: Let me finish.

Mr. Sarkozy: Just one point. I understand you, but Muslims are human beings who live in 2003 in France, since we are speaking about the French community, and you have just said something particularly incredible, which is that the stoning of women, yes, the stoning is a bit shocking, but we should simply declare a moratorium, and then we are going to think about it in order to decide if it is good... But that's monstrous—to stone a woman because she is an adulterer! It's necessary to condemn it!

Mr. Ramadan: Mr. Sarkozy, listen well to what I am saying. What I say, my own position, is that the law is not applicable—that's clear. But today, I speak to Muslims around the world and I take part, even in the United States, in the Muslim world... You should have a pedagogical posture that makes people discuss things. You can decide all by yourself to be a progressive in the communities. That's too easy. Today my position is, that is to say, 'We should stop.'

Mr. Sarkozy: Mr. Ramadan, if it is regressive not to want to stone women, I avow that I am a regressive.

Some six million French people watched that exchange. A huge number of Muslim immigrants must have been among them—the very people who might have benefited from hearing a prestigious and articulate public figure speak with absolute clarity about violence against women. Ramadan was not up to it. Here was his Qutbian moment, the moment of frisson. The seventh century had suddenly appeared, poking out from beneath the modern rhetoric of feminism and rights. A moment of barbarism. A thrill. The whole panorama of Muslim women's oppression suddenly deployed across the television screens of France—the panorama of violence that is condoned, sanctified, and even mandated by the highest of religious authorities, or, at any rate, by the authorities who are venerated by the Islamist movement. And here was Sarkozy, recoiling in horror: the bourgeoisie, shocked at last.

Sarkozy had more to say. Ramadan had written yet another preface, this time introducing a book that cites the Koranic passage enjoining husbands to beat their wives under certain circumstances—though the book maintained that beatings should merely amount to a light slap, without producing a physical wound. Sarkozy was mordant: "We are grateful for this advice and recommendation."

And yet—here is another peculiarity—some people, and not just salafi reformists, have convinced themselves that Ramadan came out looking pretty good in that exchange. There is the case of Olivier Roy, one of the France's supreme experts on Islam and Muslim culture. In his book *Globalized Islam*, Roy took the view that Ramadan's argument on stoning was more than understandable—it was positively progressive. Ramadan's argument was a blow for secularism, on the grounds that state and church ought to be separate. Ramadan had affirmed the autonomy of his own religious sphere, and he had done so against the demands of a high French government official. And yet Ramadan had affirmed the autonomy of the religious sphere with just the right touch of hypocrisy not to run afoul of secular law. From this point of view, Sarkozy, the interior minister, was the tyrannical oppressor, and Ramadan, the progressive. Such was Olivier Roy's very curious argument.

Buruma's outlook in the *Times Magazine* was cagier. Buruma wrote: "When I talked with Ramadan in London, the mere mention of the word 'stoning' set him on a long explanation.

"'Personally,' he said, 'I'm against capital punishment, not only in Muslim countries, but also in the U.S. But when you want to be heard in Muslim countries, when you are addressing religious issues, you can't just say it has to stop. I think it has to stop. But you have to discuss it within the religious context. There are texts involved. I am not just talking to Muslims in Europe, but addressing the implementation of *huddud* everywhere, in Indonesia, Pakistan and the Middle East. And I'm speaking from the inside to Muslims. Speaking as an outsider would be counterproductive.'"

And Buruma left his commentary at that, without appending any remark of his own. Still, the journalist lingered over one aspect of Ramadan's argument, and this was the matter of speaking to Muslims as an insider, and not as an outsider. A pragmatic question. A matter of political positioning. On this matter, Buruma figured that Ramadan was on to something. Buruma invited his readers to amble with him, in their imagination, down Brick Lane in London's East End—the old and traditional immigrant district, which, as he lachrymosely observed, "used to be a poor Jewish area, where refugees from Russian pogroms eked out a living in the Sunday markets, cheap clothing stores and kosher eating halls." Nowadays the immigrants on Brick Lane tend to be Bangladeshis and Pakistanis. And, against the backdrop of those colorful and touching scenes, Buruma contemplated Ramadan and compared him with another up-to-date intellectual with sharp opinions and a Muslim background.

This second person was Ayaan Hirsi Ali, a well-known personality in large parts of the world by now—someone who was born in Somalia and, as a young woman, made her way to Europe to pursue an education and have her say. One more immigrant striver. Hirsi Ali found refuge in Buruma's homeland, which is Holland. She plunged into her studies, then into political activism. She wrote books. One of those books was expressively called *Infidel*. A second book, under the title *The Caged Virgin*, was subtitled *An Emancipation Proclamation for Women and Islam*—which is to say that here, at last, is someone not afraid to proclaim her opinions openly to the world.

In the *Times Magazine*, Buruma looked on Hirsi Ali and Tariq Ramadan as parallel figures. "Her mission, too, is to spread universal values. She, too, speaks of reform"—though I have to interrupt these quotations to recall a couple of observations from previous chapters, namely that Buruma's understanding of Ramadan's universal values is based on a philosophical mistake, and his appropriation of Ramadan's word *reform* rests on a factual error. He continued on the topic of Hirsi Ali: "But she has renounced her belief in Islam. She says that Islam is backward and perverse. As a result, she has had more success with secular non-Muslims than with the kind of people who shop in Brick Lane." Ramadan, though, has avoided this fate. His prestige and popularity among the immigrant masses, his ability to address the masses and be respectfully received, have remained intact—in Buruma's estimation, at any rate.

In sum, Ramadan made the right decision in refusing to condemn the practice of stoning women to death—not for Olivier Roy's reason (a principled blow for secularism) but on political grounds: to maintain his viability on streets like Brick Lane. This ought to be a familiar argument. It is the argument that Sartre famously invoked in order to explain why he refused to condemn Stalin and the Soviet Union, back in the days when Stalin was popular in the French working class. Sartre invited his readers to think about the industrial suburb of Paris called Billancourt, where the oppressed and exploited workers, not knowing any better, kept up their old belief in communism and the Soviet future. Sartre did not want to demoralize the downtrodden, to *désespérer* Billancourt. And so, Sartre bit his tongue, and if the ignorant proletarians of France were going to learn the truth about the Soviet Union, it was not going to be from France's most famous philosopher. And Ramadan is right not to *désespérer* Brick Lane by offering a straight-out condemnation of violence against women.

Yet another positive evaluation of Ramadan's response to Sarkozy ran in Stéphanie Giry's review of Ramadan's biography of Muhammad in *The New York Times Book Review*. Giry argued that Ramadan's refusal to condemn stoning could be sympathetically regarded as, in her words, "an expression of his view that each society must decide for itself how to put into practice the values of Islam." An argument for self-determination. It is almost comic to notice that Olivier Roy, Ian Buruma and Stéphanie Giry disagree entirely about why Ramadan was right to take the position that he did, but all three commentators agree that, whatever the rationale, he was right. To go on television and unambiguously condemn the stoning to death of Muslim women—surely everyone can see how wrong that would have been, especially for any progressive and enlightened person who cares about secular values, poverty, colonialism, and the plight of the immigrants! This is amazing.

Ramadan himself was plainly stung by Sarkozy's jabs, and, in the years since then, he has never let the issue drop. In 2005 he elevated his call for a moratorium to a formal proposal, issued in his own name and directed at the entire Muslim world, proposing a moratorium on the whole range of Islamically-mandated corporal punishments. He made the case that, in our present age, the religiously-stipulated conditions for carrying out the ancient punishments no longer exist and cannot be brought back into existence. The punishments ought to be suspended, therefore, and their future status placed under formal discussion. Such was his argument. It evoked a response. He appears to have been surprised and a little hurt by certain aspects of that response. Among the twenty million or so Muslims in Europe today, a great many people, in spite of what you may read about streets like Brick Lane, have adapted perfectly well to the modern and liberal values of present-day Europe; and people with modern and liberal ideas were hardly going to burst into applause at the prospect of participating in a debate over barbaric religious injunctions that bore on their own lives not at all. Nor were they going to respond to a summons from Tariq Ramadan.

The Muslims most likely to take an interest in his proposed debate were bound to be a different population altogether—the adherents of the various ideological factions that descend from the Muslim Brotherhood, the salafi reformists and their literalist comrades, who do, in fact, approve of the barbaric practices, or at least make a point of saying they do. Naturally the literalists showed no interest in departing from literalism. But neither did the reformists show much interest. Ramadan's critics looked upon him as a man who had taken a step too far, who had succumbed to the pressures of Western liberal culture, whose proposals were bound to neutralize the beneficent strictures of Islam—meaning, their own version of Islam. Yusuf al-Qaradawi presides over a large and apparently well-financed salafi reformist website in Arabic and English called IslamOnline.net, based in Qatar and Cairo but aimed in large part at Europe (and with an office in Washington, DC). And the website, to judge from Ramadan's plaint, appears to have responded less than enthusiastically. Ramadan ended up at odds even with his own most beloved hero—at odds, anyway, with Qaradawi's allies, comrades and minions at the website. Here, you might suppose, was a fateful turn in Ramadan's career—potentially a break with his past.

He has persisted, even so. In 2009, he published a broadly elaborated fullscale rumination under the title *Radical Reform: Islamic Ethics and Liberation*. In his TV appearance with Sarkozy back in 2003, Ramadan had called for, in his phrase, "a true debate," and *Radical Reform* proposed some imaginative ways to go about conducting the true debate—not only in regard to stoning adulterers but with a variety of Islamic topics and controversial matters in mind. Who should participate in the true debate? Ramadan specifies. He argues that secular scholars should participate. Here is the apparent novelty in Ramadan's idea, or so it may seem to readers from outside the world of Islam—though, in reality, the notion of bringing together scholars of various sorts for consultation on religious topics is altogether ancient. Still, Ramadan's account of his proposed group of secular consultants does sound appealingly up-to-date. He calls for the participation of schol-

ars whose fields of study exude an atmosphere of
the latest word: "power relations, the relationship to
language, modes of expression and communication,
generational relations and/or gaps, knowledge and
behavior transmission modalities, male-female relations, group relations, collective psychology, even
'rites of passage,' established or not, which remain
present even in the most modern societies."

The schools of academic thought that descend
from Claude Lévi-Strauss, Michel Foucault and
Jacques Derrida would plainly be well-represented.
Then again, Ramadan expresses a willingness to hear
out artists and writers, too, and even to include the
kinds of rebellious artists whose art is provocation.
He leaves room for well-intentioned non-Muslims
who command an expertise on this or that question.
These people would join together in committees. The
whole idea amounts to a kind of academic utopia.
A daydream of the faculty dining hall. It is a call
for a multi-disciplinary task force on the hugest of
scales, with the multi-disciplines defined along lines
that might prove to be especially appealing to the
dining hall's political left. It goes without saying that
Ramadan intends to rely on the traditional Islamic
scholars, too—the masters of what are called the "Islamic sciences." Owing to the participation of the
Islamic-science scholars, the multi-disciplinary task
forces would end up wielding a more than academic
power. A more than secular power, truth to tell.

Ramadan bestows on these task forces the non-
university label of "fatwa committees." The fatwa
committees would train their cumulative secular-and-
sacred wisdoms on the challenges of our age. These,
too, he enumerates: the need to generate a sounder
ecology, the need to recognize the diversity of human
culture, the need to promote the individual, the need

to affirm the rights of women, the need to prevent cruelty to animals, and so on. He goes so far as to discuss the advisability of adopting tolerant attitudes even toward homosexuality, if only as a practical necessity imposed by the AIDS epidemic and the need to come up with effective responses. And the fatwa committees would presumably discuss whether stoning adulterers to death continues to be a good idea.

I notice that, even in *Radical Reform*, Ramadan never does come out with a full, roundhouse condemnation of the practice. It is not that, faced with an injustice, Ramadan is incapable of expressing indignation. He notes in this book that, in many mosques in the Muslim countries, there is no space for women, to which he responds, "This is simply not acceptable!" No such exclamation mark on stoning women to death. Still, the book leaves a distinct impression that a properly constituted modern-day fatwa committee, drawing on the scholarly expertise of researchers into power relations, language structures, and gender relations, ultimately would, in its pooled wisdom, decide to bring the practice to an end. The whole purpose of the true debate and the fatwa committees would be to come up with, in his phrase, an "applied Islamic ethics," and the applied ethics would be shaped into Islamic law. A fatwa would accordingly be issued, and presumably stoning would henceforth be deemed contrary to the properly and legitimately modernized dictates of Islam.

You might wonder: why would the Islamic scholars in Ramadan's proposed fatwa committees agree to listen respectfully or grant even the slightest authority to secular experts from the post-modern universities and even from the world of rebel culture? What reasoning would lead the Islamic scholars to do such a thing? Ramadan addresses the question. I have to confess that his answer fills me with delight, for a moment. I am charmed, almost. It is because, in presenting his argument, he invokes, not for the first time, his grandfather's preferred sage, the philosopher al-Ghazali. The doctrines of al-Ghazali turn out to be, as I had never fully appreciated before, central to Ramadan's worldview, and not just to his grandfather's. "Reformism" itself, in Ramadan's presentation, began with al-Ghazali, back in the twelfth century. And now that I see how powerfully al-Ghazali looms over Ramadan's thinking, I have gone to the trouble, all too belatedly, of digging up some of al-Ghazali's better-known books—and for this, more than for anything else, I feel a surge of gratitude to Tariq Ramadan.

Al-Ghazali, I have discovered (I am nine hundred years late in making this discovery), was a marvel. And a joy. And a puzzlement. He lived from 1058 CE to 1111 CE, mostly in Persia, though he spent many years teaching law in Baghdad, too. He wrote prolifically. He was a Sufi mystic. I am sad to report that al-Ghazali's reputation among the historians of ideas is, by and large, wretched. He is regarded as the Islamic thinker who, in the name of maintaining the purity of Islam, persuaded the Muslim world of the Middle Ages to turn away from the ancient Greek philosophers. He declared war on Socrates, Hippocrates, Aristotle, Plato and Plato's followers within the Muslim word, the neo-Platonists—the "dimwits," in al-Ghazali's mocking locution (which I draw from his treatise *The Incoherence of the Philosophers*, in the Brigham Young University translation by Michael E. Marmura). And, to be sure, in the centuries after al-Ghazali, the leading Islamic thinkers did turn away from the Greek philosophers and the Islamic "dimwits."

The lights went out on Islam's Age of Enlightenment. Islam's Dark Ages got underway. Science went into eclipse. Religious tolerance, too. In H. Graetz's telling, one of the terrible persecutions of the Jews that did take place under medieval Islam, in Morocco during the twelfth century, was inaugurated by a personal disciple of al-Ghazali's, who came to Morocco from Baghdad bearing the mystic word, which turned out to be a call for religious hatred. Such was reformism in its earliest version. Still, I wonder how much of the blame for these sorry developments should be laid on al-Ghazali's shoulders. The question does get debated.

To cite a lively instance of that debate from our own moment: Steven Weinberg, the distinguished physicist, published an essay called "Without God" in *The New York Review of Books* in 2008, pointing to al-Ghazali as one of the many religious thinkers over the centuries who have inflicted a genuine damage on science—in al-Ghazali's case, by arguing that laws of nature do not exist. (Al-Ghazali thought that God makes all the decisions, which are normally predictable, though now and then He works a miracle.) But a learned reader from Chicago responded with a letter insisting that al-Ghazali's ideas are subtler than you might suppose from Weinberg's essay, and certain of those ideas could even be seen as anticipating David Hume, from the eighteenth century. Ramadan in *Radical Reform* defends al-Ghazali along roughly similar lines. Ramadan points out that, even if al-Ghazali did set out to refute the Greek philosophers, his refutations trod a disciplined philosophical path.

He was analytically rigorous—as you can see for yourself in his *Incoherence of the Philosophers*. And in *Radical Reform*, Ramadan rehearses one more time the claim from his early book *Islam, the West and the Challenge of Modernity* about the historic place of al-Ghazali's intellectual explorations—Ramadan's insistence that, on the matter of philosophical doubt, al-Ghazali anticipated Descartes, from the seventeenth century. (And, just to show that Tariq Ramadan will yield not one inch to his hectoring critics, in *Radical Reform* he repeats a scholarly footnote, as well, from *Islam, the West and the Challenge of Modernity*, respectfully citing a relevant study of Descartes by none other than... his own brother Hani Ramadan, the defender of stoning women!)

Myself, if I wanted to gild al-Ghazali's reputation with the prestige of some admired philosopher from a later age, I would turn to William James, the brother of Henry, from the years around 1900. William James was sufficiently curious about the history of Islam to get hold of al-Ghazali's autobiography and to insert a couple of vivid pages from it into *The Varieties of Religious Experience*. James wanted to show his readers the qualities of a mystical imagination in a Muslim version. And James noticed that al-Ghazali was pretty clever at something apart from mystical reveries. Al-Ghazali knew how to put his finger on a specific psychological reality—on the subtle difference between experiencing something for yourself, and merely learning about it from other people. On this point, William James was certainly right.

The great thing about Plato's followers, the neo-Platonists, was their desire to identify different mental stages. The neo-Platonists wanted to describe the several ways you might know some aspect of the world—the way you might, for instance, *sort of* know something; or *really* know something; or *really really* know something. Or you might know something *absolutely* well, such that your knowledge surpasses mere words, and you can no longer express what you know in ordinary language, and, instead, you experience your own knowledge as an electric thrill of mystic union between yourself and the universe. The neo-Platonists of long ago were wonderfully adept at sketching those cognitive gradations. And so was al-Ghazali—even if he declared himself an enemy of the neo-Platonists of long ago.

He devoted a major work to describing the different ways you might know the universe. This was his treatise *The Niche For Lights*, or *Mishkat al-Anwar*, which I have come across in a flowery Victorian translation by someone named W.H.T. Gairdner, published in a modern edition by the Islamic Book Service of New Delhi. (Ramadan disapproves of this translation, but I notice that the Islamic Book Service also publishes Sheikh Qaradawi, which leads me to guess that Gairdner's translation cannot be utterly without merit, from a salafi reformist point of view.) *The Niche For Lights* offers a commentary on a single verse of the Koran, Surah 24, verse 35. In the verse, the light of Allah shines in star-like brilliance from a lamp, which is housed in a crystal, which is housed in a niche. And with this haunting image of light and niche invoked, al-Ghazali goes about painting his picture of the universe and the ways we experience it—a dissertation on light as knowledge and as more than knowledge, and on knowledge as a yearning. And, in the course of his exposition, al-Ghazali explains that reality itself consists of two different worlds. There is the World Terrestrial, and there is the Realm Celestial. We know the World Terrestrial through the senses, in an ordinary crude way. The World Terrestrial, though, is ultimately a text, which we cannot know through the senses. We need to read it, and to interpret what we read.

Reading and interpreting require talent, study and labor. Still, the light from Allah's lamp tumbles outward from the sacred niche upon the World Terrestrial, and, in the glow of the downward-falling light, a knowledgeable scholar can bend to the task of deciphering and interpreting. Study will reveal the hidden meaning. We will begin to see, at last, the world in its true reality. This is the Realm Celestial. Al-Ghazali's exposition of these ideas sends you clambering up and down from World Terrestrial to Realm Celestial, making your way through a divine light that is diffused by seventy thousand veils—though he concedes that maybe there are only seven hundred veils. Angels flutter past. The entire discussion could hardly be more thrilling. And the discussion ends up doubly thrilling because, in a handful of passing remarks, he halfway suggests that, for all his veils and angels, he is not entirely a fantasist.

He is a metaphorist. His arguments remind me in a general way of Plotinus, Plato's follower in ancient Rome—even if al-Ghazali must have regarded, or pretended to regard, Plotinus as king of the dimwits. And, like Plotinus, al-Ghazali evokes a recognizable set of experiences—the different levels of intensity that you might bring to your appreciation and knowledge of the world. He does this with splendid precision, too. You feel that, if al-Ghazali were asked to identify and catalogue the degree of luminous divine brilliance that passes through each of those seventy thousand veils, he could do so with ease and pleasure. You can understand why, eight hundred years later, William James found something to admire in this man's writings.

And from al-Ghazali's doctrines, Tariq Ramadan has drawn his own set of prim and seemingly earnest ideas, though with none of the poetic splendor or emotional intensity. Ramadan, too, regards the universe as a double reality—as two worlds instead of one. Al-Ghazali sometimes describes the World Terrestrial and the Realm Celestial as two separate-and-related books—the "outspread book," which is the ordinary universe, and the "written book," which is the Koran. Ramadan adopts this language for himself. He speaks of two capital-B Books—the Book of the world before your eyes, and the Book of the sacred Islamic scriptures. Both of those Books can be regarded as capital-R Revelations. Both of those Books need to be read and interpreted. And, since the task of reading and interpreting requires disciplined study by well-trained experts, the scholars who pore over either of those two Books can look upon the scholars who pore over the other as esteemed colleagues and even as equals—the way that university researchers in geological rock formations, say, might look upon the classics department. Ramadan's proposed fatwa committees, with these metaphysical ideas in mind, can make room for experts of many kinds, sacred and secular—scholars of one Book and of the other, all of them adjusting their eyeglasses and bending collegially over the texts before them.

The charm in Ramadan's exposition, by my lights, rests on its rare and even astounding antiquity. He points out that ideas like al-Ghazali's used to be, as *Radical Reform* puts it, "common in early renaissance literature." This is true. The fifteenth and sixteenth centuries were the Golden Age of cosmic speculation in Europe. The early Renaissance savants looked upon the world as a universe of cryptic symbols, and they set out to catalogue and interpret the symbols, and they expected that, with a proper application of learning and logic, they would ultimately penetrate the symbols into the secrets of the otherwise inscrutable spiritual world. Did the European savants draw in any significant fashion on al-Ghazali himself? They did. Al-Ghazali studied the ancient Greeks and the neo-Platonists, and, in the Middle Ages, Hebrew and Latin translators brought his texts into one language and the other, which allowed them to pass into the larger European imagination; and, in that fashion, al-Ghazali contributed to the larger project of rescuing the forgotten ideas of the ancient Greeks and Romans.

Ramadan makes a larger claim. Those early Renaissance ideas, he explains, "gradually changed the outlook of the world, which was seen as a space to be deciphered, interpreted, and understood: a horizon open to reason, learning, and science." Ramadan means to suggest that he himself, as an al-Ghazalian of our own era, stands in the grandest of intellectual traditions—in the current of thought that led to the progress, in his words, of "reason, learning, and science" during the early Renaissance. And, if I understand him correctly, Ramadan means to suggest that his own tradition, which is al-Ghazali's, has remained a living tradition.

I wonder, though. My eyebrow rises at Ramadan's mention of science. I think he has skipped over a crucial point. The early Renaissance savants labored assiduously at deciphering and interpreting, just as Ramadan says; and yet they never did make any progress. The secrets of the world of spirit remained secret. Progress in science was close to nil. The savants were stymied. What Ramadan describes as an open horizon remained hopelessly narrow. When science in Europe did begin to show a few signs of indisputable progress, the advances came suddenly, not gradually. And the advances came about only because the savants had decided to stage an uprising against the very ideas that resembled and even descended from al-Ghazali's theory of the two Books, Terrestial and Celestial. The scientists abandoned the notion of a two-tiered, symbolic-and-spiritual universe. They gave up on the notion of viewing the world as a text. They looked for hard facts instead of symbols. They took to measuring things, instead of interpreting things. And, lo, the horizons of learning did begin to widen. The moment of breakthrough did not come about during the early Renaissance, though. The scientists' revolt took place in the seventeenth century. Their revolt marked the beginning of the modern age.

Still, the early Renaissance doctrine about symbols and a world of spirit went on clinging to life, in plain evidence that here was a vital and vigorous intellectual tradition, regardless of various disappointments and mass defections. Ramadan is right about that. The tradition was no longer scientific, though. It was a poets' tradition. The poets began to suspect that modern science, for all its visible successes, was failing to get at some deep truths. The mechanical view of the world seemed hopelessly inadequate. And so, after the scientists had staged their rebellion against the old ideas, the poets staged their own rebellion against the scientists. The poets set about reviving the old ideas as a kind of alternative culture, independent of the scientists and critical of the scientific cult of hard facts and mechanical explanations. And the poets' alternative culture has gone on producing criticisms for several hundred years now, sometimes under one name, sometimes under another. Under the name of Romantic poetry, for instance.

American readers will dimly recall the shape and texture of the Romantic poetry ideas from the essays of Ralph Waldo Emerson—who was, after

all, the Founding Father of American literature.
Emerson was brought up to revere the mechanical
and scientific-minded doctrines that ruled Harvard
and the Unitarian Church in his time. But he re-
belled. He embraced Plato. He quoted Plotinus. He
set about reviving the whole philosophical system of
the old ideas. The visible as symbol of the spiritual
became his greatest theme. His revival was literary,
philosophical, and religious at once. Emerson even
entertained the hope that science and the grand old
heritage from Plotinus and the Plato-followers of
yore could ultimately be reconciled.

His revival drew on the Islamic past. He loved
Hafiz, the mystical medieval Persian poet. He trans-
lated sumptuous lyrics by Hafiz into stony New
England verse. He translated Saadi—yet another
Plato-besotted Persian Sufi. He quoted the Koran.
The Founding Father of American literature thought
Islam was marvelous. I wonder what would have
happened if, in the course of his library browsings,
Emerson had ever come across al-Ghazali's *The Incoherence of the Philosophers*. I think he would have
entertained some reservations. But what about *The
Niche For Lights*? I can guess. The author of "The
Over-Soul," who regarded himself as a transparent
eyeball, would have studied al-Ghazali's account of
eyesight, lightbeams and the Realm Celestial. And
the transparent eyeball would have leapt from his library chair in excitement, overwhelmed by feelings of
brotherly communion with still another distant mystic Muslim from medieval Persia. In any event, I will
confess that the Emersonian in me reads *The Niche
For Lights* with an occasional skip of the heart.

Emerson was a man of the mid-nineteenth century, though, and he and his generation were the
last intellectually sophisticated people to imagine

that science and the old ideas might resolve their differences someday and reunite. If any scientists were left in those days who still toyed with the old ideas and their analytic possibilities, *The Origin of Species* seems to have finished them off forever. And the poets went into a prolonged sulk. They were not about to abandon the old doctrine. But they bent it around a new and gloomier theme, which has remained a lasting fixture of modern literature. This is the sorrowful theme of philosophical defeat—the recognition that, however exhilarating the archaic ideas about a world of symbols and a world of spirit may once have been, or however acutely those old ideas may get at mysterious truths even now, a modern person has no alternative but to accept that science rules the day.

The archaic doctrine, in its new post-Darwin literary adaptation, became a kind of protest idea. The poets went on affirming the doctrine in order to withdraw moodily from the unappealing modern world (this was Verlaine's theme), or to weepily proclaim their own freely-chosen inebriation (Darío's theme), or to bathe in gorgeous nostalgias (Wallace Stevens's theme), or to strike a dandy pose, ironic and detached, laughing at their own absurdities (Borges's theme). And then, in the mid-twentieth century, the French post-modernist philosophers came up with still more revivals of the old doctrine, stranger still, half in earnest, half ironic, which converted the archaic notion of a symbolic world into a cult of linguistics.

I am aware that my cartoon summary of six hundred years of relations between science, poetry and neo-Platonist theorizing may lack something in nuance and detail. Still, my summary is sufficient, I think, to allow me to ask where Ramadan and his al-Ghazalian ideas stand in this history. His own revival of the doctrine of two worlds, symbolic and spiritual—how does his revival fit into the pattern of previous revivals and disputes over these past hundreds of years? Maybe I am foolish to ask. Ramadan, you could argue, has set out to revive al-Ghazali's medieval doctrine merely for rhetorical purposes, and not because he wishes to promote any particular philosophical or even literary goals. He has wanted to win a couple of arguments, and nothing more.

He has wanted to convince the narrow-minded conservative scholars of the "Islamic sciences" to open their minds to modern-day secular ideas. He would like to persuade the Islamic scholars that, if they paid a little attention to high-minded sociologists or other experts from the Western universities, no sort of treason to ancient Islam would be committed. The Islamic scholars could hear out even the most roguish of their secular colleagues, and, if anything bothersome or upsetting were uttered or proposed, the horrified Islamic scholars, clutching the walls, could steady their bearings by reflecting on al-Ghazali's capacious theory of the two Books from circa 1100 CE. Or maybe Ramadan wants to persuade the secular colleagues. He wants to convince his liberal critics that he does know how to influence opinions among the scholarly old Islamic Neanderthals. He wields a secret weapon for this purpose, which is the fabulous doctrine of al-Ghazali, and his critics should demonstrate a little patience while he puts the fabulous doctrine into effect. Either way, he wants to issue reassurances in every direction, and his capital-letter theories about Books and Revelations are merely a forensic device, and there is no point in looking too closely into the creaky old ideas. Or so you could argue, or at least, hope.

Still, when I read *Radical Reform*, I do not see any evidence that Ramadan thinks of his argument as merely a rhetorical flourish. The poets who came after Darwin knew that, in continuing to play with the ancient doctrine, they were looking at the world aslant, and they wanted their readers to know it, too. The slant was their theme. But Ramadan, in promoting his doctrine of the two Books, appears to be straightforwardly sincere—a sober researcher with a PowerPoint presentation, displaying his medieval cosmological theories on a giant screen behind the podium. He is not striking an attitude. He is presenting a brief. And yet, how is that possible, in our twenty-first century? What can he be thinking of?

Considered as a scientific doctrine, those old ideas lost a wheel sometime back in the seventeenth century. Considered as a poetry doctrine, the old ideas receded into a self-conscious protest in the later nineteenth century. Considered as a theology, the old ideas long ago retreated to a special corner of the imagination, designated for religious purposes. But Ramadan is unfazed. He speaks of the two Books and the two Revelations as if he were making ordinary sense. And so, the old ideas, in this latest of revivals, have assumed a newer form yet, which appears to owe nothing at all to the intellectual developments of the last four hundred years. In Ramadan's version, the old ideas have reemerged as crackpot ideas. They are a medieval contraption, presented as a modern gadget. And the crackpot quality in his ideas leads to consequences.

Caroline Fourest worried about these consequences as long ago as 2004, when she published *Brother Tariq*. Ramadan had already held his debate about stoning with Sarkozy, and he had already spelled out a few preliminary thoughts about his proposed moratorium and his proposed fatwa committees. He had not yet laid out any details, though. Even so, Fourest, back in 2004, raised an eyebrow at the entire proposal. She wondered who was going to occupy the Islamic side of Ramadan's proposed fatwa debate. The experts in the "Islamic sciences," the people who, after consultation with the secular scholars, would presumably issue the new and better-informed fatwas—who were those Islamic experts going to be, exactly?

She took a guess. She pointed out that, as a salafi reformist, Ramadan entertains a precise notion of who constitutes a proper Islamic expert and who does not. She figured that, in choosing the Islamic participants in his proposed fatwa committees, he was not going to select people whose credentials he disputes. And so, Fourest guessed that Ramadan's fatwa committees would end up consisting, on their Islamic scholarly side, of Islamist fanatics, and not of Islamic liberals. And the fiery old fanatics, in their fanaticism, would never decide to abandon their own doctrines. In short, Fourest predicted that Ramadan's proposal was going to turn out to be a sham—a proposal for an open debate that was guaranteed to be a closed debate. The proposal was going to be a cleverly disguised new argument for vesting authority in the leaders of the Islamist movement, who already claim authority. But that was back in 2004, before Ramadan had laid out the details.

Five years later, in *Radical Reform*, he listed the several kinds of secular experts he would like to see joining the Islamic consultation—the Foucauldians, the Derridians, and onwards to the cultural rebels. He noted the many kinds of Islamic scholars who ought to participate, the `ulamâ' in their sundry professional categories—the *fuqahâ'*, *usûliyyûn, mujtahid, a'imma,* and generally the *shuyûkh* or sheikhs and mufti, whose sundry areas of specialization he describes. In the course of the book, he serves up many admirable quotations from the Koran on tolerance and pluralism, too, and the quotations could make you suppose that, in their devotion to the Koran, these many specialized Islamic scholars must surely be the champions of tolerance. Still, in reading his account, you could find yourself wondering who exactly he has in mind. Sheikhs—which sheikhs in particular? The people who will make the crucial decisions in Ramadan's fatwa committees—who will they be? The ultimate authorities on the sacred Book?

I turn his pages with an eye out for actual names—the flesh-and-blood scholars he has in mind, and not just their formal titles and job descriptions. The ethical leaders of Islam, in his estimation. The bold new thinkers. The scholars who, after proper consultation with their secular colleagues, can be counted on to come up with fitting and modern reforms, skillful at drawing the crucial distinction between the immutable and the mutable. The scholars who will surely find new ways to reinforce and promote the old Koranic injunctions to be tolerant and ethical. And, here and there in his discussion, a sprinkling of names does appear.

Ramadan takes note of the Islamic scholars who have labored creatively to adapt the ancient principles to immigrant circumstances in the Western countries—an old and central theme of his. Who are these modernizing scholars? The reader will not be surprised, but may be dismayed, to learn that, first among them, cited as the author of a book called *Fi Fiqh al-Aqalliyât al-Muslimah*, which Ramadan describes as "seminal," is Sheikh Qaradawi. In a section of *Radical Reform* called "Reconsidering Islamic Ethics and Its Higher Objectives," Ramadan cites several Islamic scholars whose work in reconsidering the ethical quandaries deserves special mention. One of those forward-thinking ethicists likewise turns out to be Yusuf al-Qaradawi.

In a section called "An Applied Ethics of Being, of the Heart, and the Experimental and Social Sciences," Ramadan approvingly cites a number of Islamic experts on applied ethics who have argued for a broader social view. Here again he invokes the name of Yusuf al-Qaradawi. On the topic of women's rights, Ramadan praises the Islamic scholars who, in his words, "have clearly contributed to furthering the debate and reflection about the issue of women." Who are these progressive people? He mentions Yusuf al-Qaradawi (which makes sense, if I may add, given that Qaradawi is the scholar who issued the fatwa permitting Palestinian women to dispense with hijabs while committing suicide—an advance, presumably, for "Islamic feminism").

A modernized and reformed Islam will require new thinking on economics. Whose reflections and scholarship should be consulted on this difficult topic? Ramadan respectfully cites, as he has likewise done in *Islam, the West and the Challenge of Modernity*, two "classical contemporary scholars," of whom the first is a modern Egyptian cleric named Muhammad al-Ghazali, the medieval philosopher's namesake—a prominent leader of the Muslim Brotherhood who became famous for arguing, back in 1993, that anyone who resists the rule of sharia should be killed. (Two sentences from Muhammad al-Ghazali's obituary in *The New York Times* in 1996: "He also called on the

Government to appoint a committee to measure the
faith of the population and give wayward Egyptian
Muslims time to repent. Those who did not should
be killed, he said.") And the second of Ramadan's admired "classical contemporary scholars" on the topic
of economics, after the distinguished Muhammad al-
Ghazali? It is Yusuf al-Qaradawi.

Truly it is a shame, but Caroline Fourest has
been proved right, yet again. Ramadan's call for a
moratorium and a "true debate," now that he has
presented a full elaboration of the idea, adds up to a
proposal to leave the ultimate decisions to the worst
sorts of violent and obscurantist preachers—even if
the obscurantist preachers have already demonstrated
a stubborn and predictable unwillingness to engage
in anything like the broad-minded consultations that
Ramadan would like to see. Ramadan's thinking on
these topics has progressed not one whit. All these
years of philosophizing on Ramadan's part, his calls
for ethical thinking, his call for "Islamic Ethics and
Liberation" even in the subtitle of his *Radical Reform*, his repeated calls for reason and dialogue and
an open-minded spirit, his denunciations of bigotry
and unfairness—all of this has added up to nothing.

His commitment to ethical thinking turns out to
be worthless. Tariq Ramadan remains a man who
cannot see that a monstrous figure like Yusuf al-Qaradawi is a monstrous figure. "Oh Allah, count their
numbers, and kill them, down to the very last one,"
said the mufti of martyrdom operations in January
2009. And Tariq Ramadan in that same year managed to publish yet another book citing Qaradawi in
tones of veneration. Here is the worst of Islam—an
ideological corruption of the old religion, in Pierre-
André Taguieff's phrase. But Tariq Ramadan does

not see an ideological corruption. His critics point
out his error. They even predict his error. Still he
cannot see it.

Why not? If I take Ramadan seriously as a philosopher, then I would have to conclude that his understanding of al-Ghazali, the medieval sage, stands
in the way. I am a good enough reader of Emerson
to know intuitively that, if only *The Niche For Lights*
had made its way to nineteenth-century Massachu-
setts, Emerson would have seen in the mystic doctrine an exotic but recognizable argument for ever
closer attention to your own heart and thoughts. A
Koranic lesson in self-reliance. A muezzin's call for
individual conscience. But Tariq Ramadan is not an
Emersonian. Ramadan has interpreted the medieval
doctrine as a call for humility and obedience. Ramadan offers a few remarks of his own about listening
to the heart in *Radical Reform*. But his own heart
tells him to revere the authority figures who adhere
to his grandfather's legacy.

And so, Ramadan obeys and reveres. He especially reveres the people who revere his grandfather.
His method of obeying and revering is to call for
what he describes as "reform." In *Radical Reform* he
makes reform sound more radical than ever. And yet,
reform, to him, means a continuation of his grandfather's project from the 1930s and '40s. It is the call to
return to the purity of ancient times. The long-ago,
imagined past. The age of the supine. Anyway, it is a
call to return, in a slightly softer version, to the militant, sharp-elbowed atmosphere of his grandfather's
time—the atmosphere in which each new member of
the Muslim Brotherhood swore personal allegiance
to the Supreme Guide, Hassan al-Banna, whose own
shining hero was al-Ghazali, the earliest leader of an

Islamic reform, back in the twelfth century. And, in this spirit, Ramadan invokes al-Ghazali.

He cannot think his way out of this. He is imprisoned in a cage made of his own doctrine about his grandfather and his grandfather's ideology. All of his intelligence, which is considerable, and his energy, which is vast, and his literary talent, which is modest, goes into devising ever more clever ways, book after book, to paint the iron bars of his ideological cage in cheerful colors that appear to be modern and progressive. He wants to make his cage look like anything but a cage. Sometimes he cannot think of new ways to disguise the old ideas. Then he pretends that one or another aspect of his own doctrine does not exist. He mutters about *itjihad*. And yet he cannot figure out how to unlock the cage. He cannot think for himself. He does not believe in thinking for himself.

Chapter Eight
A REBEL SOUL

There is one additional pesky matter to raise in regard to the Ramadan-Sarkozy debate of 2003, and this has to do with Ayaan Hirsi Ali—the rebel soul whom a number of journalists counterposed to Ramadan in the post-debate discussion, invariably to Ramadan's advantage.

Ramadan and Hirsi Ali do seem to be parallel and even comparable figures, seen from one angle. Ramadan has his ancestors, and so does Hirsi Ali—in her case, the Osman Mahamud clan of Somalia, going back thirteen generations. Ramadan's father, Said, militated in his Egyptian homeland for the principles of Islamism and the martyred Hassan al-Banna, and the Ramadan family paid the price, which was a life of exile in faraway Switzerland. During Hirsi Ali's childhood and adolescence, her own father militated for a different set of principles, which emphasized political democracy and a liberal interpretation of Islam. Political democracy and liberal interpretations failed to prosper. And her family, too, paid the price, which was exile. There the parallel between Ayaan Hirsi Ali and Tariq Ramadan comes to an end.

Exile in Hirsi Ali's case meant a childhood and adolescence shuttling about from home to home in Somalia, Saudi Arabia, the Sudan, Ethiopia and Kenya. She saw and endured scenes of brutality and suffering of a sort that a privileged boy growing up in Switzerland could not possibly know. As a seventeen-year-old in Kenya, she followed a young people's trend and joined the Muslim Brotherhood, which, for a while, brought her into Tariq Ramadan's world, intellectually speaking. She studied the works of Hassan al-Banna and Sayyid Qutb. She learned about the worldwide conspiracy to eradicate Islam, led by the Jews and the Godless West. Then again, she read *Nancy Drew* and romance novels, from which she gleaned an alternative notion of life and its possibilities.

Her father, for all his liberal political ideas, clung to the old-fashioned cultural customs. In the mosque one day he arranged a marriage for her with a distant cousin from Canada, whom she had never met. She had no desire to marry the distant cousin, but neither did she have any choice in the matter, and she consented. Even so, en route to Canada to consummate the marriage and begin her new life, the influence of Hassan al-Banna and Qutb and family tradition seems to have fallen away, and the influence of *Nancy Drew*, girl detective, seems to have come to the fore. And, during a stop-over in Germany, Hirsi Ali saw her opportunity, and made a run for it. She got to Holland.

She was clever enough to demand asylum there on political grounds, instead of acknowledging that she was fleeing an arranged marriage. She lived in refugee shelters. She worked in factories. She studied Dutch. She mastered it. She went to work as an interpreter, helping Dutch officials and Somali refugees and immigrants communicate to one and another. She insisted on applying to a university, against the advice of a teacher. She was admitted. She studied political science at the University of Leiden (where Ramadan would later on be offered a professorship, which he turned down).

She took out Dutch citizenship. She spoke up on political issues. She raised the question of women's rights, especially the rights of Muslim immigrant women. She criticized Muslim reactionaries. She joined the social democratic party—and found that, because of her criticisms, she already needed to come under police protection. The center-right party lured her away. She ran for parliament on the center-right ticket. She was elected. Back in 1992, Tariq Ramadan entered public life in Switzerland by mounting a successful campaign to prevent a Geneva theatre from presenting Voltaire's play, *Fanaticism, or, Mahomet the Prophet* (though, as I have remarked, Ramadan has denied mounting any such campaign and considers it a lie to say otherwise). A decade later, Hirsi Ali, by contrast, came to think that Muhammad was, in truth, a fanatic. Worse, "a perverse man," as she told an interviewer in Holland, given the prophet's marriage to a child-bride. ("Admittedly I let rip in that interview," she was later to write.) And Voltaire was a hero.

The chapters in Hirsi Ali's *Caged Virgin: An Emancipation Proclamation for Women and Islam* carry such titles as "Genital Mutilation Must Not Be Tolerated" and "Stand Up For Your Rights!" Among those chapters is one called "Let Us Have a Voltaire." She nominated herself for the role (even if, as she has made clear, Locke, Spinoza, John Stuart Mill, Russell and Karl Popper have likewise influenced her thinking, not to mention Mary Wollstonecraft, the author, in 1792, of *A Vindication of the Rights of Women*). She struck up an alliance with Theo van Gogh, the filmmaker. She collaborated with van Gogh on the short and sensational film, *Submission, Part I*, which features a selection of horrendous passages about women from the Koran, graphically inscribed on women's bodies—a film that lasts eleven minutes and played on Dutch TV only once, yet enraged Muhammed Bouyeri sufficiently to prompt him, in 2004, to shoot van Gogh in the street and then ritually slit his throat.

It is sometimes forgotten that Bouyeri also left a dagger stuck into van Gogh's chest, pinning to the dead body a short poem on Islamist themes, together with a multi-page death threat entitled "Open Letter to Ayaan Hirsi Ali." The open letter was composed in the form of a fatwa, beginning with an invocation of Allah. The letter justified the murder by sketching a paranoid picture of the world. The picture was anti-Semitic. The "Open Letter to Ayaan Hirsi Ali" accused the Jews of regarding non-Jews as non-humans, and of reserving to themselves the right to deceive and lie to non-Jews. The letter accused the Jews of planning a genocide. And the letter accused the Jews of dominating Dutch politics. The letter that was pinned to van Gogh's dead body—what was this letter, then? It was a product of the political tradition that entered the world political scene with Haj Amin al-Husseini, the mufti of Jerusalem, and the German Arabic-language broadcasts and propaganda of the 1940s—the tradition of a Nazified Islam that has ended up being promoted today by any number of people, not just on the terrorist fringes of the Islamist movement. The letter expressed nothing that Hirsi Ali had not encountered before—in Saudi Arabia as a child, and in the curriculum at the

Muslim Girls' Secondary School in Nairobi, which she attended, and in the propaganda of the Muslim Brotherhood.

Only this time the paranoid worldview was aimed at herself. She was accused of being an "infidel fundamentalist," or alternatively an "unbelieving fundamentalist," which means the same thing. The "Open Letter" plucked on that one note, *fundamentalist*, in the singular or plural, repeatedly. It was a dominant note. The letter accused her of "intellectual terrorism," too, and, all in all, of being an "instrument of the true enemies of Islam." The letter invoked the Judgment Day. A Koranic verse was invoked against her—a verse about rising up against pharaoh: a key passage in the Islamist lexicon. The Netherlands, Europe and America were likewise threatened—pharaohs all, awaiting their destruction. The letter was signed with a *nom de guerre*, which left a suggestion that Muhammed Bouyeri, in performing his ritual slaughter of van Gogh, was not acting on his own, and he did have comrades, and Hirsi Ali was in extreme danger.

Ian Buruma, as the historian of van Gogh's murder, has naturally written at length about Hirsi Ali, and not just for the purpose of holding her up for invidious comparison to Tariq Ramadan. The portrait of Hirsi Ali stands at the center of *Murder in Amsterdam*. The portrait contains a number of sympathetic strokes. Buruma appreciates that Hirsi Ali has undergone difficult experiences, though he does not linger over them. He allows that, as a polemicist, she has raised worthy points in favor of secular values, though he tends not to spell these out. He applauds her denunciations of bigotry. In a post-script at the tail end of the book, oddly printed in small type, as if added in a fit of last-minute pre-publication remorse, he expresses a bit of indignation at Holland's treatment of Hirsi Ali. He reports that, in the aftermath of van Gogh's assassination and a series of other controversies, Hirsi Ali ultimately came to the conclusion that she had better leave Holland. Buruma laments her departure. "My country seems smaller without her," he remarks.

His method of portraiture, though, is to accompany each of his sympathetic strokes with a series of further, vivid, detailed, telling, multiple counterstrokes, which, through no visible ill-feeling or malice of his own, indeed entirely to his regret, happen to run in the opposite direction, with a cumulative effect. The key to Hirsi Ali's life, in Buruma's estimation, is her teenage experience with the Muslim Brotherhood in Nairobi. Buruma takes it for a certainty that, when she was seventeen, Hirsi Ali must surely have been a fanatic, even if Hirsi Ali says otherwise in her memoir. He is saddened to note that, instead of maturing in a normal way from teenager to adult intellectual, Hirsi Ali has leapt from dogma to dogma, and has done so with a convert's fervor, a narrow-minded absolutist from start to finish— someone who has failed to mature at all. In Hirsi Ali's battle for secular values, Buruma regrets to tell us, "there are hints of zealousness, echoes perhaps of her earlier enthusiasm for the Muslim Brotherhood, before she was converted to the ideals of the European Enlightenment."

People like Hirsi Ali, he explains, have come to be thought of as "Enlightenment fundamentalists," which might seem an odd and oxymoronic locution, since the Enlightenment, back in the eighteenth century, was nothing if not a protest against fundamentalism. "Enlightenment fundamentalist" might seem a cruel locution, as well, given that van Gogh's murderer had already attached the fundamentalist label, in a slightly different form, to Hirsi Ali in his death threat. Buruma's readers are not likely to notice the echo, however, if only because, in *Murder in Amsterdam*, Buruma reports that Hirsi Ali was accused in the "Open Letter" of being a "soldier of evil," a "liar," and a tool of the "Zionists and Crusaders," but he never does get around to reminding us that, most of all, she was denounced as an "infidel fundamentalist."

Buruma is a diffident man, and he speaks about Hirsi Ali typically in backward-facing sentences expressed in the negative, such that each new point is politely attached to a *not* and stated as its opposite. He wishes to present himself as rigorously fair, and fair-mindedness likewise impels him to preface his large and weighty condemnations with small, vague gestures of approval. About Hirsi Ali's secular and liberal goals, he says, "It is hard to disagree in principle," which indicates his approval, until he gets to the words "in principle," which indicates his disapproval. Then he adds, "Whether she was wise is another matter," which indicates that disapproval has deepened into condemnation. Hirsi Ali has denounced Koranic intolerance against Jews and homosexuals. Buruma applauds. "But her strident tone put people off."

He cites one of Hirsi Ali's detractors, a Dutch Muslim actress named Funda Müjde. The actress, he tells us, "admires" Hirsi Ali and even "salutes her courage"—"yet cannot hide her disapproval, not so much of what she says, as the way she says it, of her attitude, her style." About the fateful movie that Hirsi Ali made with van Gogh, Buruma explains that not even van Gogh thought it was any good. Too preachy for van Gogh's taste. "But even as a sermon it didn't work. Ayaan made it too easy for people to miss the point." The movie, Buruma concludes, failed "to challenge the beliefs of a complacent majority, the mainstream of a secure and prosperous European nation. It did not even speak for a generation." Nor did it speak for some tiny rebellious minority among the Muslim immigrants. Buruma reports in *Murder in Amsterdam* that he was unable to find a single Dutch Muslim who admired the film.

Buruma is pained to report that Hirsi Ali's personal demeanor tends to be off-putting to anyone who, like himself, sympathizes with the downtrodden. It is because of her unattractively aristocratic air of haughty disdain. The way Hirsi Ali gestured during a TV appearance in Holland disturbs him. The cameras showed her visiting a women's shelter and chatting with the frightened inmates. The inmates disliked her radical opinions. One of them protested. Hirsi Ali responded with a wave of her hand. The wave, to Buruma, was her ultimate offense. "It was this wave, this gentle gesture of disdain, this almost aristocratic dismissal of a noisome inferior, that upset her critics more than anything"—though in speaking of Hirsi Ali's critics he clearly means to include himself.

Buruma thinks that, in the fervor of her conversion to the "Enlightenment fundamentalist" cause, Hirsi Ali has come to look down upon the old-stock Dutch, as well, even if the old-stock Dutch are the very people who generously accepted her into their society. "Like all converts, she did not take her membership lightly," he tells us. And continues: "she soon felt as though she were surrounded in her adopted land by men and women who had fallen so deeply into the pit of moral decadence that they could never be counted on in the war against the forces of darkness." In Buruma's judgment, Hirsi Ali reserves her haughtiest condemnations, though, for other immigrant women, especially the women who, unlike herself, have had trouble adjusting to Dutch society—the noisome inferiors, frightened, endangered and demoralized, whom she met at the women's shelter. Buruma quotes the actress Müjde, Hirsi Ali's articulate detractor, who says about her, "I sensed aggression, a hatred almost, for the kind of people she was trying to save"—to which Buruma politely demurs by remarking that words like *aggression* or *hatred* go "too far."

He describes Hirsi Ali's relationship with her younger sister. The sister had a difficult childhood and adolescence in Somalia and Kenya. She followed Hirsi Ali to Holland. Culture shock overwhelmed her. She fell apart psychologically. She spent six months in a Dutch hospital, recuperating from a full-blown psychotic collapse. She never did recover, though. She returned to Kenya and underwent further psychotic episodes. She became pregnant. She suffered a miscarriage under horrific conditions. And she died. "This was the most difficult moment in Ayaan's life," Buruma affirms—though, if I read him correctly, he does not mean to suggest that Hirsi Ali was overcome with grief. He concludes his story of the two sisters by remarking about Hirsi Ali, instead: "The knowledge that some women, perhaps many women, couldn't break their bonds, even under the most favorable of circumstances, filled her with disappointment, but also with disgust." In *Murder in Amsterdam*, Buruma describes a Dutch literary tradition known as *scheldkritieken*, which means criticism in the form of what he calls "personal abuse."

The sentence I have just quoted, about Hirsi Ali's response to her sister's death, is surely an example of *scheldkritieken*, as practiced by Ian Buruma.

He thinks that Hirsi Ali's bravery, which of course he admires, ought not to be admired excessively. "The great thing about the Enlightenment, she said, with a spark of almost religious fervor in her eyes"—the spark is meant to remind us that Hirsi Ali has remained an incorrigible fundamentalist—"was that 'it strips away culture, and leaves only the human individual.'" Followed by this: "It takes courage for an African immigrant in Europe to say that, even if she is from a privileged class"—which suggests that even her fundamentalist fervors may require less courage than you might suppose, given her privileges (though the notion of Hirsi Ali's background as especially privileged may seem a little surprising, if you reflect on Somalia, which is one of the most wretched places on earth).

Buruma finds it galling that Hirsi Ali might identify with Voltaire. "There is a difference between the anticlericalism of Voltaire, who was up against one of the two most powerful institutions of eighteenth-century France, and radical secularists today battling a minority within an already embattled minority." The point seems to Buruma worth repeating. More than a hundred pages later: "Ayaan Hirsi Ali was no Voltaire. For Voltaire had flung his insults at the Catholic Church, one of the two most powerful institutions of eighteenth-century France, while Ayaan risked offending only a minority that was already feeling vulnerable in the heart of Europe"—which suggests that, far from displaying a significant bravery, Hirsi Ali has bullied the vulnerable.

The Hirsi Ali who emerges from Buruma's portrait turns out to be, in sum, a fanatical fundamentalist animated by crude ideas, zealous, strident, humorless, ineffective, counterproductive, contemptuous of people around her, arrogant, aristocratic, aggressive and hateful (or nearly so) toward humble immigrants, not really a feminist at all but, instead, a woman filled with disgust for women less successful than herself. She is someone who responded to the tragedy even of her own sister with feelings of disgust, someone who boasts of her own courage while merely goading the weak and the defenseless—someone who, through her taunts at powerless people at the bottom of society, plainly brought on the murder of her more talented and amusing colleague, van Gogh. A repulsive personality, all in all—though Buruma, ever courteous and amiable, would never stoop to using a strong adjective like *repulsive*, or any adjective at all, unless it were presented as a double negative. Besides, he repeatedly calls Hirsi Ali by her first name in *Murder in Amsterdam*, as if she were a dear and troubled friend, younger and less worldly than himself—therefore, not someone who could arouse in him even the slightest animosity.

Buruma has devoted extraordinary journalistic energies to expressing his lack of animosity. The first time that he wrote about Hirsi Ali, to my knowledge, was in *The New Yorker* in 2005, where he reported on van Gogh's murder. His tone was respectful. In *The New Yorker* he even reported visiting a Dutch classroom filled with Muslim and non-Muslim students, in which someone whom he described as "a dark-skinned girl with Indian features" announced in front of her classmates, "I think Hirsi Ali is really brave. She is saying things no one else has the guts to talk about." But that sort of admiring quotation disappeared from Buruma's subsequent writings. And his tone hardened.

In 2006, the Dutch minister of immigration announced an intention to strip away Hirsi Ali's citizenship, based on a legal technicality—the all-too-true fact that Hirsi Ali had claimed, upon arriving in Holland, that she was fleeing political persecution back in Somalia, instead of fleeing an arranged marriage. A parliamentary battle broke out, and the minister was forced to rescind the decision. The dispute over Hirsi Ali's citizenship became rather heated in the meanwhile, though. Buruma participated in the debate. He published an op-ed in *The New York Times*, suggesting that Hirsi Ali had brought this new round of troubles on herself. And he argued that people with a sense of social generosity ought to sympathize chiefly with Hirsi Ali's hapless victims, her fellow immigrants, who had suffered deportation as a result of her own antipathies toward the poor and the oppressed: "It would have been better if she had taken this opportunity to speak up for the people who face the same problem that she did, of trying to move to a free European country, because their lives are stunted at home for social, political or economic reasons. By all means let us support Ayaan Hirsi Ali now, but spare a thought also for the nameless people sent back to terrible places in the name of a hard line to which she herself has contributed."

The next year, in his profile of Ramadan in *The New York Times Magazine*, Buruma offered still more criticisms of Hirsi Ali's regrettable conduct. "She has renounced her belief in Islam," he wrote—and, as a result, she, unlike Ramadan, has failed to make herself popular among the kind of people who live on Brick Lane in London. A few weeks later Buruma reviewed her book *Infidel* in *The New York Times Book Review*, and, with his customary diffident cough and his passion for negative formulations, he lit into her again. He presented her as a fanatic with silly and cartoonish views: "But much though I respect her courage, I'm not convinced that Ayaan Hirsi Ali's absolutist view of a perfectly enlightened West at war with the demonic world of Islam offers the best perspective."

A few months later, the Dutch government, outdoing itself, declined any longer to provide Hirsi Ali with bodyguards, given that she had fled the country. Buruma rose to Holland's defense in the British *Guardian*. He observed that Holland was much to be admired for having allowed an immigrant like Hirsi Ali to prosper in the first place. "But the reasons for her rise are not entirely salubrious. Whatever the merits—and they are considerable—of her arguments against the bigotry of Islamic or African customs, especially those concerning the treatment of women, she lent respectability to bigotry of a different kind: the native resentment of foreigners, and Muslims in particular." In *The New Yorker* in 2009 he found another occasion, if only in passing, to draw an invidious comparison between her and someone else from a Muslim background—in this case, not Tariq Ramadan but a Dutch politician named Ahmed Marcouch, whose coalition-building talents have turned out to be greater than Hirsi Ali's. Buruma saluted Marcouch as a Muslim dissenter. "There have been a few bold dissenters, to be sure, such as the Somali-born activist Ayaan Hirsi Ali. But she had renounced her faith"—though perhaps Buruma might have mentioned that Hirsi Ali has also renounced her career as politician, which meant that coalition-building was no longer her task in life.

In *The New York Review of Books*, he accused her of "zeal," "dogmatism," ineffectiveness, and, with a flick of the word "ghostwritten," of not hav-

ing written her book *Infidel* (in the composing of
which Hirsi Ali did in fact draw on the editorial help
of a colleague, who is thanked, though not quite ad-
equately, in the "acknowledgments" section). Buruma's judgments of Hirsi Ali in *The New York Review*
were principally expressed, however, second hand by
Timothy Garton Ash, in an essay in 2006 on the
double theme of *Murder in Amsterdam* and *Infidel*.
This was the essay in which Garton Ash expressed
his admiration for Tariq Ramadan as a champion of
Islamic moderation. Garton Ash applauded Buruma's
book—"a characteristically vivid and astute combination of essay and reportage." About Hirsi Ali, on
the other hand, Garton Ash echoed Buruma: "Having in her youth been tempted by Islamist fundamentalism, under the influence of an inspiring schoolteacher, Ayaan Hirsi Ali is now a brave, outspoken,
slightly simplistic Enlightenment fundamentalist."
The freighted term "Enlightenment fundamentalist"
itself came from Buruma's book. Garton Ash added:
"It's no disrespect to Ms. Ali to suggest that if she
had been short, squat, and squinting, her story and
views might not be so closely attended to"—with the
phrase about "no disrespect" conforming to the tech-
nique, *de rigueur* among the detractors of Hirsi Ali,
of insulting her while claiming to be doing nothing
of the sort. Garton Ash's point was of course that
Hirsi Ali's successes have owed more to her looks
than to her brains.

I think that nearly any author, no matter how
privileged, tenured, pampered, safe and comfortable,
would find it vexing to be denigrated, invidiously
compared, sneered at, and generally assailed, intellectually and personally, by a single well-regarded
journalist, and by the journalist's even more highly-
regarded sidekick, in the columns of *The New York*

Times Magazine, The New York Times op-ed page, *The New York Times Book Review, The New York Review of Books,* and, in passing, *The New Yorker,* not to mention in the British *Guardian* and in the extended portrait in Buruma's own book. Hirsi Ali, though, is not privileged, tenured, pampered, safe and comfortable. She is someone who has fled from one of the most oppressed countries on earth to take refuge in one of the world's happiest and most progressive countries, Holland, only to discover that even in Holland she was forced to flee underground, dependent entirely on bodyguards, very nearly stripped of her citizenship, evicted by court order from her apartment because of a lawsuit by neighbors who found it frightening to live next door to a terrorist target, and berated in the press—until, having been smuggled from safe house to safe house, she fled yet again to the United States, where she was lucky enough to be offered a job by the American Enterprise Institute (which occasioned yet another sneer from Buruma, who made it seem, in *The New York Times Magazine,* that she had sold out to the neocons). A more classic example of a persecuted dissident intellectual does not exist. She is despised for her liberal opinions by many millions of people, and she is threatened with death by we have no idea how many terrorist individuals and groups. She is someone who will have to worry about Koran-quoting assassins for the rest of her life and who, even now, cannot confidently look upon any country as truly her own (though she gamely goes on proclaiming her loyalty to Holland).

And yet, what terrible thing has Hirsi Ali done— what dreadful atrocity, sufficient to merit this series of sneers in one magazine after another? To judge from Buruma's most widely-distributed complaint, the one in his *New York Times Magazine* article, which he repeated in *The New York Review of Books* and echoed in passing in *The New Yorker*, her ultimate sin has been, by giving up her religion, to fritter away any useful chance she may have had to promote liberal principles in the immigrant neighborhoods of Europe. But is this even true? Buruma insists. But it is easy to imagine that bookish young Muslim women in many an immigrant community in Europe and everywhere else have been sneaking glances at Hirsi Ali's writings all along ("Ten Tips for Muslim Women Who Want To Leave": a chapter in *The Caged Virgin*) and have been making brave resolutions for themselves. Anne Applebaum pointed out this likelihood in the *Washington Post*, in the course of noting what a large and nasty intellectuals' campaign has been gotten up.

In Holland, the novelist Margriet de Moor, in her own contribution to a larger debate about Buruma's journalism on these themes, came up with her own version of Applebaum's opinion: "And it was claimed that she did not reach her target group?" No: "Secretly, though, all of them swallowed what she said, their ears burning." And, to be sure, the notion that, in Europe, Muslim women's opinions are difficult to gauge has already been demonstrated, in France, by the government hearings on the headscarf law and the anonymous testimony of the schoolgirls who live in fear of the Islamists.

In any case, what if it were true that Hirsi Ali, in hurling a few high-spirited insults at her old religion, did make herself hopelessly unpopular on certain immigrant streets? Why should this arouse the wrath of the journalists? Salman Rushdie has not endeared himself either in those same neighborhoods, and this is not a count against him, given that, in our modern day, novelists have no reason to pander to the religious reactionaries. It may even be that Rushdie, in deploying those many mischievous scenes of his across the page, has had a liberating effect, here and there, on readers in different parts of the world. (Rushdie certainly seems to have unleashed a flood of Indian writers.) Besides, it ought to be indisputable by now that Rushdie, in writing impudently about fanatics and ayatollahs, has done an excellent job of describing reality. Why should Hirsi Ali, the tractarian and memoirist, be subjected to a different standard than Rushdie, the novelist? Her entire purpose in fleeing to Holland, as she has explained eloquently and at length, was to escape a life of submitting to other people's reactionary demands—beginning with her own father's demand that she marry her distant cousin—and to go bang the table on behalf of individual freedom and analytic thought. Which she has done, with gusto. But then, what can explain the attacks and sneers?

If you open either of the books she has so far published and read a few lines at random, you will discover one reality that you would hardly have guessed from the insults and criticisms in the magazines and in Buruma's book. Hirsi Ali has been presented as, first and foremost, a Voltairean rabble-rousing stalwart of the anticlerical cause. And, to be sure, she does condemn Islam. She draws her image of the religion from her own experience, and her experience has reflected some undeniable realities. The Saudi version of Islam, which is also Hassan al-Banna's version, has done rather well during the last few decades in her regions of East Africa and in some of the immigrant neighborhoods in Europe, too—the version of Islam that emphasizes the seventh century and the original sacred texts, and the worst portions, at that, of the ancient texts. She has concluded that here is the true Islam, which therefore she rejects *in toto*. Actually, not totally *in toto*, since, if you read her closely, you will notice that, in one passage or another, she grants that, in the past, Islam has sometimes been more tolerant; and certain versions of Islam display a tolerant and scarcely religious spirit even in the present (e.g., Islam in its Bosnian version); and, someday in the future, genuine reforms might come about. But the Islam she takes most seriously is the Islam that she herself has had to experience, and she does not bite her tongue.

Even so, anticlerical rabble-rousing has not, in fact, been her largest cause. In the two books, and in the little film she made with van Gogh, she has dedicated herself to something else, and this is to describe and decry the miseries of women who have had to make do with the oppressive old customs and ideas. Her *Infidel* is a moving book, and it touches on many aspects of life apart from matters that might concern a do-good committee—her childhood games and her relationship with her mother, a broken-hearted account of her relations with her father, her first kiss, her longings, her intellectual awakening. Still, no one will fail to see that, on the topic of women's oppression, she does have a lot to say.

She has written an account of her own genital mutilation as a little girl, and of the botched genital mutilation of her sister, which led, she believes, to her sister's breakdown and early death. She has described the beating she suffered as a girl in Kenya at the hands of her Koran teacher, who fractured her skull. She has written about the life of her grandmother, the Somali nomad, and the patriarchal customs of the past, which do seem to have lingered on, and about the airless miseries of traditional marriage for wives in East Africa. She has written of her sense of horror, as a girl, at seeing the women of Saudi Arabia for the first time—these women who have no faces because of their veils and whose black garments hang so shapelessly upon their bodies that, in order to know which way the women are facing, you have to look to see which way their shoes are pointing. She has written about the terrors of refugee life and about the double terrors for women—an account of her own extended family and other Somalis inhabiting a refugee camp along the Kenyan border, where women were raped and left for dead and people were expiring of starvation. She has described the lice and filth, and the baby whom Hirsi Ali herself rescued and brought back into Kenya. Nothing in these passages expresses a disgust for people who, like her sister, have been unable to cope. Nor are these the reflections of, in Buruma's phrase, a "privileged class." These are messages from the abyss.

Her critics in the intellectual magazines accuse her of making herself an outsider to the world of the immigrant Muslims—unlike Ramadan, who boasts of his privileged status as participant in the Muslim world's internal debates. But how is she an outsider? In his *Radical Reform*, Ramadan himself takes up the topic of female genital mutilation. He points out, as Hirsi Ali herself is careful to do, that genital mutilation is not, in fact, an Islamic religious injunction. Still, in parts of Africa and elsewhere, some people do think of it as an Islamic custom. Ramadan deplores the practice. But he has nothing else to say about it. He specifies, instead, that female genital mutilation and other issues bearing on the question of violence against women should be addressed, in his phrase, "from within"—addressed by the true insiders of the world of Islam and its many cultures, and not by hostile outsiders. This was Ramadan's point during his debate with Sarkozy—his reason, or at least his stated reason, for declining to denounce outright the practice of stoning women to death. But, then, on questions like these, who is the person who can reasonably claim to speak "from within"? And what shape would the speaking take, if not a tell-all autobiography like *Infidel*?

Buruma writes in *Murder in Amsterdam*: "And so Ayaan Hirsi Ali ended up preaching to those who were already convinced, and further alienating many of those whom she needed to engage." Unni Wikan, the Norwegian expert on honor killings, sees it differently, though. Wikan remarks, in the course of her own book, "Ayaan Hirsi Ali has played a crucial role in the Netherlands in alerting the authorities to the problem of honor crimes." Who is right on this issue, Buruma or Wikan? During the period when Hirsi Ali was, in fact, a politician, she campaigned, as a member of parliament, for one issue in particular. The Dutch police had never reported on honor crimes, and Hirsi Ali wanted to require them to do so. She pled her case. Parliament found it persuasive. The Dutch government ordered a reform. In short, Wikan is right, and Buruma is wrong. To shed light on social problems, to denounce what needs to be denounced, to stand up for people whose oppression, because it is enforced within the family, may well be invisible to the rest of society—this has been Hirsi Ali's particular mission. And it is easy to understand why a number of successes have come her way, even if the journalists declare her a failure.

Here, after all, is the true and obvious insider—the African immigrant, and not the Swiss professor. Al-Ghazali, the medieval philosopher, would have appreciated the difference between these two people—

the obvious distinction between somebody who has undergone experiences in the flesh and knows how to describe those experiences, and somebody who, like Ramadan, has merely learned about various things second-hand. Somebody who *really* knows, versus somebody who *sort of* knows. And, yes, a substantial public, and not just the Dutch parliament, has responded to her arguments and revelations. People do buy her books. And yet, this, too, Hirsi Ali's ability to reach over the heads of the disapproving intellectuals to a general public, has ended up figuring as one more count against her. Garton Ash, in the course of looking down his nose at Hirsi Ali in *The New York Review of Books*, pointed out that she has been awarded the "Hero of the Month" prize from *Glamour* magazine. Why was this worth mentioning? Garton Ash seemed to regard it as an amusing proof that Hirsi Ali's successes owe more to her looks than to her brains—though, in reading Garton Ash, I can't help observing that here may be proof, instead, that *Glamour* magazine nowadays offers a more reliable guide to liberal principles than *The New York Review of Books*.

The campaign in the intellectual press against Hirsi Ali seems to me unprecedented—at least since the days when lonely dissident refugees from Stalin's Soviet Union used to find themselves slandered in the Western pro-communist press (where the dissidents were accused, by the way, of whipping up right-wing fervors, exactly as is Hirsi Ali. And the dissidents were treated, too, with phrases like Buruma's "not entirely salubrious"—meaning, unwholesome, revolting, germ-bearing. "An anti-communist is a dirty rat," said Jean-Paul Sartre.) But that was long ago. In our own era we have never seen anything like this, until now. Something in these attacks on Hirsi Ali seems to me comparable to the spectacle of millions of civic-minded Britons marching in the streets in 2003 under the leadership of an Islamist organization, and comparable to the calm discussions in *The New York Times* of why it would be wrong to condemn with any vigor the stoning of women to death, and comparable to the anti-Semitic mob assault during the Paris peace march of 2003—comparable because, varied as these sundry events have been, they share one dismal point in common. These are developments that, even ten years ago, would have seemed unimaginable.

A sustained attack in the intellectual world on a persecuted liberal dissident from Africa, a campaign in the press that has managed to push the question of women's rights systematically to the side, a campaign that has veered more than once into personal cruelty, a soft vendetta, but a visible one, presided over by the normally cautious and sincerely liberal editors of one distinguished and admired journal after another, applauded and faithfully imitated by a variety of other writers and journalists, such that, in some circles, the sustained attack has come to be accepted as a conventional wisdom—no, this could not have happened in the past, except on the extreme right. Not in the recent past, anyway. Here, then, is a new development. Here is a reactionary turn in the intellectual world—led by people who, until just yesterday, I myself had always regarded as the best of the best.

Chapter Nine
THE FLIGHT OF THE INTELLECTUALS

A controversy over the treatment of Hirsi Ali in the press broke out in Europe early in 2007, and then spread to other places. The controversy was launched by an online English-language journal in Germany that bears the punny title *Signandsight.com* (the pun being on Heidegger's *Sein und Zeit*, though what Heidegger has to do with this is beyond me). And from the upper ethers of cyberspace the controversy drifted downward onto the feuilleton pages of paper-and-ink newspapers and journals in one country after another in Europe, and outside Europe. Also into a couple of books: the German anthology *Welche Freiheit: Plädoyer für eine offene Gesellschaft*, or *Which Freedom: Arguments for an Open Society*, edited by Ulrike Ackermann; and a second German anthology, *Islam in Europa: Eine internationale Debatte*, edited by Thierry Chervel and Anja Seeliger. Then still more controversy broke out over the related theme of Ramadan and his own treatment in the press—an inseparable theme, given that Ramadan's loudest admirers in the Anglophone countries, and Hirsi Ali's loudest detractors, have turned out to be the same people. And the newer arguments went spilling across the press in Italy, Holland, and into the magazines and newspapers here and there in the United States, Canada, Britain and Australia.

The debate was inaugurated by Pascal Bruckner, the French writer. This was in keeping with his own work over the years. Pascal Bruckner comes from the school of thought in France that used to be known as the New Philosophers—writers with personal backgrounds on the radical left who, back in the 1970s and early '80s, came out with a condemnation of communism and of totalitarian doctrines as a whole. The New Philosophers' condemnation turned out to be hugely effective, too—a mortal blow, as it happened, to communist and pro-communist ideas, at least in Europe. It is sometimes said of the New Philosophers that, in making their condemnation, they had done nothing especially clever or original, given how many other people in earlier generations and in other countries had already analyzed communist oppression, down to the last grisly detail. But this observation is offered chiefly by people who have never read the New Philosophers.

The New Philosophers' central theme was always the Western intellectuals, and not so much the realities of life in the faraway Soviet Union or other communist countries—though the communist realities did come up for useful discussion. The New Philosophers wanted to know why it was that, in the face of ever-growing mountains of evidence over the course of the twentieth century, so many intelligent people in the Western countries had kept on deluding themselves about the Soviet Union, and then about communist China, Cuba, and other such regimes. This was a large question. And an autobiographical question. The New Philosophers proposed a variety of interesting and sometimes novel observations. And, among those several observations, Pascal Bruckner's have remained especially fresh and useful—observations from a quarter century ago that, when you hold them up to the light today, can serve as a clarifying lens for observing any number of our own debates and controversies.

The people in the New Philosophy movement in France were, in one fashion or another, veterans of the student uprising of 1968, most of whom had taken up Marxism at one point, and set it down again, and afterwards had a great deal to say about their Marxist experiences—a main theme of autobiographical analysis. Bruckner, though, was never a Marxist. He was a disciple of Roland Barthes, and, under Barthes' influence, he adopted, in his student radical days, a leftism of a slightly different bent, in the hippie style. Barthes devoted a study to Charles Fourier, the most imaginative of the utopian socialist theoreticians from the early nineteenth century. And young Bruckner did the same. The first of Bruckner's books, which I have never seen, was called *Charles Fourier*—though I do notice that traces of Fourier and his mischievous imagination keep turning up in the pages of Bruckner's subsequent books.

The young Bruckner marched in the left-wing marches. But then, instead of enlisting in a revolutionary organization, he went on vagabond explorations of the Far East, which was the hippie thing to do. He toured ashrams. He contemplated Asian wisdoms. He preached the virtues of Taoist sexual techniques. He wrote a lively book on the sexual revolution with his fellow radical, Alain Finkielkraut, which was full of shrewd observations. He kept an eye on his fellow Western vagabonds. And, most of all, he kept an eye on the elite left-wing intellectuals back home in France, and on the peculiar ways in which the elite intellectuals kept describing exotic peoples in the rest of the world. And, after a while, Bruckner drew up a survey of what he had seen.

He inquired into the doctrine that was known in the 1960s and '70s as "Third Worldism." This was a leftism of a slightly new kind—the doctrine that looked for a new and superior revolutionary society to emerge not from the industrialized Western countries, who constituted the "First World," and not from the Soviet Bloc, who constituted the "Second World," but, instead, from anticolonial movements in the poorest regions of Africa, Asia and Latin America: the "Third World." Militants of the Third World cause gazed with veneration at leaders like Mao Zedong, Ho Chi Minh and Fidel Castro, who were communists.

But Third Worldists venerated the communist leaders because those people were anti-imperialists from the formerly colonized zones, and not because of their communism. And Third Worldists, in one of their main versions, indulged some hippie inspirations. Third Worldists looked for a spiritual revolution on top of the political revolution—a revolution that was likely to owe as much and more to Buddhist sages and the mystic gurus of India as to any of the leftist and anti-colonial political leaders. A saintly revolution, and not just a socialist one.

Bruckner understood those several notions and impulses perfectly because they had been, for a while during his student days, his own notions and impulses. But once he had gained a little distance on his own ideas, he began to notice a series of oddities, which, like his teacher Barthes, or like Fourier the utopian, he set about cataloguing with ferocious precision. His book on these peculiarities was *The Tears of the White Man: Compassion as Contempt*. Bruckner is the maestro of the subtitle. The book came out in 1983. It is a classic of modern political literature. It lays out for critical examination a lengthy catalog of left-wing European clichés about the poor and the oppressed in other parts of the world. Bruckner quoted one distinguished French or Western intellectual after another making a fool of himself, or of herself, and the quotations demonstrated all too clearly that, under a Third Worldist influence, even the most brilliant of Western intellects had proved to be absurdly incapable of recognizing everyday people in faraway places as everyday people. It was as if, in gazing at faraway parts of the world, the Western intellectuals could hardly do anything more than blink, and fall into reveries. People in exotic parts of the world were deemed to be spiritually loftier than people near at hand. They were immune to greed. They were selfless. Intuitive, instead of analytic. Sexually more at ease, or even indifferent to sexual urges. Capable of sagacious insights not accessible to the rigid and inhibited Western mind. Materially poor, but morally wealthy.

To the Western intellectuals, the poorest human beings in the poorest regions of the world appeared to be, in sum, better than other human beings, even if lacking in Western sophistication or other complexities. They were Noble Savages. Fantasies, in short. And the grand left-wing intellectuals of the Western countries never seemed to notice that, in conjuring those many fantastic images of people far away, they had ended up replicating the worst and most horrendous prejudices of the European imperialists of the past, except in a version that pretended to be admiring instead of hostile. The intellectuals pictured themselves as the enemies of racism, but somehow they had ended up as racists. They felt contempt for people different from themselves, and they packaged their contempt as compassion. They looked down, and described it as looking up. And why did they do those things?

Bruckner detected a familiar pattern: the rebellion against old and disreputable values that willy-nilly lapses into a conformism to the old and disreputable values. Third Worldism, he reflected, had set out to express a fitting and proper European feeling of culpability and repentance for the crimes of European imperialism. Repentance had hardened into dogma, though, and dogma had, oddly enough, yielded a pleasure. This was the pleasure of self-hatred. And self-hatred had joyously expressed itself by elaborating a utopian theory about the superior and scarcely human virtues of the exotic populations who were thought to inhabit the previously colonized regions of the world. A European who hated himself because of the crimes of the European past could revel in the satisfactions of imagining superior societies arising among Europe's former victims. And the satisfactions of utopian reveling led back to the even keener and more intimate and intense pleasures of despising oneself.

Bruckner had found his theme. He spent the next quarter-century contemplating the oddities of remorse and self-hatred and their perverse manifestations—sometimes in sexual life (a theme of various of his novels, notably *The Evil Angels*, which Roman Polanski made into a film called *Bitter Moon*), sometimes in European political life. He became the historian of modern unhappiness—the author of one book after another chronicling the experiences of boredom, purposelessness, envy, and sense of inadequacy among people who have no material reason to feel at all unhappy. He was the master of melancholy.

You might suppose that, given his downbeat themes, Bruckner would prove to be a gloomy writer. But, on the contrary, the topic of other people's foolish miseries appears to render him ebullient. And, to be sure, the greatest of his insights have always touched on the peculiar human quirk that allows for happiness in unhappiness, and for pleasure in pain. To desire is animal, he says somewhere, and to be perverse is human.

He has also labored mightily to record the many doctrines and ideologies that have emerged from the modern experiences of masochism and self-hatred. *The Tears of the White Man: Compassion as Contempt* was merely the first of his doctrinal chronicles. He has been updating his observations ever since, in one book after another. He has noted that doctrines come and go, and yet, from his perspective, not very much has changed. Ideologies do not die. They metamorphose. The leftist doctrine called Third Worldism disappeared long ago. Nobody dreams any longer of remote and impoverished countries in the formerly colonized regions leading the rest of mankind into a superior new phase of civilization. The fantasy of a Third World utopia disappeared in 1989, together with its elder brother, the fantasy of a communist utopia.

And yet, certain other elements of the old doctrine, having adopted new names, linger on, incognito. People who used to natter on about the Third World nowadays speak solemnly about the "south," The phenomenon formerly known as Western imperialism has ended up being described as the forces of globalization. And the main concept never seems to change at all—namely, the firm belief that wealth is theft, and Western success is the source of everyone else's difficulties, and Western prosperity means non-Western poverty, and suffering elsewhere means guilt here. And so, the spirit of self-hatred has persisted, and has even deepened and spread—a spirit of self-loathing that has come to be expressed in ever-more ingenious philosophical systems. The intellectual class, in Bruckner's portrait, has come to resemble the medieval clergy, a "penitential caste," which communicates its dogma of remorse by expounding multicultural theories of inexpiable Western guilt, and looks for ever newer ways to display its own humility.

Bruckner presented those updated ideas in the most recent of his cultural and intellectual chronicles, a book called *La Tyrannie de la Pénitence*, which came out in France in 2006 and has come out just now, in 2010, in English under the title *The Tyranny of Guilt* (an unfortunate translation because of the disappearance of the word *penitence*, with its implication of self-flagellation), but with the Brucknerian subtitle intact: *An Essay on Western Masochism*. He analyzes the Europeans, and especially the French. Error in its Parisian variations has always been his specialty. He shakes his head in dismay at the European intellectuals and their habit of thinking ever more poorly of themselves, and their habit of attributing fantastical virtues to exotic peoples faraway. He notes the oddly optimistic analyses of radical Islamism offered by Olivier Roy, the French expert on Islamic affairs, who made the mistake of predicting the failure of the Islamist movement as long ago as 1992, precisely at the moment when Islamism was blossoming more vigorously than ever before. The spectacle of Roy and other analysts getting things wrong produces in Bruckner his customary good cheer.

And then, no sooner did *The Tyranny of Guilt: An Essay on Western Masochism* appear in the

French bookstores than, in *The New York Review of Books*, Timothy Garton Ash published his remarkable essay—the one that applauded Ian Buruma, and sneered at Ayaan Hirsi Ali for having taken up the ideas of Western liberalism, and celebrated Tariq Ramadan for having done nothing of the sort. And Bruckner, in turning the handsomely designed pages of *The New York Review*, must have grown wide-eyed in delight. Buruma and Garton Ash were virtually cartoon figures from his own book, suddenly popping up in the American magazine. The Anglophone masochists, expressing their wrath at Hirsi Ali, the admirer of the West, and groveling to Ramadan, who berates the West. And, in *Signandsight.com* (and in *Le Meilleur des Mondes* magazine, in Paris), Bruckner posted what was, in effect, a solid epilogue to his *Tyranny of Guilt: An Essay on Western Masochism*.

He composed his additional commentary in his own decidedly French style, which can be described as Buruma's English style, upside down—a style of flashy epigrams, philosophical generalizations, positive assertions, and outright condemnations, instead of apologetic coughs, passive insinuations, double negatives, and an aversion to big ideas. From Bruckner's perspective, Buruma and Garton Ash had fallen into the doctrinal miasmas of the present age. Modern-day multiculturalism renders everything the equal of everything else. Buruma and Garton Ash had surrendered to that idea. And, under its influence, they had ended up committing the simplest of analytic mistakes. The Enlightenment is one of the great achievements of Western civilization. In our present era of self-hatred, though, the intellectuals have come to look upon the Enlightenment as merely a set of anthropological prejudices, no better

and very likely rather worse than other sets of anthropological prejudices—a European prejudice that,
in its arrogance, lends itself to zealotry and excess.
Buruma and Garton Ash knew very well that van
Gogh's murderer was a fundamentalist. But, in their
confusion over the Enlightenment, they managed
to convince themselves that Hirsi Ali must likewise
have been a fundamentalist, which was, of course,
preposterous.

Buruma and Garton Ash had lost the ability
to make the most elementary of distinctions. They
could no longer reliably tell black from white, a fanatical murderer from a rational debater. They had
lost the ability to make this sort of distinction especially in the case of someone like Hirsi Ali, who
came from the world that used to be oppressed and
tyrannized by the Western imperialists. Buruma and
Garton Ash thought of themselves as the enemies of
European racism. And yet, in throwing themselves
into the anti-racist cause, they had somehow ended
up concentrating their indignant energies on demean-
ing the dissident liberal from Somalia. Bruckner was
not afraid to give this error a name.

It was "the racism of the anti-racists." It was
a racism that, while pretending to fight for the oppressed, instinctively denies to someone from a
genuinely oppressed region of the world the right
to employ the same tools of Enlightenment analysis
that Europeans are welcome to use. Bruckner noticed the touch of personal meanness that seemed to
come into play whenever Hirsi Ali was discussed—
the masculine condescension, to mention one aspect,
which nobody could have failed to notice in *The
New York Review of Books*. He also noticed that
Buruma and Garton Ash were anything but marginal
writers. These writers were two of the most admired,

sophisticated, accomplished and influential intellectuals in the English-speaking world—Europeans both
of them, even if they contributed to the New York
press. And Bruckner offered his judgment.

"It is astonishing," he wrote—this was early in
2007—"that sixty-two years after the fall of the Third
Reich and sixteen years after the fall of the Berlin
Wall, an important segment of Europe's intelligentsia
is engaged in slandering the friends of democracy."
This was not a gentle criticism. Then again, Bruckner
was not alone in making it. In *Signandsight.com*, the
Turkish writer Necla Kelek weighed in with views
of her own. Necla Kelek saw in Buruma's writings
on Islamist themes a new set of stereotypes about
Muslims—stereotypes that prevented Buruma from
being able to notice the increasing problem in Europe of Muslim men preventing their own women
from receiving medical care from male physicians,
and other dangers.

Bassam Tibi weighed in. Tibi, without being
much of a fan of Hirsi Ali, likewise saw in Buruma's
journalism a prejudice against Muslims. Tibi was indignant that Buruma could not distinguish between
Islam and Islamism: between the religion and the
modern totalitarian ideology. Tibi was indignant
that Buruma had ceded to Tariq Ramadan the right
to speak for Islam. And Tibi was indignant that Buruma could not see the possibility of a genuinely new
kind of Islam arising, something not at all like Tariq
Ramadan's salafi reformism but, instead, an Islam in
a genuinely attractive and European style—a "Euro-
Islam," in Tibi's phrase, which modern Muslim liberals like himself have championed, even if non-Muslim liberals have declined to offer much support.

Buruma and Garton Ash, both of them, responded
to these criticisms and accusations—in Garton Ash's

case, with the opening statement, "Pascal Bruckner is the intellectual equivalent of a drunk meandering down the road," which was not a good beginning. Garton Ash maintained that Bruckner, in his inebriation, had failed to identify any sort of problem at all. And yet, other people, not just Necla Kelek and Bassam Tibi, did seem to think that Bruckner had made a valid point. One of those additional people turned out to be Ulrike Ackermann in Germany—the editor who eventually brought out the first of the German anthologies of the debate. Ackermann proposed a few remarks of her own, and these carried a significant weight, especially in regard to Garton Ash.

It should be remembered that Garton Ash, back in the 1980s, spent a great deal of time in East Germany and other countries in what was then the Soviet zone, stubbornly reporting on the East Bloc dissidents and their agitations—an extremely difficult story to report, given the communist dictatorships and the police surveillance. Garton Ash persisted even so. He filed vivid accounts of dissident protest and communist repression for *The New York Review of Books*. He demonstrated an intuitive sympathy for the dissidents, even if the enormous propaganda system of the communist states maligned the dissidents. Garton Ash became an unimpeachable authority on the nature and the necessity of dissidence. His contribution to public understanding was immense, in those years. In 2006 and 2007, these historic journalistic achievements of his conferred a moral weight on his easy dismissal of Hirsi Ali as a foolish simpleminded woman and his cautious applause for Tariq Ramadan—a greater moral weight than Garton Ash may have recognized (which might account for how careless he was in adopting his positions, how flippant in his phrasing, how content he seemed to be with his paucity of research).

But then again, Ulrike Ackermann was herself a heroic journalist from the later years of East Bloc communism—someone who played a role similar to Garton Ash's, though her journalism was better known in Germany than in the English-speaking world. Ackermann in those days reported from the Czechoslovak Socialist Republic. The dissidents there worked up a manifesto called Charter 77, which marked one of the early and most important stages in the development of the dissident movement. The Socialist Republic was keen on suppressing Charter 77's supporters and on making the dissident effort appear to be nothing at all. But Ackermann, in her journalism, offered an alternative account. She defended the dissidents, and she did this at a time when not too many people in her own West Germany or anywhere else in the world were paying attention. And, for her troubles, she was arrested by the authorities in Prague. She spent six weeks in jail and was lucky to get out when she did.

Ulrike Ackermann, then—here was Garton Ash's counterpart and equal, someone with her own weighty credentials on the large and controversial matter of who ought to be regarded as a heroic dissident, and who ought to be dismissed as a fake and a fool. Ackermann arrived at a judgment different from Garton Ash's. In her view, it was obvious at a glance that Hirsi Ali was a true and genuine heir of the East Bloc dissidents of the past. And it was obvious that Hirsi Ali had received a dreadful treatment from journalists who ought to have known better. Ackermann delivered a ferocious verdict on her old colleague, Garton Ash. She considered that Garton

Ash had somehow turned into the kind of person who, in the past, never did want to see communism collapse—the kind of person who, because he was unable to appreciate the achievements of liberal democracy in the West, could not detect the fundamental realities of communist rule in the East Bloc. Ackermann mulled over Garton Ash's endorsement of Tariq Ramadan in *The New York Review of Books*. She wrote: "Precisely because of his support for the Central European dissidents—which I am very familiar with—I find it astonishing that Timothy Garton Ash has clearly become a fellow traveler of Tariq Ramadan." Ulrike Ackermann was angry. *Fellow traveler* was a merciless phrase.

Garton Ash responded in the *Guardian*. His response was to heap still more criticism on Hirsi Ali. He was indefatigable. He had lately spent a little time in Egypt, and he wished to explain that, compared to Hirsi Ali, other dissidents and intellectuals in the Muslim world were infinitely preferable. He came up with a distinguished example. It was Tariq Ramadan's elderly great-uncle, Jamal al-Banna—the younger brother of Hassan al-Banna. Garton Ash visited Jamal al-Banna at his Cairo apartment. The place was stacked with religious texts—a true indication, Garton Ash meant to suggest, of Sheikh al-Banna's Islamic erudition. Garton Ash contrasted the elderly sheikh, with his magnificent book collection, to Hirsi Ali, whom he presented as pitifully ignorant.

Garton Ash quoted one of Hirsi Ali's critical comments on Islam. He quoted a stately alternative remark by Jamal al-Banna. And, comparing the two quotations, Garton Ash was beside himself with indignation at Hirsi Ali's inferiority. About those two quoted statements, Garton Ash asked the readers of the *Guardian*, "Which do you think reveals a deeper historical knowledge of Islam? Which is more likely

THE FLIGHT OF THE INTELLECTUALS 279

to encourage thoughtful Muslims in the view that they can be both good Muslims and good citizens of free societies?" Garton Ash evidently felt that he had finally unmasked the intellectual pretensions of Hirsi Ali, the ignoramus, and, like a lawyer addressing a jury, he wished to convince the *Guardian* readers to join him in making his condemnation.

Only, a pity! And more than a pity! Garton Ash's favorable comparison of Jamal al-Banna with Ayaan Hirsi Ali ran in the *Guardian* on March 15, 2007, and, on the very next day, the Middle East Media Research Institute, MEMRI, happened to issue its own report on Jamal al-Banna. MEMRI's evaluation was less admiring. This was because of Sheikh al-Banna's praise—it is terrible to have to report these things—for the 9/11 terrorists and, in Sheikh al-Banna's words, their "extremely courageous" action, which was "dreadful and splendid," in opposition to the "barbaric capitalism" of the United States. Sheikh al-Banna had signed a petition in 2001 blaming America for having brought on the 9/11 attacks. Five years later, he elaborated on his original judgment, and his new elaboration aroused a debate, which MEMRI reported—the outraged response to Sheikh al-Banna by Arab liberals, horrified at his stance. Sheikh al-Banna clung to his views, though. Mostly he encouraged the Palestinians to continue in their campaign of suicide and random terror. He was explicit about this. A few days after Garton Ash's applause for Jamal al-Banna appeared in the *Guardian*, MEMRI posted online portions of a transcript of a television debate on the question of martyrdom operations, in which Sheikh al-Banna was one of the participants.

Jamal al-Banna: "Martyrdom operations in Palestine, in particular, are justified, for two reasons. First, the Palestinians do not have weapons to defend themselves. They have no tanks, artillery, and so on. This is the only means available to them. Therefore, it is justified, especially since it is the Israeli soldiers that are targeted. When I say 'soldiers'—the entire Israeli people is recruited. The women are the most vicious of them all. Therefore, this is justified. I consider this to be martyrdom. Even if they harm a woman—all the women serve in the army. All the men serve in the army. Only the small children remain, and the fact is that these are only very rarely harmed. I believe that these are martyrdom operations, and are necessary."

How in the world did Garton Ash manage to come up with someone like this as his grand exemplar of Muslim liberalism in a superior version? Was Garton Ash so utterly desperate to find the name of a Muslim thinker, anyone at all, whom he could declare to be visibly preferable to Ayaan Hirsi Ali? There is something uncanny, almost creepy, about how often the journalistic critics of Ayaan Hirsi Ali, who happen also to be the ardent defenders of Tariq Ramadan, have ended up wandering into the zones of suicide terror and the most prominent of its theorists and champions.

Still, I do not want to be naïve about this. Garton Ash's celebration of Jamal al-Banna in the *Guardian* is not, in fact, hard to explain. Within the world of the Islamists, Jamal al-Banna enjoys, after all, a reputation for being a rather liberal person—a reformer, more moderate even than Sheikh Qaradawi, the mufti of martyrdom operations, who himself is, as I say, continually extolled for his moderation. And, to be sure, viewed from a variety of angles, Jamal al-Banna does occupy a moderate position, or even a liberal-minded position—far more moderate than Qaradawi's, even if Jamal al-Banna and Qaradawi have both gone on television to urge Palestinians to commit suicide. An Egyptian friend of mine, whom I hugely admire, a true liberal and democrat, defends Sheikh al-Banna, and, though I think my friend makes a mistake in doing this, I can understand his reasoning. Within Egypt itself, the worst of the terrorist threats—the murderous operations that assassinated Sadat and have killed all kinds of other people—have come from the followers of Sayyid Qutb. And Jamal al-Banna is an anti-Qutbist. He argues against the Qutbists of Egypt on their own grounds, which are Koranic, and, even if his arguments do not extend to Islamist terrorism of other sorts, his arguments are bound to make some of his fellow Egyptians, the true Egyptian liberals and democrats, look on him with gratitude.

Jamal al-Banna has worked up a peculiar and heretical interpretation of Islam, and his interpretation is bound to seem congenial to people with liberal and secular views. I have been able to read the English translation, not yet published, of a new book by Jamal al-Banna called *Islam and the Challenges of the Modern Age*, and I can summarize some of his main points. Jamal al-Banna looks on Islam as very nearly a secular religion, something like, say, Reconstructionist Judaism. As a proper and pious Muslim, he of course accepts the Koran as a revelation from God—and yet, even on this crucial point, if I read him correctly, he does not rule out the possibility that humans may bear the ultimate responsibility for having written the Koran.

In either case, whether the Koran should be regarded as divine or human, he does rule out the notion that post-Koranic scriptures in Islam, the sunnah and hadith, the "Traditions," ought to be regarded as divine. He regards the "Traditions" as unreliable.

Islam, in Jamal al-Banna's version, is a stripped-down affair, confined to the Koran. Nor does he grant any authority to the Islamic religious hierarchy in determining the correct interpretations of the Koran. The scholars, too, seem to him unreliable. And yet, the Koran obviously requires interpretation. And so, Jamal al-Banna encourages Muslims to come up with their own interpretations—to think for themselves. His grand-nephew, Ramadan, says likewise, of course. But Ramadan, with his incessant appeals to authority, is none too convincing on this point. Jamal al-Banna, who dismisses the "Traditions" and disdains the scholarly religious hierarchy, makes a more persuasive case.

Jamal al-Banna defends the freedom to be an apostate. He cites surah and verse to defend the principles of pluralism and tolerance. He opposes stoning adulterers to death. He opposes honor killings. And not only does he oppose these things, he actually mounts arguments against them, instead of merely proposing a future debate on these matters. In Jamal al-Banna's opinion, stoning adulterers to death runs contrary to anything the Prophet Muhammad could possibly have advocated, and the post-Koranic scriptures that say otherwise ought to be disregarded—another point on which Jamal al-Banna goes well beyond the timid ambiguities of Ramadan. Jamal al-Banna speaks his mind. He does not put his moral conscience on hold, while awaiting the decisions of some future fatwa committee that will never be formed. Then again, Jamal al-Banna declares himself undecided on whether to chop off the hands of thieves. He thinks there may be a good argument for chopping off hands, which has to do with practical consequences. The spectacle of people walking around without hands may discourage other people from becoming thieves, or so he supposes.

At least, he does not feel that Koranic authority should be invoked on this matter. The question of whether to chop off people's hands seems to him a civic issue, not a religious one. He does not want to create an Islamic state, not even in the Muslim-majority countries—another point on which he is more liberal and secular than his grand-nephew. Jamal al-Banna figures that Islamic states can only be bad for Islam—just as Christian states turned out to be bad for Christianity, and socialist states bad for socialism. On this one large point, and on some deeper philosophical points, as well, Jamal al-Banna's *Islam and the Challenges of the Modern Age* could almost be likened to the genuinely liberal arguments you can find in the book *Islam and the Secular State* by Abdullahi Ahmed An-Na'im, the Emory University professor.

Jamal al-Banna specifies, too, that a proper civic state ought to be democratic, and this, too, is heartening to see. His notion of how to construct a democratic state is a little unusual. Jamal al-Banna knows his way around the history of European leftist theory, and his ideas about democracy draw on this background. He does not approve of the conventional version of a democratic state, as it has arisen in Western Europe and North America—a democratic state in which the electoral districts tend to be drawn up geographically. He prefers to organize a representative democracy through the various professions and fields of work, with each profession or field of work electing its own legislators. This is a very old left-wing idea, dating from the years around 1900, which used to be popular among trade unionists under the name of anarchosyndicalism, and later on flourished on the British left under the name of guild socialism.

People with ideas like those came to power in parts of Spain for a little while during the Spanish Civil War in 1936. Some of the ideas were put into effect, for a few months. Then the anarchosyndicalist or guild socialist program disappeared from the world scene. In our present age, there is not the slightest chance of a revived anarchosyndicalism or guild socialism being put into practical effect. Sheikh al-Banna upholds the idea, even so, and this seems to me perfectly all right, if the idea is taken as a utopian sparkplug, useful for igniting imaginations. In my own student writings, I used to emphasize the virtues of anarchosyndicalist thinking on a regular basis, and someday I plan to advert to certain of those virtues again, in a limited context.

And so, yes, I can, in fact, see how Garton Ash came up with Jamal al-Banna, and I can see why Garton Ash imagined that he was doing a good thing in promoting Jamal al-Banna's reputation among the readers of the *Guardian*. Jamal al-Banna's attractive qualities would be undeniable, if only you could separate out the appalling qualities. And it is true that Jamal al-Banna can boast of some first-rate enemies. Qutbists the world over can only regard him with loathing. Even the mainstream conservatives of the Muslim Brotherhood must shudder in annoyance or anger at Jamal al-Banna's deviations. To reject the "Traditions" and the Islamic scholars—why, this is heresy. And yet, the attractive traits in Jamal al-Banna bring us to the heart of a problem that I have been alluding to throughout this book—the strange fact that, in a modern political world shaped by the rise of the Islamists, even some of the most attractive of thinkers tend, if they have come under an Islamist

influence, to have a soft spot for suicide terrorism.
And a soft spot for anti-Semitism.

It would be wonderful, after all, to think that
suicide terrorism today is advocated only by a lunatic fringe of wild extremists, the Qutbist ultra-
reactionaries, or by the people whom Ramadan dismisses as salafi literalists, together with the people
like Sheikh Qaradawi, whom Ramadan does not
dismiss—the hardcore champions of Hassan al-Banna. But that is not the case. People with seemingly
reasonable and even appealing views on a variety of
themes sometimes join the lunatic fringe and the al-
Banna mainstream in making those arguments. They
might do so openly and on television, as Hassan al-
Banna's brother, Jamal, does; or they might do so by
subtle implication and by burying their ideas in the
small-print footnotes, as Hassan al-Banna's grandson, Tariq Ramadan, does. But, either way, they do
it. And some very bright journalists from the non-
Islamic press seem unable to recognize these anoma-
lies, or unwilling to point them out.

Why so? It is because the Islamist movement, in
prospering, has succeeded in imposing its own categories of analysis over how everyone else tends to
think. Mainstream Islamists look on Jamal al-Banna
as a free-thinking maverick, and on Sheikh Qaradawi as a sound and reassuring orthodox moderate,
and on Tariq Ramadan as a man half-way lost to
the vapors of Western liberalism—and these judgments, which are Islamist judgments, end up getting
adopted by the Western and non-Islamist journalists,
as well, who report the judgments as fact, without
pausing to make any investigations of their own.
Timothy Garton Ash is hardly the only journalist to
have stumbled over this particular point, in regard to
Jamal al-Banna.

The New York Times, for instance—to harp on my hometown paper one last time—ran an admiring portrait of Sheikh al-Banna in 2009, under the byline of Michael Slackman, called "Hints of Pluralism in Egyptian Religious Debates." The *Times* presented Jamal al-Banna as an important figure helping to liberate religious discussion in Egypt—a man who was leading other people to think for themselves. You could hardly read the account without breaking into applause at Jamal al-Banna and his gutsy questioning of the Egyptian religious establishment's old-school rigidities. And somehow the article never did get around even to hinting that Jamal al-Banna had also found a few kind words to say on behalf of the 9/11 terrorists, or had forthrightly urged Palestinians to kill themselves in random attacks on their neighbors, the Israelis, and especially the Israeli women.

And so, Garton Ash stands in good company. But this is not an honor. I presume that Garton Ash, in extolling Jamal al-Banna to the readers of the *Guardian*, knew nothing at all about the sheikh's sympathies for martyrdom operations. But so what? Even if I agreed to remove Jamal al-Banna's views on suicide and terrorism from the discussion, I would nonetheless find it puzzling that Garton Ash has ended up persuaded of Jamal al-Banna's intellectual superiority over Hirsi Ali. I recognize that Jamal al-Banna's *Islam and the Challenges of the Modern Age* is a lucidly presented book. Someone ought to publish the English translation. Hirsi Ali's *Infidel*, though, is a riveting book—an autobiography that recounts one of the most dramatic modern-day life stories that you are ever likely to read. I am more than happy to acknowledge a value in Jamal al-Banna's interest in reviving or updating the old anarchosyndicalist and guild socialist ideas. Still, I would think it obvious, at least to anyone who considers himself liberal-minded, that Hirsi Ali's invocations of John Stuart Mill and applications of his insights are more valuable still. Valuable, I mean, from a practical point of view—valuable because of their immediate applicability to the Muslim world, and to the non-Muslim world.

Sheikh al-Banna writes movingly in favor of pluralism and tolerance, and this is marvelous—though his arguments on this matter might lead you to suppose that, in regard to anti-Semitism, which has played a fateful role in modern Egyptian history, he would offer wise and practical counsel. After all, Egypt, which has been inhabited by Jews for thousands of years, has seen virtually its entire Jewish community flee the country over the course of Sheikh al-Banna's lifetime. In *Islam and the Challenges of the Modern Age*, though, the sheikh's most striking observation on the Jews is to point out that, unfortunately, the Jews have been damned by God: "The curse of God then befell them in a horrific way." This is not how Hirsi Ali writes about the Jews.

Jamal al-Banna's opposition to violence against women is altogether splendid (leaving aside, of course, his belief that Israeli women ought to be murdered—but is this so easy to leave aside?). Even so, I find it hard to imagine how any liberal-minded person could seriously argue that Jamal al-Banna has done a better job than Hirsi Ali in raising the question of women's rights. Nor does she advocate putting anybody to death. Nor do I have to pore over the writings of Hirsi Ali to know that she is not a hand-chopper. Her own position on suicide terrorism has the merit of lacking the slightest nuance. Never once has Hirsi Ali gone on TV urging anyone to commit suicide. Why, then—I am genuinely puzzled by this—would a liberal journalist as sophisticated and experienced as Garton Ash gaze at Jamal al-Banna, and at Ayaan Hirsi Ali, and find something preferable in Jamal al-Banna?

And what can account for this repeated urge, on Garton Ash's part and Buruma's, to hold Hirsi Ali up for comparison to this or that other person from a Muslim background, who is invariably said to offer a more promising solution to the entire mass of Muslim problems? One journalist after another, following Buruma's example, has insisted on making these invidious comparisons. I suppose the comparisons express an unstated superstitious belief, held by any number of non-Muslims, that Islam and the Muslim world will be rescued from their sins by a single messianic figure, a Supreme Guide, if only we could identify who this miraculous Guide might be. Obviously it will not be Ayaan Hirsi Ali. To be the Supreme Guide is not one of her aspirations, as she has taken pains to stipulate. She wants Muslims to think for themselves—which is the true meaning of her commitment to the Enlightenment. And what can explain the tone of contempt that so frequently creeps across the discussions of Hirsi Ali—the tone that Garton Ash employed with so much relish in *The New York Review of Books* and again in the *Guardian*? Garton Ash's demolition of Hirsi Ali in the *Guardian*, or what he took to be a demolition, was written, after all, with a visible tremor of emotion.

Now, on this last point, the dismissive and patronizing tone, I am happy to report that Garton Ash, having received his share of criticism from several parts of the world, eventually glanced back at his own journalism, and he noticed at least one unfortunate phrase that, seen in daylight, might have been better chosen. Several months after the controversy over Buruma and his own journalism broke out, Garton Ash participated in a debate with Hirsi Ali at the Royal Society of Arts in London, in front of an audience of British journalists and other people and a Swedish TV camera (thanks to which I have watched the debate). Garton Ash walked to the podium and, in a brave and forthright manner, straightaway retracted the one unfortunate phrase—the words "Enlightenment fundamentalist"—with which he had taxed Hirsi Ali in *The New York Review of Books*: a "slightly simplistic Enlightenment fundamentalist."

That one phrase had led to misunderstandings, he conceded. He allowed, too, that he ought to have foreseen the misunderstandings. He said, "It did not occur to me that anyone would be so idiotic as to imagine that one was construing any sympathy between Islamic fundamentalists and Enlightenment fundamentalists"—the idiotic persons being, presumably, Bruckner, Ackermann, and a good many others, perhaps including myself, if by chance Garton Ash had seen my own essay in *The New Republic*. The remark about his idiotic critics was not so bad, under the circumstances. A man ought to be allowed an occasional dig at his critics. But Garton Ash was noble to regret his own phrase. Still, even then, he seemed not to recognize the full implication of what he had written—how cruel it was, on his part, to pick up an accusation from Muhammed Bouyeri's death threat and modify it ever so slightly (from *infidel fundamentalist*) and, as Buruma had done, fling it anew at Hirsi Ali, this time in *The New York Review of Books*.

Hirsi Ali had brought a copy of the magazine to the debate, and she pulled it out to read aloud one of Garton Ash's other passages—which she was spared from doing by the moderator. This was John

Lloyd, the well-known British journalist. Lloyd insisted on reciting the passage himself. He knew the passage from memory, without having to glance at the magazine. The passage was Garton Ash's remark about how, if only Hirsi Ali had been "short, squat, and squinting," instead of good-looking, she would not have achieved her successes. Lloyd was able to recite the passage because, over the course of the controversy, the insulting words had acquired a degree of notoriety. And, with the published sneer at Hirsi Ali hovering in the air, as recited by John Lloyd, and with the magazine lying on the table a few feet away, Garton Ash contemplated this remark, too. And he retreated from it. He explained that, in writing about Hirsi Ali's looks, he meant only to tease. He repeated his observation from *The New York Review of Books* that, after all, she had received an award from *Glamour* magazine, which evidently continued to strike him as amusing. Hirsi Ali, gracious but firm, chose to accept his comments as, in her words, a "veiled apology." Garton Ash seemed to think she was amiably joking, and he quipped that his comments were, instead, a "burqa."

He also took the occasion to reaffirm his high evaluation of Tariq Ramadan and Ramadan's contribution to the modern scene. This, in Garton Ash's estimation, consists of offering to bridge the gaps that need to be bridged—the remark that is always made by people who figure that Ramadan is doing something useful. Garton Ash's way of expressing his positive evaluation was odd, though—a portion of the debate that Nick Cohen, the author of *What Left?*, who sat in the audience, pointed out some days later in the London *Observer*. Garton Ash chose to describe religious discussions as, in his word, "gobbledygook." He said, "If it is gobbledygook anyway, and I think it is gobbledygook, then we should prefer

a version of gobbledygook that is more compatible
to a liberal society." He meant that liberals should
look with gratitude upon Tariq Ramadan because
of his useful gobbledygook. And, to this point, too,
Hirsi Ali offered a quiet rejoinder.

Her rejoinder was partly philosophical. Garton
Ash, in the course of the debate, had lectured Hirsi
Ali on the differences between John Locke and Voltaire and their alternative versions of the Enlightenment, which he evidently felt she did not understand.
But Hirsi Ali, in her reply, lectured Garton Ash on
the deeper purpose of the Enlightenment. The deeper
purpose was to find ways of speaking that are not, in
fact, gobbledygook—ways of speaking that everyone
can understand. Ways of speaking that do not rely on
the appeal to authority—therefore, ways of speaking
that allow people to think for themselves. She proposed a second observation. This observation, too,
bore on Garton Ash's comment about gobbledygook.
Muslims, she observed, were being "treated like a
child." Here again, she was admirably gracious, perhaps even to a fault. Her remark conveyed none of
the ferocity that animated Pascal Bruckner's angry
essay. Still, Hirsi Ali's observation about Garton Ash
treating Muslims like children corresponded pretty
closely to Bruckner's argument. What does it mean,
after all, to treat adults from some other culture
like children—to argue that, in speaking to them,
it is best to use gobbledygook? Bruckner's phrase,
"the racism of the anti-racists," was not Hirsi Ali's.
Still, Garton Ash's argument was an illustration of
Bruckner's point. Hirsi Ali elegantly drove this point
home. And she observed that, if you treat people like
children, they may act like children.

But let me return to Ian Buruma and his own
responses to Bruckner and his other critics in the
larger debate. Buruma's initial response to the criti-

cism took a different tack from Garton Ash's. Buruma refrained, for the moment, from heaping any additional attacks on Hirsi Ali. Buruma argued, instead, that he had never heaped any attacks at all. He wrote in *Signandsight.com*, "If Mr. Bruckner has been kind enough to read my book, I'm not sure how he came to the conclusion that it was an attack on Ayaan Hirsi Ali." And more: "I admire Ayaan Hirsi Ali, and agree with most of what she stands for"— which, to be sure, is what Buruma said about Tariq Ramadan, too, in *The New York Times Magazine*: "We agreed on most matters."

This was a congenial response on Buruma's part, or, at least, it had the look of congeniality. And yet the debate would have been furthered, I think, if only Buruma had worked up the courage to acknowledge that, whatever he may have thought he was doing in writing about Hirsi Ali in *The New York Review of Books,* *The New York Times* op-ed page, *The New York Times Magazine,* *The New York Times Book Review*, the *Guardian*, and in whole sections of *Murder in Amsterdam*, some people did think he was making an attack. Pascal Bruckner was not the only person to arrive at this judgment. Bruckner was merely the first to point it out. Buruma might have had the courage to assume responsibility for what he had written about Tariq Ramadan, as well, his anointing of Ramadan as the grand interlocutor between the liberal societies of the West and Islam—a "laudatory portrait," in Bruckner's unlaudatory phrase, that "borders on hagiography, despite minor reservations."

But I see that, in recounting these quarrels, I have, by the logic of my own narrative, ended up trotting out the dread word *courage*. This may be the heart of the matter. Bruckner thought so: "A culture of courage is perhaps what is most lacking among today's directors of conscience." Buruma appeared to think so, too, from an opposite standpoint. In Buruma's analysis, phrases like Bruckner's represent a positive danger. It is because of the word *courage*. The word conjures Buruma's own historical memories of the fascist past: not the fascist past in the Arab countries but the fascist past among the intellectuals of Europe. Responding to Bruckner's call for "a culture of courage," Buruma tut-tutted in *Signandsight.com*, "Now where have we heard that kind of thing before? The need to defend Europe against alien threats; the fatigued, self-doubting, weak-kneed intellectuals..." Buruma wanted his readers to hear in Bruckner's language an echo of the ultra-right-wing rhetoric of Europe from seventy years ago—the kinds of phrases that used to pour from the mouths of Nazi and fascist ideologues, in upbraiding the champions of reason and tolerance. Something seems to have eluded Buruma, though.

The worst single thing that Ayaan Hirsi Ali has ever done, to judge from his own book, was to behave haughtily during her televised discussion at the women's shelter in Holland—the discussion in which she offended Buruma by waving her hand dismissively at one of the other women. And yet, by Buruma's account, most of the women participating in that discussion wore disguises over their faces, for fear of what might happen to them. Buruma recounts the television episode chiefly to illustrate how disagreeable is Hirsi Ali's personality. And somehow he appears to have missed the obvious reality that, however boorish Hirsi Ali's handwave may have looked on the TV screen, Dutch television was broadcasting at that moment a scene of terrorized women, and Hirsi Ali was one of them. By the time that van Gogh was murdered, Hirsi Ali had already spent more than two years under police protection, fleeing from safe house to safe house. Then, in the panic that followed the murder, she was whisked away by the Dutch authorities to an air force barracks, a police camp, and a series of hide-aways, flown by military plane to remote hide-outs in the United States, and then back to still more safe houses in Holland and even in Germany—a woman condemned to life under permanent armed guard.

I met her at a conference called the Engelsberg Seminar in Sweden two years later, in 2006. She was protected by no less than five bodyguards. Even in the United States, she is protected by bodyguards. But this is no longer unusual. At that same conference in Sweden in 2006 I happened to meet Ibn Warraq, the author of *Defending the West* and other books, whose real name is not Ibn Warraq, but who has been forced to adopt a pseudonym out of fear that, because of his sympathy for the philosophical views of Bertrand Russell, he could be singled out for assassination. (And, to be sure, in 2008 Ibn Warraq found himself reading a call for his own murder posted on a British Muslim website).

I met Bassam Tibi at the Swedish conference— Tibi, who pioneered the concept of Islamism as a modern totalitarianism, and pioneered the concept of a liberal "Euro-Islam," as well. Tibi spent two years under twenty-four-hour police protection in Germany. I happened to attend a different conference in Italy a few days earlier. There I met the Egyptian-Italian journalist Magdi Allam, who writes scathing indictments of the new totalitarian wave in the Italian newspaper, *Il Corriere della Sera*. I discovered that Allam, too, was traveling with a full complement of five bodyguards. (This is the same Magdi Allam who went on to convert to Catholicism, at the hands of Pope Benedict XVI himself—which drew upon Allam a torrent of abuse, as if, in converting to a new religion, he had done something disgraceful.)

Then again, nowadays intellectuals and artists who are not from Muslim backgrounds likewise find themselves in danger if they are thought to have said or done the wrong thing. At the Italian conference where I met Allam, I ran into the Italian journalist Fiamma Nirenstein, who was accompanied by her own bodyguards—in her case, owing to her fiery speeches and writings in defense of Israel. It is worth mentioning that Caroline Fourest in France, the author of the first and most important extended criticism of Ramadan, had to go under police protection for a while. The French philosophy professor Robert Redeker had to go into hiding. In 2008, the police in Belgium broke up a terrorist group that had planned on assassinating, among other people, Bernard-Henri Lévy.

One evening in New York I had the pleasure of dining with Flemming Rose, the culture editor of the Danish newspaper *Jyllands-Posten*, who was visiting New York only because, at that particular moment, it was too dangerous for him to remain in Denmark. One of Rose's cartoonists, Kurt Westergaard, who satirized the Prophet Muhammad as a suicide bomber, has spent years living either underground or semi-underground, and survived the latest of the assassination plots against him, in January 2010, only by fleeing into a fortified shelter within his home, which a terrorist with an axe was unable to enter. I don't even mention the writers and intellectuals who still maintain their homes within the Arab world. On another evening in New York, I had the opportunity to engage in a public conversation at the Alliance Française with Boualem Sansal on the topic of his *The*

German Mujahid—and Boualem, in a bitter mood, ended up revealing to me and to the audience that, in Algeria, he has lately found himself living in a fearful atmosphere generated by death threats against him. And van Gogh, the filmmaker...

And so, Salman Rushdie has metastasized into an entire social class. It is a subset of the European intelligentsia—its Muslim free-thinking and liberal wing especially, but including other people, too, who survive only because of bodyguards and police investigations and because of their own precautions. This is unprecedented in Western Europe since the fall of the Axis. Fear—mortal fear, the fear of getting murdered by fanatics in the grip of a bizarre ideology—has become, for a significant number of intellectuals and artists, a simple fact of modern life. And yet, if someone like Pascal Bruckner intones a few words about the need for courage under these circumstances, the sneers begin—"Now where have we heard that kind of thing before?"— and onward to the litany about fascism. In *The New York Times Magazine* Ian Buruma held back from hinting even obliquely at the genuinely fascist influences on Ramadan's grandfather, the founder of the modern cult of artistic death—Hassan al-Banna, who spoke highly of Adolf Hitler and helped the Grand Mufti of Jerusalem escape from getting tried at Nuremburg. Yet Pascal Bruckner, the liberal—here is somebody, Buruma would have us think, on the brink of fascism!

Twenty years ago, when Rushdie came under threat and one of his translators was murdered and another was knifed and a couple of Norwegian bookstores were bombed and a British hotel was attacked by a suicide bomber, not to mention the more than fifty people killed in anti-Rushdie rioting around the world—at that terrible moment, when the dangers first became obvious, a good many intellectuals in Western countries, people without any sort of Muslim background, rallied instinctively to Rushdie's defense. A good many intellectuals reached out to their endangered Arab and Muslim counterparts and colleagues, and celebrated the courage of everyone who refused to be intimidated.

My glance happens to fall just now on a dusty volume on my bookshelf, brought out in the course of the Rushdie affair, in 1993, by the French publishing house La Découverte, which contains statements of support for Rushdie by a solid one hundred Arab and Muslim intellectuals. The book, under the title *Pour Rushdie*, is a moving display of fraternal solidarity by the publisher and the contributors both. Leafing through the pages, I stumble on the contribution by Orhan Pamuk, who nowadays goes about with his own detail of bodyguards, though in his case the danger comes from Turkish nationalists, not from Islamists. And here is the contribution by Antoine Sfeir, the Lebanese historian who later on criticized Tariq Ramadan in France, and then had to fend off Ramadan's lawsuit.

In his 1993 essay on the Rushdie affair, Sfeir recalled that, in Egypt, Naguib Mahfouz had been brutally assaulted not very long before, as part of the same wave of Islamist terror that was threatening Rushdie himself and his associates. The Egyptian intellectual Farag Foda had recently been murdered. Sfeir wrote, "We will never say it enough: to attack the Islamists, to denounce their actions and their lies, is not to attack Islam. To attack the Islamists is, on the contrary, to defend the Muslims themselves, the first though not the only victims of the Islamists."

How times have changed! The Rushdies of today find themselves under criticism, contrasted unfavorably in the very best of magazines with Tariq Ramadan, who is celebrated as a bridge between cultures—Ramadan, an alumnus of the anti-Rushdie Islamic Foundation in Britain. Ramadan, who, even in 2009, managed to commend in a single sentence of his book *Radical Reform* both Sheikh Qaradawi, the theologian of the human bomb, and the Egyptian sheikh Muhammad al-Ghazali, who publicly defended the assassination of Foda. (The sentence appears on page 349, buried all too typically in the footnotes, and without a listing in the index.) And yet, if there is a menace to society, nowadays it is said to come from Hirsi Ali or some other vocal and articulate opponent of the violent sheikhs—the European intellectuals from Muslim backgrounds who, in their unforgivable departure from the child-like image of how Muslims are supposed to behave, have arrogated to themselves the right to update a few ideas from John Locke or John Stuart Mill or Bertrand Russell. During the Rushdie affair, liberals who called for courage were applauded. Liberals from Muslim backgrounds were positively celebrated. But not today.

How did this happen? The equanimity on the part of some well-known Western intellectuals and journalists in the face of Islamist death threats so numerous as to constitute a campaign; the equanimity in regard to stoning women to death; the journalistic inability even to acknowledge that women's rights have been at stake in the debates over Islamism; the inability to acknowledge how large has been the role of a massively reinvigorated anti-Semitism; the sneering masculine put-downs of the best-known feminist intellectual ever to come out of Africa; the striking number of errors of understanding and even of fact that have entered into the journalistic applause for Tariq Ramadan and his ideas; the reluctance to discuss with any frankness the role of Ramadan's family over the years; the unwitting endorsement in the *Guardian* of a champion of martyrdom operations; the refusal to discuss or even acknowledge the Nazi influence that has turned out to be so weirdly venomous and enduring in the history of the Islamist movement—what can possibly account for this string of bumbles, gaffes, timidities, slanders, miscomprehensions and silences?

Two developments account for it—two large new realities that, condensing overhead, have altered the intellectual atmosphere down below, almost without being noticed. The first of those developments is the spectacular and intimidating growth of the Islamist movement since the time of the Rushdie fatwa. The second development is terrorism.

INDEX OF NAMES